DANIEL YANKELOVICH

CHASING THE SOCRATIC DREAM

BLUEFISH PRESS

SAN DIEGO, CALIFORNIA

Bluefish Press
www.bluefisheditorial.com

Book Layout ©2013 BookDesignTemplates.com

Parts of this book also appear in Daniel Yankelovich's *Wicked Problems, Workable Solutions: Lessons from a Public Life* (New York: Rowman and Littlefield, 2015)

Chasing the Socratic Dream / Daniel Yankelovich —1st ed.
ISBN 978-0-9974216-3-7

3

TABLE OF CONTENTS

INTRODUCTION: Philosophy in a Minor Key 1

PART ONE: AN EVENTFUL CHILDHOOD

Becoming an Outsider 11

One Damned Foster Home after Another 21

The Pumpernickel Bread with the Hollow Center 35

A View from the Fringe 43

An Outsider's Consolation Prize 47

The Boston Latin School 49

PART TWO: ON MY OWN

A New and Exciting World 59

The Long Vomick 67

Grenoble, the Guildhall, and the Girl 81

Back to Harvard 95

Girls 105

"Oh, hello there." 109

The Worst "Bright Idea" I Ever Had 115

The Rue Servandoni 119

Stumbling into Marriage 125

Life in Paris 131

A Respite in the Mountains 137

"You Will Need a Suit" 141

Return to Reality 145

My Job Search...149

My First Full-Time Job..153

Marti Rejoins Me in New York...............................157

Taking Refuge in Work 163

My Philosophy "Sabbatical"..................................169

Screwed 173

PART THREE: STRUGGLING TO TURN MY LIFE AROUND

Facing Up to the Mess 179

Applying Philosophy to Life 185

A Head Makeover..189

A Shift in Perspective 195

Breaking Up 201

The Next Big Step 207

Engaging in Public Life 213

Launching My Own Firm 219

A Welcome Change... 223

An Instructive Failure... 233

A Unique Opportunity.. 237

Becoming an Insider's Outsider 241

Other Chutzpah-Filled Adventures 247

The Shah and I 257

PART FOUR: AN UNEXPECTED TURN

My Life Turns Upside Down 267

From Walking to Mentoring to Loving 275

The Safety Valve Fails 279

Caught Unprepared 283

How Do I Defend Myself without a Shell? 287

Together 293

Picking Up the Pieces 297

Taking Stock 319

Finding Closure in Philosophy 323

A New Love 331

*I dedicate this book to Laura, Nicole, and Rachel
and to all of the many friends I have come to cherish.*

You have been the greatest sources of personal fulfillment in my life.

I conceive this book as part of the legacy of that quintessential Amercan philosopher, John Dewey.

Dewey believed passionately that our democracy had to be more than an aggregation of individual citizens. His abiding theme was the need for Americans to bring a strong sense of civic virtue to the task of creating community. "Democracy," he wrote, "is the very idea of community itself."

He refused to confine philosophy to academia and insisted that it have a practical purpose in strengthening the communal aspects of our democracy.

INTRODUCTION:
Philosophy in a Minor Key

MY MOTHER DIED IN the early years of the Great Depression and my father was unable to hold our family together. As a consequence, I was sent to live in a series of foster homes from the age of eight to eighteen. It was in these foster homes that I began my life-long love affair with philosophy.

I didn't, of course, call it by that name. I didn't know what the word meant until I was in high school. And indeed, my boyhood conception of what I called philosophy bore little resemblance to the academic discipline that became my college major.

The philosophy I studied at Harvard (after a three-year stint in the army in World War II) concerned itself with highly abstract subdivisions of philosophy such as logic, epistemology and metaphysics. The version of philosophy I struggled with in my day-to-day foster home life concerned itself with deep emotional questions of caring, love, dependency, and what one should expect from oneself and others.

My abrupt transition from an intact, loving, caring family to poorly paid foster homes cut the ground out from under me. I lost the compass that had guided my life. My reflections about what was happening to my life became a bewildering preoccupation.

In my late high school years, I started to use the word "philosophy" for those musings. When Harvard accepted me on scholarship,

I couldn't wait to study the real thing. But it took me a long time to reconcile what I meant by philosophy with what the Harvard philosophy department meant by the term. When I finally unscrambled the differing meanings and how they related to each other, I decided to abandon academic philosophy but continue to pursue what *I* meant by philosophy.

There must be many other people, possibly millions of them, who pursue their own flirtations with philosophy, mostly without labeling it as such. It is, after all, a quest for the kind of wisdom that people cherish and yearn for. Yet, at the same time, philosophy as practiced in our colleges and universities has morphed into a forbidding subject, conspicuously lacking a welcome mat for outsiders.

Despite setbacks and frustrations, my lifelong love of philosophy has proved to be deeply satisfying. Over the course of decades, engaging in philosophy as I conceive it restored the grounding that I lost in my foster home years. It provided me with clues to the haunting question of how best to live.

I learned to rely on philosophy to maintain a sense of perspective—an overview of how all the pieces fit together. I found the "examined life" indispensable to my sense of well-being. And I discovered that the philosophical values of stewardship added a *strong ethical dimension* to my life.

I came to realize that philosophy has a distinctive value to impart, one that is more closely linked to sound judgment than to scientific information or cleverness in manipulating logic. Philosophy's breadth of judgment is desperately needed in a world of increasing specialization. It is needed if we are to keep the whole in sight at all times, to separate the truly important from the trivial, and to maintain a balanced perspective on our chaotic world; it prevents us from losing the ethical anchor that keeps the extreme self-centeredness of today's individualist culture in check. We need philosophy if we are to sustain the sense of wonder and astonishment all of us experience at one time or other at the sheer fact of existence.

Present-day philosophy as taught in universities reflects a huge and confusing divide that dates back to its earliest days. The era of Socrates, Plato, and Aristotle in ancient Athens witnessed a great flowering of philosophy, but it also set the stage for a deep confusion of identity. Contrary to superficial appearances, Socrates and Plato, the founders of Western philosophy, pursued different conceptions of that subject.

Socrates saw philosophy as the quest for how best to live. He pursued this goal through dialogue with the citizens of Athens he encountered in his daily life. This all-too-public quest troubled many Athenians who saw his relentless questioning as an invasion of their space and privacy. In 399 BC, Socrates was condemned to death by hemlock, essentially for being so pesky and intrusive.

Plato, on the other hand, saw philosophy as a search for universal truths about the nature of reality. His conception was austere, scholarly, and disdainful of the views of the average Athenians. Plato equated philosophy exclusively with the rational products of the mind rather than the non-rational output of the senses. For example, he mistrusted all forms of poetry.

He famously identified the experiences of our senses as the misleading shadows on the wall of a cave that its occupants, deprived of the light of the mind, falsely perceive as reality. He contrasted these distorted impressions unfavorably with the ideas that our rational minds produce. At the highest level of abstraction, Plato's *Ideas* define the nature of *being, reality, courage, justice,* and other so-called Universals. For Plato, these alone constituted genuine philosophy.

Over the centuries, these two different conceptions of philosophy coexisted uneasily, with the Platonic conception becoming ever more dominant.

In the modern era, professional academic philosophers rarely go back to the Socratic question of how best to live. In mainstream academia the Platonic conception goes unchallenged. (Philosopher Alfred North Whitehead was hardly exaggerating when he described contemporary philosophy as "a series of footnotes to Plato.")

It is mainly outsiders who practice the Socratic quest for how best to live. Today, professional academic philosophers address the Socratic question of how best to live only when are taking a breather from their more serious duties. Consider philosopher Robert Nozick's book, *The Examined Life*, written in 1989. While Nozick wrote most of his books in the formal Platonic tradition, he wrote this one in the minor-key Socratic tradition, and he wasted no time in explaining his deviancy.

In his introduction, Nozick distinguished clearly between the Socratic and the more professional Platonic conceptions of philosophy. He acknowledged the professional philosopher's preference for the latter, stating that: "Life or living is not the sort of topic whose investigation philosophers find especially rewarding."[1] I was astonished that a leading philosopher of our day should admit that life and living are not suitable subjects for philosophy!

Nozick suggested that with this book he was taking time off from serious work. Rather self-mockingly he remarked that professors of philosophy like him prefer the Platonic approach because they enjoy elaborate intellectual structures that display their brilliance.

My own personal discussions with academic philosophers suggest a more down-to-earth motivation for avoiding the Socratic tradition.

---

1   Robert Nozick, *The Examined Life: Philosophical Meditations* (New York: Touchstone Publications, 1990), 12.

Philosophers in universities are, first and foremost, teachers. They need teachable subjects with which they themselves are comfortable. Plato and the history of philosophy are teachable subjects that they feel fully qualified to pass on to others. Professors are uncomfortable with the Socratic goal of teaching others how to live—a task that calls for wisdom they are not sure they themselves possess.

There is a major obstacle to engaging the Socratic goal of how best to live. If you are like me, you will want to learn what outstanding thinkers have to say about the subject. In searching the literature, however, I found it difficult to find many philosophers who attack the subject directly. They appear more comfortable approaching it indirectly through its various aspects.

One prominent aspect of the how-best-to-live theme concerns *how to be.* Heidegger, Sartre and other existentialist philosophers identified *being* with *caring.* You exist in the world as an autonomous, responsible self only to the extent that you care. Caring is your path to connectivity with the world. The existential theologian Paul Tillich writes about the *Courage to Be.* His insight is that it takes courage to assert one's being in the face of the terror of non-being that hovers over the lives of so many people.

John Kaag, a philosopher who specializes in early American philosophy, has described the deep agony suffered by the philosopher Josiah Royce, a contemporary of William James at Harvard. According to Kaag, Royce was terrified of being an anonymous nobody—a nothing, a random mound of earth. Eventually, through philosophy, Royce found his salvation: "a heartfelt sense of belonging to a greater whole. " It is this conviction, Royce came to believe, that saves individuals from "their feelings of quiet desperation."[2]

---

2   John Kaag, *American Philosophy: A Love Story* (New York: Farrar, Strauss and Giroux, 2016), 169.

How to think is another key aspect of the Socratic quest. It is an area where scientific knowledge has deepened greatly in recent years. The work of the psychologist Daniel Kahneman has documented many ways our minds tend to mislead us when making judgments and decisions. Our conscious mind is not nearly as reliable a guide to judgment as many of us assume it to be.

Freud preceded Kahneman in pointing to the distorting power of unconscious mental processes. Kahneman's work tends to ignore Freud, possibly because the two men were concerned with different kinds of judgment—Kahneman focused on economic thinking while Freud focused mainly on how we handle our instinctive drives of sexuality and aggression.

My day-to-day professional work brings me into constant contact with yet another aspect of the Socratic quest, one that concerns *public* as distinct from *private* life. This is the dimension of *how to engage* with the larger society. My field of research is to track and analyze the role that individual citizens play in democratic decision-making in politics, the workplace, and the community.

In today's American society, so-called "experts" play an outsized role in these decisions, squeezing the public out of the policy process. Philosophers like Hannah Arendt have argued that the public's disengagement is a threat to freedom.

Arendt stressed that individual engagement is vital to the preservation of our freedom as a democracy. She stated that genuine freedom for the individual always involves the larger community—the society and culture to which all of us belong. This is the public aspect of our lives, as distinguished from purely private life. Our freedom requires having an active public voice in shaping the decisions that impact our lives.

If others—experts, elites, politicians, policy makers, company officials (however benign their intentions)—make those decisions for us, Arendt says, we may be liberated but we are not truly free.

An active and effective public voice is an indispensable aspect of freedom.

My personal motivation for being drawn to philosophy is rooted in the disorientations of my foster home years. They shattered my everyday expectations and left me ungrounded—a very disconcerting feeling. I eventually discovered that a Socratic philosophy for living permitted me to rebuild a foundation for my life. Philosophy supplied the ground that had crumbled beneath my feet in the years that followed my mother's unexpected death.

In the chapters that follow, I recount some of the most memorable moments of my life. Starting with my unstable childhood, I interweave the story of my long affair with philosophy as it interacted with mundane, everyday experience.

PART ONE

AN EVENTFUL CHILDHOOD

Becoming an Outsider

LOUIS AUCHINCLOSS, A GIFTED novelist from a socially prominent WASP family, writes about his life as a consummate insider. He describes his youth with his strong-willed mother and his indulgent father as a period of great inner security. "I had all my life," he said, "a curious sense of immunity, that nothing could happen to me...And nothing ever did."[3]

My own family came from the opposite end of the social spectrum, though I too had a strong-willed mother and an indulgent father. But my early life experience was the opposite of Auchincloss's. It bred a conviction that all sorts of mishaps would intrude on my life and throw it out of whack...and they mostly did. These early experiences shaped me as an outsider.

I first began to feel like an outsider when I was eight years old, after my mother died unexpectedly in the early years of the Great Depression. My father wasn't able to keep our family together. The double whammy of hard economic times and my mother's death were too much for him. After her death and the breakup of our family, my sisters and I were sent to live in foster homes.

For the following ten years I drifted from one foster home to another, initially with my younger sister, Libby, but mostly by myself. The transition from the unqualified love of a doting mother

---

3. Quoted in Larissa MacFarquhar, "East Side Story: How Louis Auchincloss came to terms with his world," *New Yorker*, February 25, 2008.

and father to the indifference of poorly paid and unfamiliar foster parents was brutally abrupt. The serial foster homes made me wary of the conventional life choices and identities that were available to me. Our culture directs most young American males on autopilot into conventional social identities. I came to feel that the culture's standard identities didn't fit my circumstances and early on I began to hack out a special path for myself.

My father was fourteen years old when he arrived in the United States as an immigrant from Russia before World War I. He came from the small town of Chernikov, not far from Chernobyl. My mother came from another small town in the same region of Russia, as a child of five or six.

My father lived with his uncle's family in Boston, working hard and going to night school to learn English, which he came to speak fluently but always with a Russian accent. When the United States was drawn into World War I, he volunteered for military service and fought with the American infantry in Europe.

He suffered lung damage through exposure to the poison gas the Germans used, and thereafter received a modest disability pension just large enough to pay for the cheap Cremo cigars he liked to smoke, an irony that was lost on him.

His first wife, one of three Gellerman sisters, died shortly after giving birth to a baby girl, my half-sister Florence. Florence was four years older than me, and I had a strained relationship with her even when we were both little children.

My father married my mother a few months after his first wife died. He was in a hurry to remarry so that his baby daughter would have a mother to care of her.

Until my mother died, he was almost always cheerful and full of jokes and stories. He was neither practical nor shrewd and was easily taken in. He was a loving father and I always took his side against the criticisms my sisters leveled at him in later years. They felt that with just a bit more practicality and effort he might have kept our family together after my mother died. I didn't see it that way. I was always convinced that if he could have, he would have kept us together.

When my father and mother married, his uncle loaned him enough money to open what was known then as a "dry goods" store—a store that provided fabrics and sewing materials to people who made their own clothes and other household items. My mother and father both worked in the store, and my father also did maintenance work for some neighborhood houses.

We were poor, but there was no stigma attached to it because everyone we knew was poor. My sister Libby and I were left on our own a lot. I remember happy days playing with the boxes downstairs in the basement of the dry goods store. I would fit boxes together the same way kids today fit Lego pieces together, and then cover my edifices with the bolts of fabric stored in the basement.

As the Depression gained momentum, my parents lost their store. Pa continued to do maintenance work, but he sometimes didn't earn enough to support the family. I always knew when things got really bad. Gloom would settle over our household and both my mother and father would bemoan the fact that Pa would now have to go to work for Mr. Schneiderman, who owned a lot of property and was notorious for exploiting the people who worked for him.

I was never very clear exactly how Mr. Schneiderman exploited my father, but in our house the mere mention of his name created an atmosphere of foreboding. Being obliged to work for Schneiderman just to be able to feed his family was one of the very few things that could shake Pa's placid acceptance of fate. Schneiderman came to symbolize for me the brutality of impersonal economic forces.

While I have never had any strong urge to make a lot of money, I did develop a fear of becoming a victim of economic forces. I vowed that I would never be forced to undergo the kind of degradation of the spirit Pa suffered on those occasions when he was obliged to work for Schneiderman.

One of the more gratifying outcomes of my life has been that I have managed to avoid ever having to work for the likes of Schneiderman. In later years I realized that my father's humiliating experience had instilled in me a deep aversion both to victimhood and to exploitative people.

This was earliest building block of my evolving philosophy for living. There seemed to me to be something profoundly unfair about being at the mercy of people you mistrusted and disliked, who were free of scruples about exploiting you solely for their own advantage.

I came to believe that in a just society, an ethic of *stewardship* obliges those who have power, access to resources, and influence to care about the welfare of the people who depend on them.

Before my mother died, our home was warm and undemanding. My mother doted on me, her only son. In the Russian Jewish culture of their era, sons were favored over daughters by both parents.

One of my most vivid memories of those early years is my recollection of my Uncle Isaac, my mother's older brother. He was a lawyer by training and education—the best-educated member of our extended family. He would often come to our house in the afternoon and share a glass of sugary tea with my mother. As soon as he said hello, with a warm hug for each of us, he would start arguing with my mother.

The arguments were never over personal things but rather over politics and religion (he attacked Judaism and my mother defended it). Whatever the subject, the arguments were intense and ferocious because both brother and sister felt so passionately about everything.

In the neighborhood, we often would see Uncle Isaac striding down the street in a coat that descended to his ankles. He seemed to wear the coat all the time, regardless of the weather. As he walked he talked out loud to himself. Though the streets were often crowded in our densely populated, largely Jewish neighborhood, no one seemed to pay much attention to his eccentric behavior.

Late in his life he converted to Catholicism. His oldest son, my cousin Jack, was a pilot and was killed when his plane was shot down in the early days of World War II. My uncle died shortly thereafter, I believe of sheer grief. When he died, he left everything in his will to the neighborhood children so that they would not want for candy.

He may have been eccentric, but I loved him and I think he loved us. (I used to play with his youngest son, Morton, and his middle son, Danny, was my favorite cousin.) I enjoyed listening to him and my mother argue. Even when he came at night after my bedtime, he and Ma could not prevent themselves from launching into their emotion-laden debates. From my bedroom nearby, I could hear my uncle talking at the kitchen table in his loud voice.

I would get out of bed and sneak behind the closed kitchen door to eavesdrop on their conversation, something Ma had explicitly ordered me not to do. Most of the time, she was too engaged in arguing with her brother to realize that I was there, and I got away with it and went back to bed when I got sleepy or bored. But one night I couldn't help coughing while I was hiding behind the door, and she heard me.

"Oh, that boy!" she exclaimed as she leapt out of her chair, "Is he going to get it!"

My father, as usual, tried to intercede on my behalf. I heard him say, "He's not doing any harm, Sadie. Let him be. He is just a boy and he wants to be in on everything."

"He's just a boy, all right," my mother answered. "But someday he is going to be a *mensch* if I have anything to say about it."

She made this standard pronouncement in a loud voice so that I could hear her; she started to lunge after me as I made a quick retreat back to my bedroom. She caught me, and it turned out that she had quite a lot to say about it.

Before my mother became ill, I was mostly moderately well behaved. My father rarely had any problems with me and intervened when my mother, who had a fierce temper, came after me determined to wallop me. If I disobeyed her in some sneaky way, which I found irresistible, she would grab me and give me a vigorous whack on my bottom, noisily exclaiming, "What did I do to deserve such a naughty boychick!"

My father never succeeded in stopping his strong-willed wife, and Ma always prevailed. Thank goodness!! My mother and I had an unspoken pact that benignly excluded my father but worked quite well for the two of us. I don't know what I would have done had she ever failed to catch me. It would have provoked enormous anxiety in me. I would have had to be responsible for my own behavior. This way, she was responsible for my behavior and fortunately she knew what she was doing. After all, she was Ma.

As her beloved son I was free to play, to experiment, to misbehave to my heart's content. The only consequence was a spanking full of sound and fury that didn't hurt much. Besides, after Ma's anger subsided, she would hold me close and tell me how much she loved me, while expressing bewilderment at the variety of ways I found to misbehave; and then, with a hug, she'd say: "Go play!"

And off I would go until some new spasm of irrepressible energy got me entangled in some new form of naughtiness and the familiar cycle would start again.

While I was never sure exactly *how* she would respond, the one thing I could count on was that she *would* always, inevitably, unfailingly respond. Even when my father would say to her, "Ignore him,

Sadie, he's just trying to get your goat," she would shout, "Well he's got it," making a vigorous grab for me.

I vividly remember two childhood illnesses that were sufficiently serious to hospitalize me. One was an appendix operation. The other was a serious bout of scarlet fever. My sister remembers our going to Boston City Hospital on the streetcar, with me blazing hot with a temperature of 105 degrees. The hospital was a huge cavernous place, and my mother and Libby both cried when the nurse separated us and took me into the large children's ward. The only thing I remember is when they came to take me home, bringing presents and love.

It was shortly thereafter that Ma fell ill. To my eight-year-old self, the transformation could not have been more confusing and frustrating, especially Ma's unresponsiveness as her illness worsened. My Ma had always been as quick with her approval and praise as she was with her anger. Most of the time, I made her laugh or at least smile with my antics and horsing around and imaginings. She would exclaim with pride to whoever was around, "Look at how smart my Danele is," usually accompanied by a huge all-enveloping hug.

Then, abruptly, it didn't seem to matter to her what I did, good or bad, funny or pesty; she just looked at me listlessly. Even at that age I would have understood if someone had said, "Mama is sick." Having been hospitalized twice, I understood sickness. When you are very sick, as I had been, you go to the hospital. When you are just plain sick, you go to bed and people stick thermometers in you and urge you to have some nice chicken soup, it will do you good.

To my recollection, until the day of her death, she never spent any time overnight in a hospital. Nor do I recall her staying in bed at home as an obviously sick person. She was not sent to the hospital until the day before she died. For several months before then, she had grown paler and weaker by the day. But she was always fully dressed, and so surely not that sick (when you are really sick, you are supposed to get undressed for bed). She also grew more unresponsive to me and to my actions, whether good or bad.

I was desperate to get her attention and to recreate the status quo that gave me my safety and security. My Ma was the touchstone to which I turned for approval and validation, the ground of my emotional security and boyhood freedom.

In the weeks before she died, I remember going to extremes of acting out to get her attention. Once I angrily threw a handful of her cooking flour at her and it landed on her apron. But instead of the expected whack followed by hugs and reassurances, she just shook her head sadly and said, "Stop it, Danele."

I was totally bewildered. Our unspoken pact no longer operated. I could misbehave and nothing would happen. Nothing. No anger. No fury. No chasing. No punishment, but also no hugging and approval. Just a look of sadness and utter fatigue. Even when I deliberately provoked her, she would just shake her head and close her eyes. Sometimes she would mumble in a barely audible way, "What is to become of you?"

Then, one day, she was gone. The doctors at Boston City Hospital had told her to rest, but failed to tell her that she was sick unto death. When she died in the hospital in the cold bleak winter of 1932, my grief-stricken father ran through the halls of the hospital, shouting and screaming uncontrollably, "What have you done with my wife?"

My guess is that if our daily lives had returned to their familiar routine after Ma died, the terrifying impact of her death might have dissipated somewhat. But she died when the Depression had fully settled in, playing havoc with people's lives. All the relatives on both sides of the family were struggling with their own problems and couldn't offer us much help.

This series of shocks undermined the reality on which my stability depended: the abrupt end to my mother's unfailing attention, love and care; being obliged to live in homes where my existence was marginal instead of the center of attention; a father who became unable to perform what he regarded as his number one mission in life—providing for his family and keeping them together.

In retrospect, I think I am lucky to have avoided some the worst consequences of these kinds of shocks—delinquency, criminality, depression, addiction, and more. My father was sure that these horrors would take over my life, due to his supposed negligence.

I am sure that there are many reasons I was able to escape with just a few inconvenient neuroses. My own conviction is that in the long run, it was the grounding power of philosophy that helped me regain stability and a sense of direction.

One Damned Foster Home after Another

ON THE GRAY SHIVERY March day of my mother's funeral, my younger sister Libby and I went to stay temporarily with distant relatives. (My older half-sister from my father's first marriage went to live with other relatives.)

The Liebermans. Aunt Kate and her husband, Uncle Bill, were childless, and they welcomed us warmly. I have an enduring memory of their kindness to us. They lived in a large apartment in the run-down Dudley Street section of Boston, under the tracks of the elevated streetcar, constantly blocked from the sun. At that time, Dudley Street was almost entirely black. I was the only white kid in my class, and the only white boy in the entire school.

I had known a few black kids in my old school. I got along with them and didn't think much about race differences. I didn't realize that, as the minority student in the new school, I was supposed to act with deference to the others. And I guess I must have failed to do so, because during one afternoon recess, I pushed back at a black kid who had pushed me, and the struggle between us quickly escalated.

It soon involved all the kids in the playground, who were shouting insults and threats at me. Two teachers hustled me off of the playground and into the principal's office, where I was kept until Mrs. Lieberman was summoned.

At the time, my behavior at the school seemed entirely natural to me. One of the kids pushed me, so I pushed back. No big deal. Except that it turned out to be a big deal.

I had no sense of being in danger during the incident, but the adults took the matter more seriously. The principal told Mrs. Lieberman that it would not be safe for me to return to the school the next day. A few days later, Libby and I took our leave of the Liebermans and went back to live with Pa, who thought he could manage to take care of us, though he had to work most of the time.

I don't remember how long we stayed with Pa, but it was at least several months. I do recall that we were alone most of the time. We were free to do whatever we wanted, which wasn't as much fun as I had expected it to be because I didn't know what it was that I wanted to do with my new-found freedom. (Libby recalls us staying out in the street until after nine at night.)

The one clear memory I have of that period—a pleasurable one— is related to my Cousin Frieda. Frieda and her brother Ben were our second or third cousins, considerably older than Libby and me. Ben was a large man, warm and friendly. He was a master plumber and made a decent living. His sister Frieda was about eighteen or nineteen at the time. She often took me to school and to the apartment she shared with Ben, who was away at work most of the time.

One afternoon after school I remember Frieda insisting on bathing me in her bathtub and soaping me with her hands all over my body. I recall having an erection when she washed those parts, and being embarrassed and fascinated at the same time. My mother had frequently bathed and washed me, but Frieda's ablutions were different. It was my first conscious encounter with erotic life, and I discovered it to be exceedingly agreeable. My recollection is that Frieda laughed at my embarrassment and approached the whole bathing experience with much gaiety.

Shortly thereafter, Libby and I were hustled off to our first paid foster home under the auspices of the Jewish Child Welfare Agency.

The series of foster homes to which I was sent after Ma died never felt like *home*. My desperate quest for home (one of the easiest things to take away from someone) coexisted side by side with the fierce desire for something that could *never* be taken away. I constantly lived with the anxiety that those on whom I most depended might disappear overnight. That anxiety stirred up all sorts of heavy-duty questions in my eight-year-old mind.

- Why Mama and not someone else?
- Was she really in heaven, as I was repeatedly assured? If so, what was it like? Did she have anyone to keep her company? Did she miss us?
- Was *I* responsible for her death? (More than once in her frustration, she had yelled, "You will be the death of me!")
- Why did something called the Depression make my father unable to keep our family together? Why was the Depression happening and why did it hurt our family so badly?
- Were we being punished? If so, for what? And why was the punishment so terrible?

Over time, these childish questions gave rise to broader, less personal ones:

- Do life-shattering events like my mother's death happen by chance or are they part of some broader scheme of meaning? What could that meaning be and must it be so cruel?
- How should a person live his (or her) life so that he understands what is happening to him?
- Is there any way of living that gives one a bit more control over fate?
- What is fate anyway?

- Is there any part of life that one can depend on, that can't be arbitrarily taken away?

It was this last question (a yearning for something that can never be taken away) that eventually nudged me in the direction of the world of ideas. My possessions, my home, and even my loved ones might be snatched away. But the ideas in my head could never be. That was my barely conscious assumption in response to the anxiety of losing home and mother's love.

The years from ages eight through twelve, the five unstable years following Ma's death, form a large blur in my mind. All the foster homes in those years are jumbled together, as are all of the various reasons my tenure at some of them was short-lived. My sister Libby has an equally blurred recollection of those years (she was only six when Ma died). We cannot recall the number of foster homes that took us in, together or separately, or how long we stayed at each. Libby estimates that there was a total of fourteen. My count is much lower, closer to five or six.

My memory of those years is not one of painful unhappiness. I really don't think I was constantly unhappy. Confused, yes. Anxious, yes. Difficult to manage, for sure. But I was not actively miserable, as I was in the few months preceding Ma's death and several times in later stages of my life.

THE MAZURS—MY FIRST FOSTER HOME

My father's older sister, my Aunt Rica, insisted that my father call the Jewish Child Welfare Agency for help in placing us in homes where we could be properly cared for. When Pa resisted, she said she would take Libby, her "darling," into her own home, and that the welfare agency would find a "nice home" for me where I would receive the care I needed. (This rejection didn't surprise me. I expected it, but it hurt anyway.)

A week or so later, a young woman from the agency, Miss Luftman, came to visit us and when she left she took me and my suitcase with her to my first foster home.

I got to know Miss Luftman fairly well over the next few years, as she transferred me from one foster home to another with some regularity. She was unfailingly supportive and friendly, even though I knew that some of the foster parents had complained about my being "unmanageable" and "too much for them to put up with."

My recollection of the "parents" at that first foster home is that they looked gray and defeated and that their house smelled. I don't think anything dramatic happened to separate me from them. We hardly spoke to one another. I didn't know what to say to them and they didn't know what to say to me. I was probably somewhat sullen and withdrawn. Whenever my father came to pick me up on Sundays, though, abruptly I became transformed from an unresponsive lump into a laughing, happy, active boy.

Not that Pa and I spent Sundays doing fun things. We would alternate between visits to his sister Aunt Rica and his older brother, Uncle Morris. We couldn't visit the two of them together because they were carrying on an unrelenting feud and had not spoken to each other for decades.

I never learned what the feud was all about, because Pa didn't want to talk about it. Aunt Rica was the most affluent member of the family. Her husband had built a successful business, the Crystal Coal and Oil Company, which I believe still exists. She would occasionally press ten or twenty dollars on Pa, who hated to take it but swallowed his pride and did so.

Uncle Morris was not affluent, but not poor. He owned a small candy store, an attraction that was far from negligible in enhancing my visits to him. He had arrived in the United States a decade or so before my father did. He had left behind a considerable debt that he owed to people in Russia. A man of honor, he insisted on paying every kopek of it over a period of years, even though he could have sloughed it off.

I was impressed by the fact that right after Sunday "dinner" at two o'clock, he would remove his clothes, take to his bed, and enjoy a two-hour nap.

At the time it seemed like an eccentric thing to do.

The Silvermans

Miss Luftman had said that the Mazur family would provide a good foster home. But it didn't feel like a real home to me. It just felt like a place I didn't belong, where I had been parked because there was no other place for me. I was relieved when Miss Luftman arrived unexpectedly one weekend and took my suitcase and me to my next foster home with Dr. and Mrs. Silverman. (Dr. Silverman was a dentist.)

The Silvermans were an improvement. They didn't seem as old and gray and removed from life as the Mazurs, and their house didn't smell. Best of all, Libby joined me and came to live with the Silvermans.

On our first night, Dr. Silverman sat us down in their living room, where all the furniture was draped in covers, and told us that we were charity children and that we were supposed to do everything Mrs. Silverman told us to do.

Thereafter, Libby and I both tried our best to do Mrs. Silverman's bidding, but she didn't really have very much to say to us, nor did we have much to say to her. At dinners, Dr. and Mrs. Silverman would talk to each other, but Libby and I would mostly eat in silence. We would ask permission to leave the table at the earliest opportunity, and permission was granted almost before it was asked.

I had the impression that in taking us into their home, Dr. and Mrs. Silverman were carrying out some sort of implicit obligation. They weren't comfortable with children and didn't have any of their own. Unlike later foster parents, they didn't seem to be taking on the foster home burden solely for the welfare money—twenty-five dollars a month per child. But being at ease with children was emphatically not their strong suit.

Though my memories of the Silverman months are blurry, I recall one incident with striking clarity. It was an act of kindness on Mrs. Silverman's part. One Saturday she explained to me that since the welfare agency had provided a small budget for our clothing, she would take me shopping and let me pick out a sweater and a pair of pants for myself. I was overjoyed. I tried on endless sweaters, liking all of them.

Finally, I chose a soft blue woolly angora sweater that I thought was the ultimate in sweater chic. I wore that sweater in all seasons and on every conceivable occasion and did not abandon it until it was in shreds. It instilled in me a love of sweaters—the only article of clothing to which I am partial. People who know me know that if they are looking for a gift for my birthday, they can't go wrong with a sweater. To this day I have accumulated more sweaters than any other article of clothing.

The sweater was not even the highlight of the shopping trip. The pants claimed that honor. Up to that day, at age nine, I had never worn anything but short pants or knickers, so I was overjoyed when Mrs. Silverman gave me permission to pick out a pair of long pants for myself—my first ever. Those long pants came to symbolize for me that I was no longer a little kid, and that I could at last begin to shift for myself.

In fact, during my foster home years I experienced many acts of kindness. One other memory of kindness from that era, a much more affectionate one, was linked to school.

My fourth grade teacher, Mrs. Ellis, totally won my heart and loyalty. All teachers of that era (except in mechanical arts) were women and all were called "Miss." Only Mrs. Ellis was a "Mrs." She must have loved children. I know of no better explanation for her unfailing kindness to all the kids in her class. We all loved her.

Even when we were in the fifth grade and no longer in her class, we visited her—in her home as well as in her classroom. I have no memory of what she did, or said, or taught. I just remember the warmth of her smile and her interested way of talking with each of us, as she beamed at our answers to her questions, however childish they may have been. She was a wonderful human being: an adult who loved children and was in turn loved by them.

I integrated these acts of kindness into my attitude toward the wider world. I knew that a vast world existed beyond my immediate experience, a world largely indifferent or often hostile to my interests and desires. We were constantly made aware of the anti-Jewish feeling that existed in the larger Boston community outside of our small ghetto-like neighborhood. And even as children we were made aware of the anti-Semitism in the larger world, as Hitler's fascism took hold in Europe.

Experiences of random kindness, like these from Mrs. Silverman and Mrs. Ellis, were oases that slaked my camel-like thirst for affection and attention. They may have been rare, but they did exist and they remain alive and fresh in my memory. Rotten things can happen to you without warning, but so can good things.

Libby and I did not always know why we were moved from one foster home to another. Apparently, the welfare agency wanted to keep us together, and it's likely that Libby had to schlep from one foster home to another because of my misdeeds.

I have no recollection of how long Libby and I stayed with the Silvermans or the reason for our departure. My guess is that it had to do with my "violence." Somewhere along the line, I seemed to have been labeled as having "a tendency toward violence." The phrase sticks in my mind, as if someone informed me that I was now officially labeled as such in the records of the welfare agency.

The violence consisted of me losing my temper, using foul language, and sometimes throwing things. I am sure that this description is correct, though I don't think my temper outbursts ever hurt anyone except myself.

Unfortunately, whatever effectiveness my temper might have had as a survival skill was undercut by my tendency to close my eyes when I was really angry. When I got into a street fight with other boys—not an infrequent occurrence—closing my eyes put me at an enormous disadvantage, and I lost most of the time. These losses lowered my self-confidence even further, making me even more prone to lose control of my temper.

I do remember Mrs. Silverman telling Miss Luftman that she was concerned about the bad influence some of the boys I played with might have on me. They were older than me; some of them smoked, and they sometimes got in trouble with the police. I played ball with them and I liked them, without being tempted to do the things that got them into trouble. Mrs. Silverman seemed genuinely worried and I appreciated that, but I resented her bad-mouthing my friends.

I felt Miss Luftman and I were friends, and I came to learn the routine of being moved from one foster home to another all too well. On one of her frequent visits to see how we were doing, I seized the opportunity to talk to her.

As she was leaving, I went outside with her and asked if we could be moved to the home of distant relatives: my "aunt" Kate Lieberman's sister, Rose Friedman, and Rose's husband Jack. Miss Luftman said in her usual considerate way that she would look into it and try to make it happen. And indeed within a matter of weeks she proved successful.

For taking us in, Aunt Rose received twenty-five dollars a month for each of us from the welfare agency—a nontrivial amount of money in the midst of the Depression.

For the first time since Ma's death three years earlier, I felt that I had played a role in shaping our fate, and the experience made me feel less like a victim and more like someone able to take action on his own behalf.

It was a good feeling.

Aunt Rose and Uncle Jack

I assumed that Aunt Rose would be as kind to us as her older sister, Aunt Kate, had been immediately after my mother's death.

Libby and I were overjoyed with our first few days. The Friedmans lived in a large house on a wide tree-lined street in Mattapan, at that time an older, relatively affluent section of Boston. I shared a room with their son, George, who was about three years older than me. Libby shared the girls' bedroom with her two cousins: Frances, who was her own age (nine), and Devorah, who was my age (eleven).

Aunt Rose overwhelmed us with her enthusiasm at our arrival. She kept repeating how happy it made her that we had come to live with her. And she really seemed happy to have us—an experience we had not enjoyed at any other foster home.

After a few days, however, some minor tensions erupted. Uncle Jack was a gloomy, largely silent presence who lived in the shadow of his dynamic wife. He had a bulbous nose and a rotten disposition, and he was strikingly ugly as well as morose. At dinner, the only time he spoke was to tell me that I was eating too much bread. It was a humiliating experience and it made me self-conscious thereafter whenever I reached for a piece of bread.

His older daughter, Devorah, looked like her father (alas) and took after him in temperament as well. We took an instant dislike to each other.

Several months after I moved into his bedroom, George got into the habit of coming over to my bed and touching various parts of my body. I didn't like it at all, and I made my dislike unmistakably clear. I don't think George was homosexual. I think he was in an experimental phase, trying things out. But I had a strong aversion to being fondled by a boy. (Cousin Frieda had been an entirely different matter.)

George treated my rejection of his advances as a rejection of him personally, which it really was not. I liked George and would have liked to be his friend. But after I repelled his advances we grew quite distant from one another.

It soon became apparent that Uncle Jack and the three Friedman children were bit players in the household. The center of attention, the superstar in the family, the sun around whom the other planets revolved, was Aunt Rose.

To say that she had a strong personality is to understate by orders of magnitude. To everyone who would listen, she explained how good-hearted and generous she was. Good-hearted to a fault. Generous to the detriment of her own family and her own health. She explained how willing she was to sacrifice herself for the sake of those two poor motherless children who couldn't appreciate everything she was doing for them.

Her rave reviews of her own selflessness and generosity went on unrelentingly, and somehow she managed to develop a chorus of yea-sayers in addition to the immediate members of the family. The chorus sang her praises, marveled at her generosity and goodness, and encouraged her recitative, which became ever more elaborate. She could have walked out of the pages of a Molière satire.

Happily for us, she believed her own self-appraisal and most of the time did go out of her way to be considerate, especially if it made for a good story that she could share later with her sisters (a key part of the chorus) and others.

In my daily routine, I avoided Uncle Jack as much as possible. George and I had our own friends, and though he never forgave me for rejecting his advances, we found it possible to go our own ways without conflict. I liked the school I attended. I loved the neighborhood and had lots of friends with whom I skated, played ball and checkers, and hung out.

But the older Friedman daughter, Devorah, clearly resented the fact that Libby and I were taking up physical and emotional space in her home and were receiving attention from her mother that was rightfully due her. She knew I had trouble keeping my temper, and she constantly goaded me, cleverly saying or doing things she knew would get under my skin.

One day I got into a shouting match with her. She kept taunting me, calling me a liar and a coward and an ungrateful, selfish pig who took advantage of her mother's goodness. Agitated, I picked up the nearest object at hand, which happened to be a heavy wooden bookend, and threatened her with it if she didn't stop. Of course, the threat egged her on and she dared me to throw it.

"I dare you," she screamed. "You are too much of a coward to throw it, aren't you? You are the orphan boy coward, aren't you? The liar coward, aren't you? The sneaky coward, aren't you? Coward! *Coward! COWARD!!*"

So I obliged and threw the bookend at her.

She easily ducked and it fell to the floor. But now she had the proof she needed to convince her mother that I was too violent and uncontrolled to live with them, because the next time, I might not miss. It was a powerful argument that made a deep impression, even on me.

I felt that Devorah had prevailed through cunning, and I had been her naïve dupe. If I were ever to gain some control over my life and destiny, I certainly had chosen the wrong way to do so. No more impulsive loss of temper. Ever. No further adherence to the assumption that I would receive equal treatment even though I was an outsider. I became permanently disabused of that illusion.

It took the lesson of Devorah's cunning a long time to sink in, but it eventually did: if you want any hope of shaping your own destiny, you have to keep your cool.

And Devorah accomplished her goal. A few days later, Miss Luftman appeared. Libby stayed with Aunt Rose and Uncle Jack and I was off to my next foster home, carrying my slightly larger suitcase with the blue angora sweater.

My new foster parents were to be Mr. and Mrs. Smith.

The experience of lurching from one foster home to another inevitably raised a series of questions in my young mind. I didn't know it at the time, but they were essentially philosophical questions. What do I really care about? What is truly important in life? What could I expect from myself and from others?

The reach of one's caring is an ideal philosophical starting point. That reach may encompass family and friends, old neighborhoods, ethnic and religious bonds, core values, ideals, attachments to schools and colleges, your immediate community and "tribe," and patriotism to the nation. I eventually came to learn that a key purpose of a philosophy of life is to keep you focused on what really matters. In a brief lifespan, it is not easy to discover the core essentials of life. And it is even more difficult to stay focused on them without distraction.

The Pumpernickel Bread with the Hollow Center

BEING BANISHED FROM THE Friedmans' household to a new foster home with total strangers was a painful and humiliating experience. I felt a shameful sense of failure. I did not arrive at my new foster home with the Smiths in a sunny state of mind.

At the same time, I also felt the thrill of starting a new life chapter. Any novel experience stimulated and excited me. Now there would be new friends to make, a new school to try, a new neighborhood to explore, and who knew what other promising possibilities.

Most important in reducing my anxiety and sense of shame was the warm way in which my new foster parents welcomed me into their home. Mr. and Mrs. Smith were both in their late forties. With their daughter, Ida, who was twenty-two years old and engaged to be married, they lived in a five-room walk-up apartment on the top floor of a three-story building. Their apartment was located in the heart of Dorchester, near Blue Hill Avenue, the vibrant and teeming nerve center of what in the 1930s was still a mixed Irish and Jewish lower middle-class neighborhood.

Both Mr. and Mrs. Smith had come to the United States from Russia in their teens when they were still single, and both still spoke with heavy Yiddish accents. Both had come with unpronounceable Russian Jewish names that the immigration authorities on Ellis Island decided to change. He became "Sam Smith" and she became

"Mary Rosen." When she and Sam married, she automatically became Mary Smith. Rarely has there existed a more improbable "Mary Smith." She was matronly, unfashionable, and distinctively Yiddish in her manners and outlook.

She was quite matter-of-fact in taking me into her home. She explained that Ida would soon be married and move to her own place, freeing up a bedroom that she felt should not go to waste at a time when people had to struggle to survive. She told me that she and her husband owned a small bakery. She took care of it, and Mr. Smith handled bakery deliveries between six and eight in the morning before going off to his full-time job at a furniture repair shop.

Mr. Smith was warm and friendly, but uncommunicative. He had a large potbelly that went with a hearty laugh whenever he found life funny, which he often did. But he was so busy and absent most of the time that I felt I hardly knew him, though I liked him a lot.

Mrs. Smith told me that they would be very busy and she hoped I would be able to look out for myself and not expect a lot of attention. I assured her that I could take care of myself. I wanted to find some part-time work to earn a little spending money for myself.

True to her word, both she and Mr. Smith were busy all day, from before sunrise until they fell asleep exhausted shortly after their supper. Except, that is, for Sunday mornings. On Sundays they would sleep late (until about eight o'clock in the morning), whereupon Mrs. Smith would go about preparing an unbelievably scrumptious brunch. She would sauté eggs and hash brown potatoes together and serve them with blintzes and sour cream, plus generous helpings of smoked salmon, whitefish, pickled herrings, and bagels fresh from the bakery.

For the Smiths, those Sunday brunches were just about their only indulgence and luxury, a time when they could recuperate and prepare themselves for another arduous week. For me, they were just plain delicious. They came to represent the archetype of *what brunch should be*, and it has taken me decades to scale down Sunday mornings to ordinary human breakfast proportions.

I was surprised to find myself immediately at home at the Smiths, even though I had to sleep on a sofa in the living room because Ida Smith was not due to be married for another four months. I had the delightful prospect of eventually getting my own room. Also, the Smiths seemed to accept me more readily than the other foster homes had, and they didn't seem to have been told that I was a troublemaker with an uncontrollable temper. Or if they had, it didn't seem to matter to them, which was even better. So my mood cheered considerably as I settled into my new home.

I liked my new neighborhood, though it was a socioeconomic step down from the Friedmans'. No tree-lined streets. No spacious house with lots of nooks and crannies. In fact, no single family houses at all, only three- and four-story apartment walk-ups. But there were more kids in the neighborhood. And it was easy to get into a touch football game in front of the apartment houses. We played in the middle of the road, but there were so few cars that traffic rarely interrupted our game. In fact, at any given time, there was almost always some sort of ball game going on in front of almost every house. Only freezing weather kept the players indoors. And newcomers like myself were automatically welcomed into the game.

I did, however, have a problem at school. When I was living with the Friedmans, the local school had put me in the "mechanic arts" track, which unbeknownst to me was the bottom of the academic barrel. Students who were college-bound were assigned to the top academic track. Those not deemed college material were assigned to the "commercial," or middle track. Students who didn't seem to qualify for either of the upper tracks were dumped into "mechanic arts" where they learned how to saw wood, screw screws, and strip and splice electric wires. I think I was tossed into mechanic arts because when they asked me what I wanted to be when I grew up, I had answered "engineer," because my father had suggested it.

My new junior high school near the Smiths' apartment had the same tracking system. I requested a transfer to the academic track, but was turned down on the bureaucratic grounds that no student could be permitted to jump two tracks without undermining the entire Boston school system.

The authorities did agree to let me advance one step up to the commercial track, but I was unhappy with that decision. My math-inclined cousin, Danny Mostow, had made me aware of the world of higher education (his father, my Uncle Isaac who used to argue with my mother all the time, was a college-trained lawyer). I had come to the conclusion that it would be great to go to college. Provisionally, I settled into the dull commercial track (mechanic arts had been far more engaging), but kept inquiring of friends and teachers as to how I might find a way to attend college eventually.

After school every day I had to go to Hebrew school to prepare for my bar mitzvah. It was to take place at the end of December, approximately four months from the time I was sent to live with the Smiths. The Hebrew school was in the basement of the local synagogue, in a dreary room filled with uncomfortable metal folding chairs.

The Hebrew teacher carried a strong wooden ruler that he used to rap the knuckles of any boys who were not paying attention or were talking to each other or were mispronouncing the unpronounce-able Hebrew words whose meaning forever remained a mystery to all those boys on the cusp of manhood (for that is what "bar mitzvah" signifies).

Needless to say, the cracking sound of knuckle-rapping and the accompanying student howls were a constant accompaniment to the Hebrew lesson. The knuckle-raps really hurt. The sadistic and poorly paid Hebrew teacher vented his frustration on us mercilessly. If his aim was to instill religious fervor in us, he couldn't have planned a more perverse effect. Indeed, the combination of my father's skepticism towards religious rituals and the Hebrew school preparation for my bar mitzvah turned me off to all sectarian forms of religion.

After school, I sometimes hung around the Smiths' bakery, graciously agreeing to consume a piece of chocolate seven-layer cake or a custard-filled éclair before walking home.

I noticed that sometimes after a customer had left the store Mrs. Smith would go to the back of the bakery and take a round pumpernickel bread from the top shelf. She then proceeded to open the pumpernickel which, like a jack-o'-lantern, turned out to have a hollow center. The center was stuffed with small pieces of paper. Mrs. Smith would then add a new piece of paper to the slips of paper already in the pumpernickel.

Once, when she saw me observing her, she smiled and put her finger to her lips: *Shhhh!* I later learned that the Smiths augmented their meager income by dealing in the numbers game. One of the very few recreations for the hard-working men and women of Dorchester was to bet on the numbers. You bet a dime or a quarter or a half dollar on a four-digit number that changed daily. (The winning number was reported in the local newspapers because it was somehow related to the horse races.) If you "hit" the number you had selected, the odds were terrific, something like seven hundred to one. Lots of conversations revolved around how Mr. Horowitz or Mrs. Bloom had hit the number a few weeks ago and had been richly rewarded.

Playing the numbers was of course illegal, but nobody thought it was wrong. There was a clear difference between the two concepts.

One day while I was lollygagging around the bakery, a big Irish cop came in. My heart was pounding, and I was afraid that he was about to arrest Mrs. Smith.

But he just paused to "buy" some rolls. He walked out of the bakery with a large bag of rolls and a blueberry pie. No money changed hands. Then, just as he was leaving, he said, "Oh, I almost forgot." He mumbled something to Mrs. Smith, handed her a quarter and left. Whereupon Mrs. Smith hastened to take out a small piece of paper, write something on it and stuff it into the pumpernickel.

The enforcer of the Law had almost forgotten to play his number for the day.

I have two vivid memories of my bar mitzvah—one sad, the other joyful.

My father had scraped together enough money so that we could celebrate my bar mitzvah in style. Since Pa didn't have a home of his own to host the celebration (he was reluctant to impose on the Smiths), we would have it at the synagogue. The rabbi had assured him that it was the right thing to do. On the day of the ceremony Pa had paid the synagogue caterer to stock the basement reception area with enough delicacies so that immediately after the service, all the guests could come downstairs for a festive lunch. So, almost immediately following my traditional "today I am a man" bar mitzvah speech, we all went down to the basement to celebrate.

I was busy being congratulated, so I was a little late in coming downstairs. As soon as I saw my father's face, I knew something was dreadfully wrong. He looked almost as grief-stricken as he had when Ma died. And just minutes earlier he had been happy and jovial.

It took me a while to realize what had happened. The synagogue was a haven for destitute old men who hung around because they had no other place to go. For some reason or another—the rabbi was not able to explain what happened—no one was guarding the food during the bar mitzvah service. So while I was busy speechifying about my new exalted status as a "man," the hungry old men had wolfed down all the pickled herring and bagels and kugel and rugelach and other Yiddish goodies Pa had paid for with his meager savings.

He took it very badly. Pa believed in signs. And here was yet another sign that his Job-like travails were not yet done, despite all of the suffering and loss he had already experienced. He had been treating my bar mitzvah as a sign of redemption—a change for the better in his luck—and it made him happy. Now, once again, Fate had kicked him in the ass when he least expected it.

The loss of food for the reception didn't trouble me particularly. I enjoyed being the center of attention, and I was thrilled that I would never have to go to Hebrew school again. I did feel bad for my father because I knew how much it meant to him, even though it would be many years before I was able to understand fully the pathos of the event as seen through his eyes. But whatever sadness I may have felt disappeared the moment I walked into the Smiths' apartment after the services were over and saw standing majestically in the middle of the living room the most gorgeous and awesome bicycle that had ever been built!

The Smiths knew how I had yearned for a bicycle, and for my thirteenth birthday—a few months after I came to live with them—they bought me just the kind of bike I wanted. Never had I been more surprised and delighted. The joy I felt was not just for the bike. I realized right away that the price of the bike had to exceed the monthly stipend the Smiths received for taking care of me. And that meant that they had taken me into their home not just for the money, and that they really cared about me.

It was the first time I had felt that way since my mother had died five years earlier. I rushed into the bathroom where no one could see me sobbing with relief and joy. Every day when it wasn't freezing cold, I took my bike to nearby Franklin Park and rode it as long as time permitted. I learned how to ride without holding onto the handlebars and took pride in my ability to balance myself just with my feet on the bike's pedals. Some of my happiest days were spent riding my bike in the wooded areas of Franklin Park.

A View from the Fringe

SOON THEREAFTER MY HOPES for acceptance as a full-fledged member of the Smith family suffered a setback. Instead of Ida leaving the apartment when she got married, she decided to remain there with her new husband Mike, an auto mechanic.

Out the window went my chances of having my own room. Moreover, Ida's attitude toward me was much less benign than her parents'. She regarded me as a nuisance who didn't belong in the house and who was often in her way. When I wasn't in the living room, she would talk about me in a loud voice that she knew perfectly well I could hear. I began to feel uncomfortable when she was around, and as a result I spent less and less time in the Smiths' apartment.

Eventually, Ida and Mike did move out, and at last I had a room of my own. But a few months later, to my surprise and dismay, Mrs. Smith informed me that they were bringing new boarders into the apartment—a recent widower and his two sons. And they were to have my room, since there was no other place to put them.

I took this announcement badly. I didn't say much in response. What could I say?

If I had been the Smiths' real son, not a foster child, I was sure that they would have found a way for me to keep the room, or at the very least talked to me in advance about their intention of renting it. I had lulled myself into a false sense of belonging and security.

Sleeping on the living room couch was not a genuine hardship. I had been doing it for several years, and it didn't inconvenience me in any serious way. It was the meaning I attributed to the event that was the crushing blow. I had grown very comfortable at the Smiths. I had come to feel that I was a real member of the family. The Smiths' action brought me back to reality.

My response, which permitted me to continue to live amicably with the Smiths, was to become less dependent on them emotionally. But I grew more anxious about the future and about my relationships with others. I tried to see my father more frequently, and I spent as much time as possible with friends whom I came to regard as family.

After Mr. Robbins and his two sons moved in, the apartment became impossibly crowded, and I spent even less time there. My main recollection of Mr. Robbins was that he owned a classy 1935 Buick with marvelous grillwork.

Gradually, my relations with the Smiths became strained. We were cordial with one another, but I felt a subtle but definite distance grow up between us. I'm sure the fault was mainly mine. In my eagerness to recreate a real home, I had leapt too far too fast. I had lulled myself into a false sense of security, of feeling like a real member of the family. My expectations had grown unrealistic. It wasn't the Smiths' fault. But as a consequence, I found myself growing more inward and reserved in my feelings.

This was a brutal lesson in reality; it created a decisive shift in my psyche. Without being wholly aware of it, I began to give up on finding love and home again, and instead shifted my focus to self-understanding.

I didn't realize at the time that I was making an existential decision. I was changing what I cared about: a key philosophical shift in the nature of my Being.

The search for self-understanding is less familiar than the search for love and home. For me, in many ways it proved as intense as the quest for love and home, perhaps because it was a partial substitute for them. It took me many years to recognize that sublimations are substitutes.

At every stage of life I confronted choices between what I wanted and what I was obliged to accept as a substitute. Often the substitutes were satisfying and even lifesavers. But one should see them as substitutes, and be prepared to embrace the real thing should the opportunity arise.[4]

It was at about this point in my teens that I began to think of life as a quest. For a long time the object of the quest was inchoate, more expressive of raw feelings than coherent thought. The desire for love and home is hardwired into our being. No values are more deeply human or more universal. The only variation among people is the intensity of their striving. Those fortunate to have enjoyed a happy childhood strive to replicate it later in life, more often than not with success. They know what they want and move toward it on automatic pilot. Those with unhappy childhoods have a harder time: they are less clear about how to create the conditions for love and the emotional security of home.

There is, sadly, nothing unusual about having had a stressful childhood because of a broken home. Millions of people can look back on childhood traumas far worse than mine. But even mild childhood traumas mark one for life, especially when changes in circumstances at an impressionable age fling a child from one extreme to another.

This time, I believe, marked the beginning of my interest in philosophy. Self-understanding grows along with a need for autonomy. Being dumped into the school's mechanic arts track and labeled as "non-college material" did not have to be my destiny.

I also came to appreciate the many sources of satisfaction as well as frustration. The kindness of Mrs. Silverman and Mrs. Ellis were

---

4   Cited in *Wicked Problems, Workable Solutions: Lessons from a Public Life* (New York: Rowman and Littlefield, 2015), 196.

not one-off affairs. I kept encountering acts of kindness throughout those foster home years. The grandest of all the many acts of kindness was the bicycle that the Smiths purchased for me.

I gradually came to realize that randomness is not necessarily bad. Random acts of kindness, out of the blue, taught me that not every surprise spelled disaster. On the contrary, life could be exciting and full of positive as well as negative surprises.

The thrown bookend, and Devorah's manipulation of my emotions, proved an unforgettable learning experience. It taught me that my anger, however justified in my own eyes, could be used against me.

The Irish cop playing the numbers at the Smiths' Jewish bakery was an eye-opener. It was one of my first insights that the "system" was flexible on many fronts—a lesson that was to be repeated in the army time and time again.

I also discovered that once I accepted the role of outsider I was no longer in danger of slipping into defeatism and self-pity. My life had become too interesting for the total self-absorption that self-pity requires.

I developed what one might call a *view from the fringe*, a view that provides an alternative way of connecting to reality. The sense of connectedness that gives meaning to the lives of most people comes from their relationships to others, from the hard-earned decency they bring to life's everyday problems, and from the religious beliefs that give them comfort and guidance.

People on the inside have less need than those on the fringe to formulate a specific social philosophy for relating to the larger society. Outsiders like me are obliged to develop explicit philosophies for ourselves.

An Outsider's Consolation Prize

BEING SHUNTED FROM ONE foster home to another raised questions in my mind about what my various foster parents really wanted and expected. Questions about the world and relationships of my foster parents—their motives, my own self-identity, the meaning of virtue and character, the goals of living, the things that are really important in life—these big questions took hold in my mind in rudimentary form in those chaotic foster home years.

I found these attempts to understand what was happening to me consoling. Pondering these larger questions dulled the pain of loss. When I reflected on them, it was as if I were able to shift to another plane of existence, a place of serenity rather than turmoil.

I discovered that I could contemplate chaos in the outside world without being overwhelmed by chaos within. From these early years of boyhood, I experienced the world of thought and philosophy as a gift, a consolation prize.

Throughout my life, that gift has kept on giving. The home-and-love aspects of my quest proved elusive for many long years. But from the boyhood onward, I found the thinking aspects of life deeply absorbing, intensified as they were by my exposure to philosophy in college some years later. I am astonished when I think of the many benefits I received from my passion for philosophy over long spans of years and decades.

When I reflect on the benefits of a philosophical perspective for me personally, the following come to mind:

- Emotionally, my pursuit of philosophy may well have saved me from depression as I was banished from one foster home after another and came to feel increasingly isolated. Thinking philosophically became a way for me to overcome isolation and rejection.
- It helped make not finding home and love tolerable.
- It helped me avoid self-pity—the most corrosive of all emotions. I found the need to understand the plight I was in so compelling that I was constantly deflected from feeling sorry for myself.
- Over time, it led me to an abundance of writings and ideas that I have come to cherish and to which I return over and over again.
- It encouraged me to develop a broad synoptic worldview, rather than a narrow specialist's perspective.
- It helped me to develop cognitive skills that have enriched my work as well as my life: for example, skill in conducting dialogue, in bringing unexamined assumptions to the surface, in listening attentively to others, in remaining open to a wide range of points of view, and in integrating perspectives from a variety of disciplines.
- It helped me develop the empathy I needed to help others understand when they were trapped in narrow, self-destructive frameworks, and how to escape from them.

My attachment to philosophy gradually gave rise to a desire to make my own distinctive contribution to the world of thought.

The first step in preparing myself came in an unexpected form.

The Boston Latin School

AS I WITHDREW EMOTIONALLY from the Smiths, I made more friends in the neighborhood and spent as much time with them as possible. One day my friend Hersh told me that he was planning to leave our local school to attend the Boston Latin School. He explained that the Boston Latin School was a public school that had been in Boston forever. (It was the oldest public school in the United States, having been founded in 1636, the year before Harvard was founded.) Hersh had discovered that it was free to any Boston resident who could pass an entrance exam.

The Boston Latin School, Hersh said, was a hard grind because it prepared boys for college. Since he wanted badly to go to college, he had taken the exam and passed it. So the following semester he would be leaving our school for the Boston Latin School.

I punched him in the arm and asked him why he hadn't told me about it earlier, since it was just what I was looking for. He was a bit sheepish in his response, saying he wasn't sure that someone like myself from the mechanic arts and commercial tracks could pass the exam. So I punched him in the arm again.

The next day Hersh brought me the information about when and where I could take the exam. I was nervous before the exam, because I was afraid that Hersh might be correct and that the mechanic arts and commercial tracks had doomed me. But the exam itself proved to be easy, and I knew as soon as I completed it that I was going to be OK. One semester after Hersh's departure from our junior high, I too felt the excitement of taking the streetcar for the long ride to the Boston Latin School.

Once again, I had escaped from what seemed like a dead end—the commercial track at school—and was able to savor the prospect of possibly going on to college.

Admission to the Boston Latin School meant that I had to pay carfare every day for streetcar and subway rides. They didn't cost much, but I had zero money and knew that I would have to find part-time work. Mr. Smith suggested that I accompany him on his deliveries from six to eight each morning and said he would pay me for running up and down the steps of the three-family houses where he had to make deliveries. I went with him for a few weeks, but after falling asleep in class almost every day, I figured that I had better find some after-school work.

My closest friend, Nat Hentoff (who subsequently became a noted jazz critic and civil rights writer), suggested I take an exam to qualify me to work where he himself was working, in a candy store named Sunday's Candies.

At first I thought he was joking. Take an exam to serve customers in a candy store? For what purpose? To multiply the number of chocolates with fudge centers by the number of those with caramel centers? When I finished my sarcastic juvenile rant, Nat assured me that he wasn't kidding and that he wasn't too sure I could pass the exam.

A few weeks later I found myself taking the exam in the back room of S2, near Franklin Park. (Mr. Caploe, the owner of Sunday's Candies, had taken a course in business administration and had named his three stores S1, S2, and S3, so sure was he that S4, S5, and S6 would follow.)

To my astonishment, I found the exam for the job of waiting on chocolate-buying customers much more difficult than the exam for admission to the Boston Latin School. But I managed to pass, and shortly thereafter found myself employed after school along with Nat and a remarkable set of boys, most of whom were paid like myself at the rate of 32.2 cents an hour—and all the chocolates they craved. A few of the older boys, including a Harvard divinity graduate student, had been promoted to store manager and were paid an extravagant 35 cents an hour.

Between unlimited access to the Smiths' bakery and Sunday's excellent candies, I grew a bit chubby. In his delightful book, *Boston Boy*, Nat Hentoff has written memorably about those many months we all worked together at Sunday's Candies. So I won't repeat his yarns of that remarkable era except to say that rarely has there existed a weirder alumni association than the graduates of Sam Caploe's chocolate "university."

The job at Sunday's Candies was one of a number of ways I earned money while going to Boston Latin. I also worked as a floorwalker at a W. T. Grant five-and-ten-cent store. It was my job to supply the sales-girls with change and services whenever they needed assistance. The salesgirls were quite capable of providing their own assistance, but the system that prevailed at the time required the floorwalkers to be male, however callow and inexperienced, and those who served cus-tomers to be female.

My favorite part-time job by a wide margin was selling lemon-ade and candies in theatres during the intermissions of a play, or in the case of the Old Howard Theatre, during the intermission of their burlesque shows.

I not only got to see many legitimate shows in their Boston try-outs, but also the Old Howard's strippers doing their burlesque num-bers, usually including at least one stripper who twirled tassels from her nipples in imitation of the famous Sally Keith.

Whenever I went backstage to replenish my supply of candies and lemonade (it's astonishing how often I needed to replenish them), I invariably received a pat or two from the performers as they rushed about, changing their skimpy costumes.

The only drawback to that job was that I dragged home late at night on the grimy, gloomy, semi-deserted streetcar. The Smiths had gone to bed hours earlier. But Mrs. Smith always left a glass of milk and a piece of cake in the icebox for me to have before I fell exhausted into bed.

Somehow, I also played in the Boston Latin School orchestra and band, under the supervision of its director, an excitable and colorful musician whose memorable name was Fortunato Sordillo.

Mr. Sordillo had a thick Italian accent, and he had a lot of trouble with my name. I was often late for rehearsals because of my heavy work schedule. Looking around for me, he would shout querulously, "Where's that *Yank...* that *Yank...* that *goddamn piccolo player?*" Of course, this broke up my friends who would insist on imitating his high-pitched whining voice (when he was safely out of earshot).

In fact, I almost never played the piccolo. I was the band and orchestra's flutist, pressed into piccolo service only when the band had to play "Stars and Stripes Forever."

During these years at the Boston Latin School, some of the raw materials out of which I would construct a philosophy for living began to take shape.

I felt myself growing ever more independent. I had learned to navigate the streetcar that carried me to all parts of the city. I juggled several part-time evening jobs in downtown Boston and had dinner by myself in restaurants. I managed to do all of my homework and also play in the band and orchestra.

I also had lots of friends and valued them greatly. My friends meant everything to me. My self-confidence grew. I was managing my life on my own, and I sensed that I would be able to cope with life without having to depend on the Mr. Schneidermans of this world.

Beneath it all, I felt a vast sense of wonder about life, always groping for a pattern to give it meaning.

I don't recall when I became preoccupied with girls. Unfortunately, my interest was often unreciprocated, leading to several painful rejections. At age fourteen, I fell in love with Evelyn Davidoff. More accurately, I fell in love with her family.

The Davidoffs were a warm, close-knit musical family. Evelyn played the piano. Her younger sister, Judith, played the cello (and subsequently became a world-famous cellist). Evelyn's mother sang. And her father played violin professionally with the Boston Symphony Orchestra. Their home was a place where young people liked to gather.

The Davidoffs were unfailingly welcoming of their daughters' friends. Moreover, unlike most of my friends' parents, Mr. and Mrs. Davidoff spoke fluent and excellent English and were well adapted to Boston's dominant WASP culture. Almost uniquely, they were free of the ethnic immigrant awkwardness that characterized the other parts of my world.

Evelyn herself was petite, with straight black hair, a stunning smile, a natural intelligence, and a generous attitude toward one and all. Her manner toward everyone and everything was polite—except for her piano. She attacked the piano with ferocity. Her mastery of it, and her musical self-assurance, filled me with wonder.

Whenever I visited the Davidoffs, I felt that I was in the presence of the ideal home and family. They became the object of my deepest yearnings. I wanted to belong to them. I wanted them to accept me as part of their lives and their family.

Disappointment was, of course, inevitable. To them I was just one of Evelyn's many friends and admirers, all of whom they treated with equal courtesy and hospitality. I suspect that my neediness and eagerness showed. Not that any of them ever made me feel unwelcome; they were always warm and friendly toward me. But Evelyn herself managed to convey that she didn't feel the same ardor toward me as I felt toward her. Ironically, many years later she married my cousin, Danny Mostow, and raised a family with him.

I am sure that the Evelyn I idealized was not the real Evelyn that Cousin Danny married. I think she realized that I was in awe of her intelligence, gracious manner and piano virtuosity and it made her uncomfortable. People, if they are honest, prefer to be liked for themselves, not for some idealized distortion of themselves.

Even after my unrequited infatuation with Evelyn, I was unable to give up the habit of idealizing the girls I cared most about. From a distance, I idealized the lovely, cheerful, and very popular Charlotte Zimmerman. I often traveled on the streetcar with Charlotte when she was en route to the Girls' Latin School (just across the street from the boys' school). I admired her, but was so awed by her that I rarely got beyond a few words of casual greeting.

Not only was she popular with the boys at my school, she was also two years older than me, which meant that she could hardly have taken a boy her younger sister's age seriously. (That younger sister, Barbara Epstein, went on in later years to cofound the *New York Review of Books*.)

I had somewhat better luck with a girl named Pearl Kahn, whom I idealized much less. Pearl's father was the lead flutist in the Boston Symphony Orchestra. After I got to know him well, he sold me his old Haynes silver flute for a pittance. (It is one of the very few possessions I still have from that period of my life.)

Pearl was a big girl, a sharp contrast with petite Evelyn. She was an easy-going, fun-loving person who enjoyed necking with me (which I adored doing with her). We spent a lot of time on her family's living room couch. I didn't know where her parents were, but since she seemed to understand the lay of the land, I didn't worry much about them. We remained good friends and spent time with each other off and on until I graduated from the Boston Latin School and went on to Harvard.

The other Pearl, Pearl Levin, was the most traditionally feminine of the girls I dated in those Boston Latin School years. She quickly grew serious about our relationship. She encouraged the physical part of it (I didn't need much encouraging), but always on the condition that the more intimate we became, the stronger the commitment had to be. If I agreed to go steady (and gave her a pin or some symbolic piece of jewelry to signify our attachment to each other), she would place fewer limits on how far my sexual advances could go.

At the time, I was still in love with Evelyn, and I felt it would betray her if I were to go steady with Pearl. So, with enormous reluctance, I did not accept Pearl's condition, though she overwhelmed me with physical desire and a thrilling sense of erotic awe. A full-blown sexual relationship with a desirable girl like Pearl seemed to me the ultimate in the wondrous mysteries of life.

The girls I cared about the most, I tended to idealize. Perhaps for that reason, they didn't reciprocate my feelings: being put on a pedestal was not what they really wanted. I had better luck with girls I didn't idealize, but the physical aspect of my relationships with them was not as soul-satisfying as it would have been had I been truly in love with them.

In my senior year at the Boston Latin School, I was admitted as a freshman to Harvard's class of 1946. The prospect of going to Harvard filled me with eager anticipation, not least because I knew I would soon be meeting some attractive college coeds.

PART TWO

ON MY OWN

A New and Exciting World

I SPENT A YEAR at Harvard before being whisked into the army and sent overseas to fight the Germans. Even though it was just a year, it was packed with intense experiences.

By subway, the trip from the Smiths' apartment in Dorchester across the Charles River to Harvard in Cambridge took only about an hour. The subway ride from Dorchester to the Boston Latin School took almost as long. Dorchester and the Boston Latin School were spiritually linked: they shared a common culture and ambiance. Both were provincial, couth-challenged, and familiar to the poor Irish and Jewish boys who rode the subways and the streetcars that connected the two parts of Boston.

Harvard was different. It certainly was not provincial. As for couth, it breathed it in and out, theoretically transforming us callow Dorchesterites from poor boys into "Harvard gentlemen." Socially and intellectually, Harvard was exotic foreign territory for us children of poor immigrants.

My friend, Warren ("Buddy") Bennett got the full impact of the culture shock. Buddy was a year older than me and had graduated from the Boston Latin School the year before I did. He was one of the first high school students in the nation to win a National Merit Scholarship to Harvard, with a stipend that paid full tuition plus room and board plus expenses. It even included spending money.

From my Depression standpoint, the munificence of his scholarship was awesome. And if anyone deserved it, Buddy did. Not only had he graduated first in his class at the Boston Latin School with higher grades than any student had achieved for decades, but in his senior year he won just about every award the school had accumulated in its three hundred-year history.

I visited Buddy in his first few months of residence in Elliot House, a posh dorm close to the Charles River. Buddy shared generously sized quarters with a preppie roommate from Virginia. The Elliot House dining room made me realize how far from Dorchester he had traveled. Lunch was served at small dining room tables fitted with elegant tablecloths and heavy silver place settings. It was opulent, and Buddy was having a bit of trouble getting used to it, as he was to his academic courses.

He had excelled in his course work at the Boston Latin School. But he did not feel that his work at Harvard stood out in the same way. He thought that this was because the Harvard courses placed less emphasis on memory than his Latin School courses, and he knew that he had an excellent memory.

My visit to Buddy whetted my desire to go to Harvard. I was not concerned about being admitted. In those days, admission was not nearly as difficult as it is now, and the top 10 percent of the class at the Boston Latin School was virtually guaranteed admission. What worried me was the tuition. Harvard's $400-a-year tuition seems ludicrously low by today's standards (even though it adds up to the equivalent of many thousands of dollars), but as it turned out, I didn't have to worry about it. Eventually, I was awarded scholarships that covered it. (The largest one was the Burroughs Newsboys Scholarship, although I had never delivered a newspaper.)

My transition to Harvard was a lot easier than Buddy's. For me it was only intellectual, not social, for the simple reason that I could not afford to live in any of Harvard's residential dorms. Like most of my Latin School classmates who had been accepted at Harvard, I commuted by subway, exactly as I had commuted to the Boston

Latin School. I didn't have to get used to being lavishly waited upon. I didn't have to worry about the expectations of preppie roommates. I didn't even need to acquire proper dining room manners.

As it turned out, Buddy's freshman year was the last year that Harvard student residences actually offered waiters and tablecloths to their students. Pearl Harbor put an end to the elegance and upper-class treatment enjoyed by earlier generations of Harvard students. From then on, self-service cafeteria-style dining on naked Formica-topped tables became the default mode of student dining at Harvard.

For commuters from the Boston area like myself, Harvard provided a comfortable facility where we could meet, hang out and eat the sandwiches we brought from home. Dudley House, the commuters' center, was conveniently located in Harvard Square. It was a warm, noisy, and cheerful place, full of armchairs and bridge tables for playing checkers, chess, and cards. Almost every day when I attended classes, I found time to play chess with two classmates, my cousin Danny Mostow and Danny Gorenstein (both of whom became noted mathematicians).

The improbable coincidence that all three of us were named Danny amused onlookers. But it was not really a total coincidence. Danny Mostow (who eventually married Evelyn Davidoff) was my first cousin, and both of us were named for the same maternal grandparent!

I did, however, experience a culture shock in the transition from the Boston Latin School's academic course work to Harvard's. The Latin School's curriculum at the time was grindingly boring—a monotonous mix of Latin and Greek and German and French and English, with a smattering of math and history taught in uninspiring ways. Moreover, we were offered almost no choice. (I chose German over Greek—not because I wanted to learn German but because I didn't want to learn Greek. Latin was enough antiquity for me.)

My transition to Harvard was a joy. Harvard afforded such an abundance of enticing choices that I had a hard time confining myself to a manageable number of courses.

Of the five courses I took in my freshman year only one, English A, was obligatory. I grumbled at having to take it because I knew it was a remedial course, designed to bring our stiff Boston Latinate writing style up to a level comparable to the better-prepared students from Andover, Exeter, Choate, and other private schools.

Because Harvard admitted a large number of public school plebes like me, many English A sections (with no more than twenty students in each section) were needed to accommodate us. Low-level "section men," graduate students without PhDs, taught the courses.

A slim, shy teaching assistant in his twenties taught my English A section. His name was John Berryman.

Of course, no one knew at the time that he would become one of America's foremost poets. As a teacher, he was extraordinary. His tense enthusiasm for the texts he assigned drew us into the orbit of his complex imaginative interpretations.

In retrospect, the books he assigned, like Edmund Wilson's *To the Finland Station* (the autobiographical story of the noted literary critic's flirtation with Marxism), were odd choices for a remedial English class. But they were perfect for me. They fit neatly with my political theory and philosophy courses. They proved essential to my introduction to the history of Western ideas.

I believe that Berryman himself had a mental stature equal to those giants of thought he shared with us. I've often wondered whether, if he had chosen a career in philosophy rather than poetry, he might have avoided being sucked into the depression and suicide that prematurely ended his life and brilliant career. (Or maybe he would have become depressed even sooner.)

My most enjoyable course was Music One, not so much taught as *performed* by a professor named Archibald Davidson. Davidson gave his lectures at the piano, and he expertly demonstrated the different styles of great composers from Buxtehude to Stravinsky. Davidson's performances made the three days a week when the course was taught a form of play rather than work.

Professor Raphael Demos's introductory philosophy course was my most important course; it turned me on to philosophy and gave me a name for my search for something that couldn't be taken away from me.

Demos devoted the first semester to the ancient Greek philosophers—primarily Socrates, Plato, and Aristotle. He recreated the vivid freshness with which these founders of Western philosophy confronted the grand questions of how to gain genuine knowledge and how to live a good and virtuous life.

Officially I was taking only one philosophy course. In effect, though, I ended up taking three. My political theory course, with its focus on Locke, Hobbes, J. S. Mill, and Bentham, was a logical extension of Demos's philosophy course, and John Berryman covered the Marx/Freud/Darwin thought revolutions of the nineteenth and twentieth centuries.

So even as a freshman, my exposure to the history of ideas was surprisingly broad. Each of these courses supplemented the others, and I found myself engaged in the history of Western ideas over a three-thousand-year expanse.

That first year at Harvard was the most intellectually absorbing experience I'd ever had.

What did I take away from the intellectual feast at which I stuffed myself before going off to war? The first impressions I gained from exposure to the philosophical canon were that:

- Philosophy is a subject of enormous breadth.

- Philosophy is not confined to any one academic department, but plays a useful role as an intellectual underpinning to many fields.
- Philosophy's real mission is the quest for truth. (How appropriate that the single word *veritas* is emblazoned on Harvard's emblem and shield.)
- The search for truth not only yields empirical knowledge about the world, it also yields moral knowledge about the nature of virtue.
- The ultimate use of this search for truth is insight into how to live one's life.
- The method of choice for finding knowledge and truth lies with the disciplines of reason and logic.

In subsequent years, I grew disillusioned with some, though not all, of these early idealistic impressions. I quickly discovered that other fields do not look to philosophy to validate their underlying frameworks. I also learned that reason and logic were far less powerful than I had supposed. I discovered that they play a surprisingly minor role in scientific inquiry and an even more peripheral role in gaining the kind of moral insight that science cannot supply.

Nor, I eventually realized, did the quest for *veritas*, certainty, and academic learning yield much insight into how best to live one's life.

On the other hand, I also learned that some of these early first impressions of philosophy were correct.

- Philosophy is a subject of enormous breadth that cuts across many specialized disciplines.
- Philosophy's quest for truth does respond to the deepest human strivings, and it should not be abandoned simply because so many thinkers have gone about looking for philosophical truth the wrong way.

- Most importantly, the goal of gaining insight into the truths of living is a noble one, even if unreachable by the traditional methods of logical reasoning.

By the end of my freshman year, I came to the heartening conclusion that thinking about ideas and philosophy engaged and excited me more than anything I had ever tried to do previously.

I began to feel that perhaps I had found a direction in life, and I thought how wonderful it would be to return to Harvard to study philosophy once I had completed my military service.

The Long Vomick

FOUR MONTHS AFTER MY eighteenth birthday, in the middle of my second semester at Harvard, I received my formal government "Greetings" instructing me to report for duty in the military service of the United States in two months. I was able to finish my freshman year before going into the army, and that pleased me greatly. Out of my Harvard class of twelve hundred, more than a thousand of us served in the military in World War II. The vast majority of us came back unharmed.

Many of us had a hard time adjusting to military service. I know I did. For me, the first few months in the army felt like a new, particularly inhospitable foster home.

In my three years of military service, I didn't do much conscious thinking about myself. The examined life was on hold. Yet after the war, I realized that my experience in the army had taught me a number of important lessons related directly to my search.

In the foster care years, I had been engaged in a constant struggle to assert some degree of control over my own life and destiny. My pre-army year at Harvard was particularly satisfying; never before had I felt as much in control.

The first few months in the army were a major setback. In my foster home years, I had developed an antagonism toward authority. I didn't like my foster parents telling me what to do because I didn't feel they had my interests at heart. My resistance to military authority was stronger than I expected. It took me almost a year to learn that the army was not an inexorable machine, but a system managed by fallible human beings. It offered greater flexibility and control than I first realized.

Unlike some of my friends, I wasn't a rebel in principle. I didn't automatically oppose what authority demanded. But when I felt that the authority was arbitrary or wrong-headed or obsessed with chickenshit regulations, I bridled and avoided obeying as much as I could get away with.

As a consequence I was demoted several times from corporal to private. The demotions were for trivial offenses; each time I was re-promoted to corporal shortly after. At the time of my honorable discharge, I held the honorable, though low, rank of corporal.

Several days after reporting for duty, I was sent to Camp Wheeler for basic training. Camp Wheeler was located a few miles from Macon, Georgia. I had never traveled outside of New England and I couldn't believe that any place on earth could get as fiery hot as rural Georgia in midsummer.

The oppressive heat was, however, the least of my troubles. Our ragtag unit of raw recruits was placed under the command of a native-born Georgia redneck, Sergeant Humphries. (I never knew what his first name was. Maybe he didn't have one. Maybe it was Sergeant.)

Humphries was a mean bastard—civil to the Southerners in our unit, vicious toward Easterners, especially those with foreign sounding names like mine. His motto was "train them by breaking them," and he did so with furious energy. His power over new recruits was nearly total.

He knew he had trouble pronouncing words, and he imagined that those who did not come from the rural south were mocking him and laughing at him behind his back, and it drove him wild. I first became aware of his problem with pronunciation when he told us that we would be likely to "vomick" on long marches when the temperature was over one hundred degrees. And indeed, several days later, when a lot of us did vomick, I realized that his prediction was correct, even if his pronunciation wasn't.

Initially, I was confused when he insisted that we wear our "hemlets" at all times. I soon realized that he was referring to our helmets. Then, on one particularly choice occasion, he told us that we should "never, never, *never* vomick in our hemlets!!" He was correct that some of us regarded his pronunciations with wonder, but wrong about our laughing at him behind his back. We were too scared shitless to do so.

When he heard that one of us, Larry Armour, had attended Princeton, he singled him out for particular abuse. I had confided in Larry that I had been to Harvard (for my self-preservation, I hadn't told anyone else). Larry, for reasons I never understood, told Sergeant Humphries. And I then became the sergeant's favorite target: East Coast, Jewish, Harvard, lax in dress code, and an innocent in matters relating to guns and bayonets. He couldn't ask for a more perfect object for his scorn, abusiveness, and punishment (in the form of latrine cleaning and endless pushups).

I think he might have broken my spirit if it hadn't been for Seth. Seth was a recruit like the rest of us, except that he was from the South and had attended a military academy in Virginia. He carried himself with erect military bearing, in contrast to our urban slouch. He could strip and reassemble an M1 rifle with his eyes closed. And he was courteous to everyone. Seth and Sergeant Humphries came to symbolize the two faces of the South for me—one displaying petty arrogance and cruelty, the other, courtesy, grace, and helpfulness.

I think Seth knew what Humphries was trying to do to me and had made up his mind to prevent it. He showed me how to strip and clean my rifle, how to polish my boots so that even Humphries could find no fault with them, how to fade into the background so that I wouldn't be noticed, how to be early for six A.M.. roll call, when Humphries would be on the lookout for stragglers to harass. Seth and I were unlikely friends, but we were friends. I liked, appreciated and admired him, and I think he liked me. I think he knew I was determined to hold on no matter what Humphries did. He wanted to help, and he did.

The most practical aspect of thinking philosophically is learning how to cope with a world largely indifferent to your own desires or fate. Those times when others opened their hearts and minds were particularly precious. They expressed caring, and caring meant everything to me.

The crisis with Humphries came about midway through my three-month basic training. We were scheduled to take the longest march of our training: a twenty-mile march wearing full field pack with rifles and bayonets. It was early August; the temperature was 101 degrees. Before the march, staring directly at me, Humphries told us that some of "you girls" wouldn't make it and would drop out from heat exhaustion.

What really astonished me was Sergeant Humphries. He kept running alongside us, making sarcastic remarks about whether we were ready to faint yet. I had trouble putting one foot ahead of the other, and here he was running back and forth. If we covered twenty miles that day, he must have covered fifty or sixty. I wanted desperately to drop out, but I kept saying to myself, "I am not going to give that cocksucker the satisfaction of dropping out if it kills me." (And I was sure it would.)

About 10 percent of our group finished the march. Sergeant Humphries never acknowledged that I was one of them. He never gave me the courtesy of a friendly look or gesture. But he stopped picking on me. From that point on, I was just another grunt, an anonymous soldier. And gradually my self-confidence returned. I no longer awoke every morning feeling like I had a huge stone lodged in my gut.

Seth, of course, finished the march with no visible signs of stress. Maybe he knew better than I did that I was not going to drop out of the twenty-mile march. After the ordeal, as we were walking back to the barracks, he tapped me lightly on the shoulder. That was all. No words. No jokes. No comments about the heat or Humphries. I responded to his tap with profound gratitude. I never grew accustomed to the charms of Macon, Georgia. But I knew that my spirit was intact and that I was going to survive.

"Hurry up and wait" is the one constant of life in the military. At Camp Wheeler we were told that we had to finish our basic training quickly because we were needed overseas. But as soon as the hellish summer of basic training in Macon was over, we were then told that we were not needed overseas at the moment and that some of us would be temporarily parked in a military education program. The program, called the Army Specialized Training Program (or ASTP), was designed to educate potential scientists and engineers.

The specialized training turned out to be two months of unspecialized academic courses at the University of Ohio in Columbus, followed by two months of equally unspecialized courses at the University of Alabama in Tuscaloosa. We wore our uniforms, but otherwise the contrast to life at Camp Wheeler could not have been greater.

A song current at the time had the title: "Take Down Your Service Flag, Mother, Your Son Is in the ASTP."

I had a splendid time in both places, though I remember nothing of my course work. I loved both places because I found a girl in each one, Harriet Rothstein in Columbus and Sarah Douglas in Tuscaloosa. Harriet was sexy, cheerful, outgoing, and fun to be with. Sarah was slim, quiet, gracious, and lovely to behold. Both were innocent flirtations and I enjoyed them hugely, especially the friendship and flirtation with Sarah Douglas. The same deep-rooted Southern culture that had shaped my friend and lifesaver Seth had also graced Sarah Douglas.

Parietal rules at the University of Alabama, where Sarah was also a student, were quite strict, so we were rarely alone. I spent a large part of my two months in Alabama in the semi-public formal sitting room of Sarah's dorm. We took advantage of those times when we were alone together there to smooch and talk and talk and smooch.

On Christmas Eve 1943, shortly before I was due to leave the ASTP program, Sarah took me to a large party. After dinner one of the guests, a heavy-set woman, sang "O, Holy Night." Never had I heard a more awesome, purer voice. It was also my first exposure to "O Holy Night," and it made the hairs on my neck stand up in wonder and astonishment. My association with my own religion was full of bad vibes, like the knuckle-rapping Hebrew teacher and the maniacal rabbi inveighing against the butcher who had dared to open a non-kosher shop a block away from the synagogue. And here was someone from the alien (to me) Baptist community singing an expressive religious melody. It reinforced my conviction that sectarian distinctions are arbitrary and often bizarre—a conviction that has grown stronger over subsequent decades.

I was then transferred to my second basic training program at Camp Claiborne, Louisiana. Camp Claiborne did not train raw recruits. It was a staging arena for sending troops overseas. I was assigned to an office that organized groups for their overseas assignments. Each day our office received detailed specs for assembling a unit (a company or battalion) that would be shipped out in the following days or weeks.

It was here that I began to understand how a seemingly powerless enlisted man could find wiggle room in an authoritarian military structure. One day one of the other clerks in the office was in a panic. He had run afoul of a captain awaiting assignment who had threatened to court-marshal him. The captain was claiming (falsely, we all believed) that our buddy had called him filthy names, rather than just swearing out loud. We knew that the captain was serious and that our friend was faced with the prospect of serving time in the brig and/or a dishonorable discharge.

So we arranged to send the captain to Alaska. We didn't particularly want to send him to Alaska, and he didn't particularly want to go there. But Alaska was the only destination available for shipping troops the next day, so off to Alaska it was. He went as a badly-needed "communication specialist" added at the last minute.

We neither celebrated nor did we indulge in *mea culpa*. We were engaged in a long military tradition in which enlisted men in an army of free citizens use their ingenuity to achieve a balance of power that equalizes army life just a wee bit. This was a far cry from the tyranny and absolute authority of Sergeant Humphries. The army chose to draft young men from every level of American society, including many with a fierce independent streak.

In the rigid hierarchy of the army, the lowly enlisted grunts like me were at the bottom, but we were not brain-dead. Inevitably, we found ways to defend against the arbitrariness of the hierarchy. These ways were not always praiseworthy. But they opened a sphere of freedom that became a valued part of my personal philosophy of life.

Captain John Hartshorne was one of the officers stationed at the camp. He had been there for over a year. We saw a great deal of him because he was in charge of putting together the groups for overseas assignments. He was very friendly and many of the enlisted men in the office liked to chat and joke with him.

One day he came into the office waving a piece of paper and said, with a huge grin on his face, "This is it. This is the command I've been waiting for." At first we thought he was kidding but soon realized that he was serious.

I was surprised when he sat down next to me and started to talk. I didn't know him as well as the others did. He said, "I'm told that you are pretty good with those punch cards. Do you think you can make sure I don't have any real dummies in my new company?"

I said, "Sure thing, Captain."

He asked, "How exactly can you do that?"

I told him that we could pick an IQ score of 100, 110, 120, or 130 and choose only those above that level.

He said, "Well, don't go too low. I'd like to start out with a smart bunch of men."

Hartshorne explained to me that he had been waiting for orders to form a company that would not be part of a larger unit: an unattached company that didn't require a rank above captain to command. Those orders, he said, came few and far between, which was why he had waited longer than he had intended. But now he had orders to form the 1567th Engineers, an independent unit that could go wherever it was needed to do whatever bridge-building and demolition work was called for. It sounded a lot like my grammar school mechanic arts class.

I suggested that if he wanted men who could learn fairly quickly, he not go below an IQ of 110. He said, "Then let's go for 120."

I told him that I would start working on a list for the new unit right away. He said, "Good." And as he stood up to leave, he said casually, almost as an afterthought: "By the way, you can include yourself, if you can pass the test." I gave him a disapproving look, but I was delighted.

Within a week we had screened 150 soldiers whose sole common denominator was their moderately high IQ.

❧

The following week we found ourselves on a ship, totally unprepared for the harrowing ocean crossing to the Normandy beaches on the shores of Northern France.

The voyage was a nightmare. To avoid German submarines, we took an extra-long northerly route. We crossed the Atlantic during a cold and stormy season, and it took us an endless twelve days. Sergeant Humphries's idiosyncratic pronunciation kept rolling around in my head: the entire trip seemed like one agonizingly prolonged vomick.

After a few days of unremitting seasickness, none of us cared how dangerous our landing on the Normandy beaches might be: death in combat was vastly to be preferred to death by vomick.

Our landing in Normandy was a huge relief. By the time my unit landed on the beaches, the troops that preceded us had established a safe beachhead.

Our landing in Normandy was uneventful, except for some unnecessary discomfort for me that was no one's fault but my own. Before going overseas we were each issued a half-tent. If we were required to make camp, we would choose a buddy with his own half-tent. Affixing the two halves together would provide some degree of shelter for the two soldiers.

I had turned down the opportunity to carry a half-tent. Each half weighed umpteen pounds, and it seemed to me an intolerably heavy burden to be carrying about on top of a full field pack. I figured I would never need it, so why carry the extra weight? And if by chance I did need it, I was sure I would work something out.

I had five long, cold, damp nights on the beaches of Normandy to regret my off-hand decision not to inconvenience myself. On any one of those nights an observer would see spread before him on the beaches of Normandy a vast sea of neatly arrayed tents, plus one shivering soldier wrapped in a raincoat to shield him from the elements.

Yet by the time our unit was ordered to leave the beach, I felt fine and relieved to be travelling light.

Five days after landing we received our orders to proceed to a military barracks in Liège, Belgium, close to the base of the First Army. I was assigned to a three-man mortar team. It was our job to keep enemy troops from getting too close to those assigned to repair bridges.

A World War II mortar is an amazingly simple device. It consists of a barrel mounted on a mechanism that can lob an artillery shell a certain distance. Using three people to man the mortar is a little like using three people to change a light bulb. One of the three soldiers peers through a telescope to locate a target and informs the mortar operator whether the shell has fallen long or short or at a wrong angle. From the instructions of the telescope scanner, the operator then calibrates the angle and distance of the next shell to be fired.

It is the job of the third man on the team, upon a signal from the operator, to carefully place the shell in the barrel of the mortar, drop it in, and remove his hand with a certain dispatch.

That was my assigned task, one for which my mechanic arts training in grammar school had exquisitely prepared me.

I also drove a two-and-a-half-ton truck to various parts of the countryside to collect products and deliver them to other units stationed nearby. I have never been a comfortable driver of large vehicles, and to this day I am astonished that I was actually able to drive a large truck for months without mishap.

It was on this assignment that I acquired my jeep.

My truck had broken down in another military base in Belgium and I was told that it needed a few days to repair. I was eager to get back to my own base, and since the truck was empty I was not obliged to stay with it. One of the mechanics working on the truck said to me, "The last guy who drove for the colonel left a jeep behind when he and the colonel were shipped out last week. If you sign these papers, you can take the jeep and turn it in at your own base. I'll take care of the paperwork on the truck and see that it gets sent back. We do that all the time."

I couldn't wait to sign the papers, assuring the mechanic that I would return the jeep in good order. Which, indeed, I did—though not exactly right away.

Driving the truck made me nervous and I didn't always feel in control. I felt that I was more likely to die from ramming the truck into a tank or driving it into a minefield than from combat.

Driving the jeep came at the other extreme of my comfort spectrum. I loved it. It gave me a sense of exhilarating freedom. The minute the jeep hit the road, I felt as if I were back in Franklin Park on my bike.

The jeep was amazing. Visibility was perfect since the jeep was totally open. It was so much more responsive than the truck that after a while it felt like part of me, an extra limb, and, like one of my own limbs, I took it everywhere.

And I mean everywhere. Liège had a library that the military had taken over. To get into the building, one had to climb a number of steps, not unlike Widener Library at Harvard. At first I parked my jeep close to the library stairs, but then I found that I could create a bit of a stir when I drove the jeep up the stairs and parked it by the front door in the ample space the architects had provided (not, I think, with that particular usage in mind.)

My possession of the jeep illustrates the familiar "don't ask, don't tell" outlook of the military. No one ever asked me where I got the jeep and why it seemed to belong to me and not to the army. In the first week I had it, I thought many times of turning it in, on the assumption that the papers I had signed would be sent to the base and someone would want to re-acquire the jeep.

But as days and weeks passed and no inquiries were made, I assumed (correctly) that no one except myself had any interest in the jeep. And so overnight I had acquired my own wheels in a town graced with many fair Belgian maidens, two of whom—Janine and Josette—became friends and often graced the jeep with their presence as passengers.

My most thrilling experiences with the jeep came on a handful of weekends when we had no assigned duties. After dark on those Friday nights, I would set out for Brussels, about forty miles away. Ordinarily, the trip would take about an hour (there was no traffic). But in the pitch black of night, it took a lot longer because the military situation called for total curfew and we were forbidden to use our lights. Other vehicles had experimented with their dimmer headlights, with disastrous consequences.

Staying on the narrow road while driving in total darkness was a challenge I think I would not have tried to meet if I were a few years older. But at nineteen, I assumed total invincibility.

Unlike Liège, which was like an American military barracks, Brussels was a largely civilian city, civilized and almost unbruised. It had plush inexpensive hotels and wonderful restaurants. I loved riding around the city in my jeep, eating at posh restaurants where they treated American soldiers with lavish attention and good wine on the house.

One night at the hotel, a prostitute who liked American service men offered me a freebie. I was too flustered and embarrassed to accept. I was still a virgin and thought I would make a fool of myself. So I turned down an opportunity that I had long dreamed about. It was common for soldiers to boast about their exploits with prostitutes and receptive Belgian ladies. But I was still too much of a romantic to want to have my first "sacred" sexual experience with a total stranger.

Life in Liège itself was fraught with tension, both for its civilians and for us American soldiers stationed there. This was because of the "buzz bombs"—V1 and V2 rockets that the Germans launched to destroy property and kill soldiers and civilians alike. They arrived constantly, hour after hour, day after day, week after week. To this day, when I close my eyes I can still hear the distinctive drone (or buzz) from which they derived their name.

As long as you could hear them, you knew you were safe. The dreaded moment of vulnerability came when the buzz abruptly stopped. That meant that the missile was no longer flying and was about to fall to the ground, destroying whatever it hit. And the hits were all around us.

When the buzz stopped, you couldn't help wondering whether you were about to be obliterated. The dread didn't last long: it didn't take the buzz bombs long to fall to the ground since they were not flying that high. So after a few moments, you knew you were safe. It was their constancy that got on your nerves. Just when you were beginning to relax, the dull, menacing buzz started again and you found yourself listening apprehensively for that sudden cessation of sound that spelled mortal danger.

Despite the buzz bombs and mortar assignments, I felt a lot luckier than the infantry troops on the front lines. They often appeared at our base looking haggard and stressed from combat with the German troops. In mid-December 1944, however, instead of our being sent to the front lines, the front lines came to us. Several weeks before Christmas, Germany's General von Rundstedt launched a major counterattack on our troops that came to be known in history as the Battle of the Bulge.

Germany was losing the war. The German high command had decided that their only chance of staving off defeat was to counter-attack. From Eisenhower on down, the American military command had been lulled into complacent optimism about impending victory in Europe and was particularly lax and overconfident during the Christmas season. So the German military machine was able to catch us off guard and to achieve almost total surprise.

The German plan was to invade Belgium through the weakly defended Ardennes forest, and then with blitzkrieg speed drive north, cross the Meuse, and sweep through Liège on to Antwerp, thereby salvaging victory from what otherwise seemed inevitable defeat. It was a bold plan, carefully prepared and skillfully executed. For eleven days the world held its breath as the Germans pressed forward relentlessly and the American military seemed to falter.

The Battle of the Bulge claimed 81,000 of our soldiers, dead, wounded, or missing, plus 3,000 French and Belgian civilian deaths. On March 7, five weeks later, our forces crossed the Rhine and exactly two months after that, on May 7, 1945, the Germans surrendered. It was finally VE Day—victory in Europe.

Grenoble, the Guildhall, and the Girl

I WAS ALMOST TWENTY-ONE when peace returned to a devastated Europe. I had been in the army for two and a half years, shuttling from place to place without much say over where I was sent or what I was to do.

Now, gradually, I felt a new freedom and a mounting excitement about what the future held. I knew I would not be going home soon. I was stationed in the heart of Europe, close to Paris, London, and Rome. I started to fantasize about visiting each of these great cities of Europe, just as I had snatched a quick taste of Brussels on my weekend jeep excursions.

For most of my life I have looked forward to change with excitement. I always assumed that there would be new experiences to savor, new relationships to cherish, new understandings of life. And rarely has this expectation been more fully realized than in the months leading up to and following my twenty-first birthday.

At first the waiting period was frustrating. Without a war going on, there wasn't much for us to do in Liège except the make-work the army excelled in creating. Unfortunately for me, my friend John Hartshorne, captain of the 1567th Engineers, returned to the United States. There were more troops ready to be shipped home than there were boats to accommodate them. So, even though I had served long enough to be sent home, I was low on the list for an available boat.

I had heard rumors about a gigantic college program the army was developing in Biarritz for soldiers who had enough points to return home but no transport to cross the Atlantic. I qualified for the program and I was about to apply when by accident I learned that several French universities had agreed to accept American soldiers who had a rudimentary grasp of French. Suddenly, I was overcome with gratitude to Mr. Levine, my pedantic French teacher at the Boston Latin School. Instead of joining the army's Biarritz program, I had the prospect of whiling away the waiting time in a real French university. The prospect was thrilling.

I was told to report to the University of Grenoble in the south of France in early September. I left Liège at the end of August, with travel plans that permitted me to spend the first few days of September in Paris en route to Grenoble.

Paris in the fall of 1945 was quiet, grey...and gorgeous. The clouds hovering over the city were thick and ominous. The famous boulevards were virtually free of traffic. The cafés were half-empty and the stores poorly stocked. People were dressed shabbily. But there was an undertone of relief and barely suppressed joyfulness that communicated itself to me, even though I was only a young, awed observer.

I spent my few days in Paris walking around the city and sitting in the cafés. The sheer beauty of Paris overwhelmed me. On the first night of my visit I attended the Comédie-Française where an actor named Louis Jouvet was performing a Molière play. I went mainly to test my French language skills in preparation for enrolling at the University of Grenoble.

It took me a while to catch the drift of the play. But as soon as Jouvet appeared, I was mesmerized. His acting possessed a charismatic theatricality I had never experienced before (and rarely since). I'm sure it was one of the events that brought me back to Paris several years after the war. I learned that Jouvet was one of France's most famous film actors, and eventually I tracked down every movie he ever made. I was never disappointed.

When I left Paris for Grenoble, I was so over-stimulated that I could not sit still on the train or read or even look at the scenery. Though I was still in uniform, the war and the army that had totally enveloped me for so long seemed to have disappeared into thin air. The lurch from combat to Paris-at-peace was one of the most welcome ever. I was about to enroll in a French university that was sure to be full of new people, new ideas, new sights and sounds, new adventures. I loved the idea that life could be so unpredictable and so full of wondrous possibilities. This experience, too, found its way into my philosophy of life.

When I arrived in Grenoble I registered at the official army unit that had been set up to oversee the American soldiers who had won admission to the University. I was assigned a hotel room and a roommate, a corporal like myself, named Thomas Dabney Wellford. Dabney, as he preferred to be called, was from Virginia and had served in the infantry. But unlike most Southerners I met in the army, his military bearing was as ungainly as my own.

He was tall, stooped, and tilted slightly to the right. His walk was more like a shuffle than a walk. He wore glasses and a look of immense kindliness and acceptance for one and all. If it hadn't been for his grin, he might have been regarded as ugly. But the grin was so all-encompassing that everyone who knew him automatically smiled when they spoke of him.

We became good friends and after the war were graduate students together. During our time at Harvard, I visited him in Virginia. I was not surprised to find that his ancestral home with its Greek columns plainly said, "old aristocratic South." His mother was very much in the *grande dame* tradition. She tolerated me, but she clearly did not approve of me.

Oddly, she was as resistant to outsiders as her only child, Dabney, was tolerant and accepting. She found my name unpronounceable and offensively ethnic. But she put up with me for Dabney's sake, on whom she doted. Dabney later became an Episcopal minister. Eventually we lost touch with one another. But for more than a decade, during and after the war, we relished each other's company.

My recollection is that about forty of us American GIs occupied rooms in the Grenoble hotel and attended classes at the university in the fall semester of 1945. On our very first day, the director of the courses organized for the American soldiers, Professor Armand Caraccio, told us slyly that the culture of Grenoble was to be found in its cafés even more than in its formal university courses. Some of us, including myself, were grateful for the hint and took full advantage of it.

The University had a student orchestra and I joined it as a flutist. After our first rehearsal, I was invited to accompany a chorus that was practicing a program to be played at Christmas. Bach's "Jesu, Joy of Man's Desiring" was to be one of the centerpieces of the concert. It has an enchantingly lyrical flute accompaniment, and I was thrilled to perform it.

At rehearsals I noticed a French woman student who looked particularly pale and gaunt and who constantly wore the same tattered rain jacket. She had a bristly hairdo and a sad, vulnerable expression. Unlike the other women students, she rarely chattered and laughed with the others. I finally introduced myself to her.

Her name was Rosine Bernheim. She told me that she had been in a prisoner of war camp up to VE day and had decided to enroll at Grenoble rather than return to her family home in Normandy. She had been in the French Resistance for years, had endured a fairly brutal life as a POW, and was not yet emotionally ready to go home.

She, Dabney, and I became daily companions, hiking in the mountains and frequenting the cafés at night to sip green Chartreuse (a sweet liqueur made in a local monastery) or Armagnac (favored by Rosine). Dabney was sometimes absent, since he was wooing an appealing female student. Rosine and I were never romantically attracted to each other and, perhaps for that reason, became lifelong friends.

I didn't realize it at the time, since she always avoided talking about her life in the Resistance, but she apparently had been one of its genuine heroes. Decades later, on the fiftieth anniversary of the Resistance movement, the French government made a handful of videos featuring its outstanding heroes and heroines. To the astonishment of her husband, her three daughters, and her psychoanalytic colleagues, Rosine was the subject of one of them. Afterwards she herself wrote a memoir of that era of her life, called *La Traîne-Sauvage*. The book's cover features a picture of the twenty-year old Rosine as I knew her in Grenoble, wearing the same worn rain jacket.

Those few months at the University of Grenoble, when Rosine and I both celebrated our twenty-first birthdays, were among the happiest of my life.

I came to know a number of French students and faculty as well as my American soldier buddies. I felt completely at home in Grenoble, even though the circumstances could hardly have been more improvised. Among my few possessions of that period, I treasure the official letter that Professor Caraccio wrote toward the end of my sojourn.

Shortly after our Christmas performance of "Jesu, Joy Of Man's Desiring," my Grenoble sojourn came to an end and I was ordered to return to my military unit. In my absence, the company had been ordered to move from Liège to Frankfurt, Germany. En route to Frankfurt, I wondered what had happened to my jeep. I had entrusted it to a fellow GI in the company, but I had no way of knowing whether he was still with the company or had been sent home or had been obliged to give up the jeep.

My first reaction on rejoining my unit in Frankfurt was relief at finding both buddy and jeep intact. But the relief turned to unease when I realized that Lieutenant Gorski (Captain Hartshorne's replacement) had great power over me...and intended to use it. Gorski had bitterly resented my closeness to Hartshorne. As soon as I rejoined the company, his first words were: "I've been waiting for you to come back. Now we will see who is really in charge."

His tone was ominous and I took him seriously.

Gorski was a real bastard. He knew that Hartshorne and I had been friends despite the difference in rank. But Hartshorne was gone now, and Gorski was in command and ready to take revenge.

The situation called for quick action. The day after I arrived in Frankfurt, I took my jeep (graciously returned to me) and sought out the headquarters of the office in charge of sending soldiers like me to academic holding pens like Biarritz and Grenoble. I found the office and told the sergeant at the desk that I needed to be sent to another school ASAP. He told me I wasn't qualified for the only place available at the time. I asked him to explain, and he informed me that the army still had one or two slots open at the Guildhall School of Music in London, but only for fully qualified music students.

I told him he was looking directly at a genuine true-blue ipsy-pipsy music student. He grinned cynically, sensing my desperation. "Nice try," he said. "But without proof that you are a serious music student, there's no way I get to liberate you from whatever trouble you happen to be in." I asked him if he would do so if I could provide the proof that I really was qualified for the music student opening. "Sure," he said dismissively. "You really must be desperate."

I drove back to the barracks, got my flute out of my duffel bag, drove back to the sergeant and, to his amusement and astonishment, proceeded to perform for an audience of himself and two others in his office, the second movement of Bizet's *L'Arléssienne Suite*—a piece I had memorized for my graduation from the Boston Latin School. With a straight face and without comment, he pulled out the requisite forms and handed them to me. I filled them in. He signed them and said, "You'd better hurry, soldier. You leave for London tomorrow."

I drove back to the barracks, gave the jeep keys to my friend, and the next morning he took me to the station where I caught the train for London. I have no idea what happened when Gorski learned that I was gone, nor have I ever wasted any time worrying about it. I was en route to London and the Guildhall School of Music.

In sharp contrast to the University of Grenoble, London's Guildhall School of Music was a charmless grimy urban brick establishment whose administration couldn't have been more indifferent to the handful of GIs it had accepted for enrollment. From time to time a few young men in American uniforms could be seen wandering the halls of the school. I don't recall meeting a single one of them.

The school had little interest in me and even less in my flute playing. If it had an orchestra, I was not invited to join it. It did, however, offer piano lessons. So, twice a week for an hour or so, I appeared there for piano lessons. All I can remember now are the finger exercises. I learned a lot about finger exercises, but not much about piano playing. But I cherished my time at the Guildhall for two big reasons.

One was that it left me free to roam about in London for a glorious three months. I hung around the London School of Economics, freely wandering into courses. The highlight of each week was the Wednesday evening soirees over which Professor Harold Laski presided. I didn't realize that Laski had an international reputation as an intellectual and political scientist until much later, after I had returned to the United States and Harvard.

I found him very impressive. Each Wednesday, after serving a light dinner to the mix of Brits and American GIs who swarmed into his well-stocked library, he would deliver a thirty-minute lecture on some aspect of political culture, usually American, full of quotes recited from memory, without ever once referring to a note or book.

I remember one occasion when someone questioned one of his quotes and he replied in his crisp British accent, "I think you will find it on page 364 of Henry Adams's *Mont-Saint-Michel and Chartres*." Whereupon he walked over to his book shelves, fumbled a bit, found the book, opened it to page 364 and read the quote out loud, adding a few sentences for emphasis. It was a spectacular theatrical performance. He was apparently gifted with a photographic memory, to which he added more than a trifle of academic showmanship.

The other reason my stay in London proved memorable was the comely, if strange, Anne Blyth. Anne was a singer studying at the Guildhall, whom I met when our lesson times coincided. She had long brown hair, a spectacular figure, an appealing giggle, and was readily approachable. I suggested going out for coffee, and she cheerfully accepted. When we parted after coffee, she invited me for dinner on Saturday at her parents' home in the suburbs. She gave me the train instructions and said she would pick me up at the station when I arrived, which she did. I was delighted.

That dinner initiated one of the oddest sets of relationships I have ever had—both between Anne and myself, and her father and myself. Indeed, my most vivid memories of my London stay were of Anne and her father. I spent almost half of the next three months in their company and, as the relationship grew more intense and time-consuming, the only way I could resolve it was to take advantage of an opportunity to return to the United States a month earlier than my orders called for.

Our first dinner together was informal and amusing. Anne's mother said hardly a word, except to give directions to the maid who served the roast beef (a wonderful treat). Anne's father, an attorney, dominated the conversation with witty anecdotes about the eccentricities of the British court system. After dinner, Anne's parents retired, leaving the living room to us.

As soon as they left, Anne immediately cuddled up to me on the couch. I was most agreeably surprised. When I started to say something, she put her fingers to her lips suggesting that I not speak. We remained on the couch plastered against one another for a very long time. From time to time I sought a more direct access to her under her dress, but she gently rebuffed my initiatives. She encouraged all moves, however, that left her clothing intact. It was a stimulating—and frustrating—evening.

After a repeat dinner the next Saturday that followed the same script, Anne's father invited me for lunch at his club. Throughout the lunch, he was chatty and cheerful while I was feeling a bit tense. I sensed that he had invited me to lunch for a purpose, and if so, it remained hidden from view. As we were having coffee after lunch, he started to talk about Anne. I couldn't have been more attentive. He said he was very pleased that we had met and were getting along so well. She didn't seem to go out much with people her own age, he said, and he added that he was delighted that she now had an American friend.

After a long pause, as if he were trying to make up his mind about something, he said that from the time Anne was a baby he had gotten into the habit of reading to her at night and lulling her to sleep. He no longer read to her but she still needed those few moments every night of his lulling her to sleep. Ever so casually he added, "I think that may have gone on too long, and I'd be so grateful to you if you were to take over that delightful chore. It would be so much more appropriate for someone her own age to do so, since she really is no longer a little girl."

I was unclear about what exactly he meant by "that delightful chore," but I sure agreed with him that Anne was no longer a little girl.

Saturday night's dinner followed the same script as the previous two, with one exception. After dinner, to my disappointment, Anne's father didn't excuse himself. So the three of us—Anne, father, and myself—found ourselves making small talk over a brandy in the living room. Anne sat next to me, very close by but without touching.

I expected her father to finish his brandy and make a graceful exit, but he seemed firmly and comfortably settled in. On the other hand, Anne kept making gestures indicating that she was about to take her leave. And then she did so. She said she was tired and was going to turn in for the night. As she was leaving, she looked directly at me though she addressed her words to both of us. "I hope that at least one of you will tuck me in for the night," she said cheerily, and she walked out the door.

I was sure that father and daughter had had a conversation. But I was still quite unprepared when, a tense half-hour or so later, father said, "Well, she'll be getting sleepy about now." He rose from his worn leather armchair and, directing me to follow him, led me to Anne's bedroom. He knocked lightly on the door. When Anne said we should come in, he said to her, "Good night, dear Anne. Dan wants to lull you to sleep."

Whereupon, he patted me on the shoulder and left. Anne, wearing two-piece blue flannel pajamas, shifted from the center of the bed to one side and said, "I'm so pleased that Daddy convinced you to take over. It's so much more appropriate." Exactly the same words that Daddy had used at our luncheon earlier in the week.

I sat on the side of the bed. She put her head on my lap. I stroked her hair. She said, "Climb in beside me and hold me." I quickly followed her instructions. A lot more instructions followed, none of them verbal. Whenever I stroked her she purred, with her eyes closed and a blissful expression on her face. But she wouldn't let me kiss her, and she firmly rebuffed my efforts to get inside or remove her flannel armor.

Admittedly, the flannel pajamas were a vast improvement over her street clothes. And she was indiscriminate about where she wanted to be stroked. Eventually, my hands got to know every nuance, nook, and cranny of the girl under the flannel pajamas. Daddy and I were both correct. She sure was no longer a little girl.

I stayed with her for about an hour as she gradually got sleepier and sleepier. As she dozed off, I gave her a light good night kiss and left her bedroom in a state of acute frustration. Daddy took me to the train station without much conversation. As he took his leave, he said quietly, "Thank you. I trust you."

At school on Monday, Anne greeted me warmly and said how much she and Daddy had enjoyed our dinner and that I must come and have dinner with them at least once or twice during the week as well as on the weekend, and that she would take the train with me on the days we had classes at the same time—Mondays and Thursdays.

I quickly accepted her invitation, certain that the flannel pajama could not conceivably prove be more than a temporary obstacle. But I was wrong. She had a repertory of flannel pajamas, red and pink as well as blue. They could have been a second skin as far as I was concerned, because I could find no way to strip them away.

After a few weeks, the ritual grew so frustrating for me physically that I was desperate to find a way to end it. I liked Anne. I liked her Daddy. I liked her mother too, even though we hardly spoke. But I was a twenty-one-year-old male fearful of being driven insane from sexual frustration.

In March of 1946, I was assigned a spot on a boat returning to the United States. I opted to take this early departure, even though I still had a month to go at the school. The lovely and voluptuous Anne and her Daddy chased me out of London.

Curiously, I have never before described these events. I usually told people, "I had a wonderful time in London at the Guildhall School of Music, but I had to leave London early because of a beautiful girl." No one ever pressed me to elaborate in detail. They made their own surmises, and I'm sure that all of them were wildly off the mark, since the situation was so truly extraordinary that it would have been hard to surmise correctly.

Whenever I pondered it over the years, which wasn't very often, I came to the conclusion that Anne and her Daddy were locked in a drama that bordered on incest. Daddy knew it. I don't think Anne did, though she knew enough to draw her own rigid lines. I suspect that at the time her sexuality may not have fully developed along adult lines, and that she was—at least at the time—still in love with Daddy, partly emotionally, partly physically.

I didn't ever feel used or exploited. I thoroughly enjoyed cuddling with Anne. She was lovable, and exceptionally cuddle-able. I think I did feel embarrassment...for all of us. Mostly for Anne's mother, who must have known but was helpless to act. But also for Daddy, who knew he was on the edge of Big Trouble but wasn't sure how to deal with it, to the point of not realizing how odd it was for a father to be pushing a foreign soldier into his beloved daughter's bed. I was embarrassed for Anne, who had somehow to reconcile her big girl's body with her little girl's desires.

And finally, I was embarrassed for myself. I had found myself in a situation that had gone far beyond the experience of a callow twenty-one-year-old virgin. I knew that I was being asked to play a bit role, though an important one, in a family drama that raised issues with very deep roots. And I didn't know whether I had played my part properly.

On the boat back to the United States and civilian life, I reflected on my army experience in Europe. On the whole, I felt I had acquitted myself honorably. I had helped to blow up some enemy bridges and to defend others similarly engaged. I had been involved in the Battle of the Bulge in the last months of the war in Europe. And I had endured and learned to cope with army life. The army was a rough foster home. But I had developed adaptive and survival skills in other foster homes and was able to use them to advantage.

When I was demobilized in April 1946, I felt good about myself and about having served as a soldier in the army of the United States, just as my father had served in a similar capacity in World War I.

Back to Harvard

IN MY FRESHMAN YEAR at Harvard, before my military service, the Socratic concept that the goal of philosophy is to reveal how best to live one's life had seized my imagination.

Yet, during the War, it seemed to me that I had not spent even an hour pursuing an examined life. Staying alive, driving in the dark, learning how to cope and survive in the military—that was the content of my army brain. And I was tired of it.

I looked forward to exploring various aspects of the examined life, as elaborated in Bertrand Russell's classic, *Problems of Philosophy.*[5] In Russell's view, confining our observations to the domain of proven scientific knowledge is like imprisoning the self in a tiny room, cut off from a world full of wonders. Examining life in an unfamiliar aspect, says Russell, opens up "many unsuspected possibilities."The questions that philosophy raises, he says, "enrich our intellectual imagination...Through the greatness of the universe which philosophy contemplates, the mind is also rendered great, and becomes capable of that union with the universe that constitutes its highest good." The questions of philosophy are "of the profoundest interest to our spiritual lives."[6]

I was eager to dig more deeply into these questions, and I learned that doing so can yield valuable guides for living. On the other hand,

---

5   Bertrand Russell, *The Problems of Philosophy* (London: Oxford University Press, 1912). See especially Chapter XV, "The Value of Philosophy."
6   Ibid., 240

it didn't surprise me that Socrates' fellow citizens had decided to rid themselves of an annoying gadfly (as he described himself). Socrates himself may have been brutally silenced, but his preaching and reasoning profoundly influenced me, along with countless millions of followers throughout the centuries.

Now that I was back from the war, I had a clear objective and a strategy for pursuing it. I would study for a doctorate in philosophy with a view to becoming a professor of philosophy, preferably at Harvard.

I no longer would have to commute to Harvard from the 'burbs of Boston—a form of second-class citizenship. Thanks to the GI Bill, I found myself comfortably housed along the Charles River in a residential Harvard dormitory, Dunster House, a five-minute walk from Harvard Square and all my classes. My roommate was an old friend from the Boston Latin School, Arthur White, who in later years became my business partner as well as a life-long friend.

I had a rough plan: through philosophy I would learn how to live the good life. I would grow wise and learned and reveal the path of wisdom to future generations of naïve students like myself. I would find a home at Harvard and happily settle there.

It seemed like a grand idea at the time.

I plunged eagerly into my philosophy courses. I was particularly interested in American pragmatism. A half century earlier, William James and Charles Peirce had developed pragmatism as a distinctive American philosophy. These seminal thinkers emphasized the social character of the self and, along with John Dewey and George Herbert Mead, made social philosophy central to thinking about pragmatism.

I soon discovered, however, that in my absence, Harvard's philosophy department had turned its back on the founders of pragmatism as outmoded and amateurish (even including their own most famous thinkers like William James). Its professors had virtually banished the societal aspects of philosophy. The leading thinkers in the department were now primarily interested in logic and epistemology, not in the human condition. The entire field of Anglo-American philosophy was trapped into not knowing how to respond to the demands that it become ever more scientific, and I believe it lost its way.

I took two philosophy courses in my first semester back at Harvard. One was a course on epistemology given by Professor C.I. Lewis. The other was a course on ethics, the province of Professor Henry Aiken.

I enjoyed both courses but they raised troubling questions in my mind. The course with C.I. Lewis was fascinating. He immediately focused on the philosophy of Immanuel Kant and what Kant called the "problem of the synthetic a priori." I was surprised to learn that this arcane phrase harbored an issue of prime importance for philosophy and for our quest for human knowledge.

Kant was exploring the question of whether we humans had access to any genuine knowledge that was not based on what we had acquired from experience. In other words, can thought alone and logical analysis alone lead to genuine knowledge, or must we depend on science and other forms of empirical investigation for all of our meaningful knowledge?

Kant's historic conclusion was that yes, there exists at least one form of knowledge that is prior to experience. It is possible, Kant concluded, to advance *mathematical* knowledge without depending on empirical testing.

The implications were clear: both philosophical reflection and logical argumentation—the major tools of philosophy—did not, could not, lead to knowledge, much less to wisdom. Math, yes; the truths of living, no.

This conclusion troubled me. It implied that philosophical reflection and logical reasoning could contribute little, if anything, to a valid understanding of how best to live.

If that was the case, why was I immersing myself ever more deeply in these cognitive pursuits?

Henry Aiken's course on ethics also stirred doubts in me. It was far less rigorous than C.I. Lewis' course on epistemology. Aiken was vague about the rationale for people's belief systems and ethical values, relying heavily on logical reasoning, while ignoring cultural and psychological influences.

Neither course had anything compelling to say about how best to live. I had begun to question my own assumptions about philosophy. Was I letting my own desires about what to expect from philosophy distort my thinking? Had my enthusiasm carried me away? Was my conception of philosophy as the quest for how best to live a naïve one? Was I giving too much credence to logic?

I began to wonder whether the problem was not just my own naïveté, but the academic discipline of philosophy itself. Something seemed to have gone astray in this ancient tradition. I suspected that philosophy as an academic discipline had become dysfunctional by attempting to meet an existential challenge through becoming more scientific—a plausible but inappropriate response.

In searching for an explanation of the bleak turn taken by academic philosophy, I was particularly drawn to one faculty philosopher, Willard Van Orman Quine.

Professor Quine, then a promising young assistant professor in the Philosophy Department, eventually became one of the world's most outstanding logicians, in the grand tradition of famous Harvard philosophers.

Quine was the most concise thinker I had ever met. He could express in a single sentence what others would take paragraphs to say. He was an artist of thought and language, a Picasso of verbal expression, conveying complex thoughts in the most parsimonious manner possible. He was, moreover, a friendly and agreeable person with a warm smile, although he often seemed a bit remote—at least to me as a student.

In several of his courses, Quine had demonstrated persuasively that logic by itself was incapable of establishing empirical truths— truths about existence. Such truths had to be introduced through the back door, as it were, through "existence premises." Logic had nothing to contribute to the truths of living.

If philosophy's major methods for finding truth were reduced to logic and reasoning, was it not logical to conclude that its limitations were far more narrow and unenlightening than I had ever imagined?

I suspected that Quine might be able to answer the question that most bewildered me. What, I wondered, was the relationship between "logic" as a tool of reasoning and discovering answers to the existential question of how to live? If applying logic provided valid answers, Quine, the virtuoso of logic, would surely show me how to connect the tool of logic to the Socratic question of how to live the good life.

Quine and I had developed a casual relationship, and I was thrilled when he invited me to dinner. I spent most of the week before the date of our dinner thinking about how to ask him my questions. The trick would be to phrase them so that they wouldn't come across as a criticism of his work.

After dinner, sitting out on his porch on a warm Cambridge July night, I screwed up my courage and said to him: "Van, I hope you won't mind if I ask you a personal question—not to pry into your life but to help me with a decision I'm trying to make."

He said, "Sure," and poured both of us another cup of coffee.

"Well," I said, drawing a deep breath, "Here goes. My impression is that so many disciplines have broken away from philosophy that it hasn't been left with much distinctively its own. Logical reasoning is philosophy's only remaining proprietary tool. When philosophers argue with one another and logically prove that one or the other position is wrong, they are in pursuit of truth.

"Now you and other logicians," I said, "are depriving philosophy of the one method left to it: the tool of logic. You, along with Russell and Whitehead, have demonstrated that logic by itself adds no new knowledge or information about the world. Sure, logic may be useful in helping us to clarify our thinking and perform other mental operations. But by itself logical reasoning can never lead to truths about the nature, purpose and meaning of life and its values."

I told Van that I had found his boldness in exploring the foundations of math and logic to be one of the most impressive intellectual feats I'd ever encountered, but that at least for me personally, it led to a bleak conclusion: it had put the final nail in the coffin of philosophy.

Van Quine sipped his coffee quietly.

I plowed ahead. "The history of philosophy," I said, "has been one long process of stripping philosophy of its unique methods for gaining knowledge, insight and wisdom about life. If this is true, what is left? Why would anyone want to devote his life to the remnants?

"And here I come to my personal questions. Am I even approximately correct in my inference? And if so, why do you, Van Quine, continue to work in the field of philosophy?"

For a long time, Quine did not answer.

Finally, he did speak. He thanked me for grouping him with towering figures like Russell and Whitehead and said modestly that he did not see himself as having that sort of stature. He said he thought my summary was overstated, that there was much that remained distinctive to philosophy.

But he went on to say that no one could disagree that philosophy's grand pretensions of the past had been radically diminished.

Speaking for himself personally, he said, philosophy continued to interest him. He had discovered he had a flair for it, and a career in Harvard's philosophy department suited his temperament extremely well.

At the end of that memorable evening, I thanked him, left his house, and strolled back to my apartment in a bemused state, convinced that I had to abandon my plans for dedicating my life to academic philosophy.

Several years ago, I had occasion to open my old Quine textbook for Mathematical Logic 19B. The book opened to page 205, which I had underlined and annotated as a graduate student.

Here is what appears on page 205:

§ 37   ABSTRACTION OF RELATIONS   205

— the class of all those members of x which are pairs of elements. It is the largest relation included in x, and it coincides with x only in case x is itself a relation. It will be referred to briefly as $\dot{x}$. When we are concerned with a complex expression in place of 'x' the superior dot may conveniently be placed at the beginning; e.g., "$(x \frown y)$'. The following definition is accordingly adopted.

D26. $\ulcorner \dot{\zeta} \urcorner$ or $\ulcorner \cdot \zeta \urcorner$ for $\ulcorner \hat{\alpha}\hat{\beta}(\zeta(\alpha,\beta)) \urcorner$.

The following theorem and metatheorem reveal positions from which the dot is suppressible.

†436. $(x)(y)(z)$ $\dot{x}(y,z) \equiv x(y,z)$.

Proof.   *433 (& D26) $\dot{x}(y,z) \equiv .y, z \in V . x(y,z)$
          *100 (& D24) $\equiv x(y,z)$

*437. $\vdash \ulcorner \cdot \hat{\alpha}\hat{\beta}\phi = \hat{\alpha}\hat{\beta}\phi \urcorner$.

Proof. Case 1: α is not β.
       *433, *188 $\vdash \ulcorner \hat{\alpha}\hat{\beta} \ L433 = \hat{\alpha}\hat{\beta} \ R433 \urcorner$
       *100, *188 (& D25) $= \hat{\alpha}\hat{\beta}\phi \urcorner$.   (1)
       *171 (& D26) $\vdash \ulcorner [1 \equiv] 437 \urcorner$.

Case 2: α is β. Let γ and δ be new and distinct.
*137, *188 (& D25) $\vdash \ulcorner \hat{\alpha}\hat{\alpha}\phi = \hat{\delta}(\exists \alpha)(\alpha, \alpha \in V . \delta = \alpha;\alpha . \phi) \urcorner$
*234b, *188 (& D25) $= \hat{\alpha}\hat{\gamma}(\phi . \alpha = \gamma) \urcorner$ (1)
*437 (Case 1) $= \cdot \hat{\alpha}\hat{\gamma}(\phi . \alpha = \gamma) \urcorner$
(1), *227 $= \cdot \hat{\alpha}\hat{\alpha}\phi \urcorner$.

Use of †436 and *437 will be tacit; dots will simply be dropped, without comment, from the positions $\ulcorner \dot{\zeta}(\eta, \theta) \urcorner$ and $\ulcorner \cdot \hat{\alpha}\hat{\beta}\phi \urcorner$. (Cf. proofs of †446, †447.) This practice is still followed when the relevant context $\ulcorner \dot{\zeta}(\eta, \theta) \urcorner$ or $\ulcorner \cdot \hat{\alpha}\hat{\beta}\phi \urcorner$ is concealed under definitional abbreviations. E.g., the second dot in '$\ddot{x}$' would be dropped by tacit use of *437 on the ground that it has the position "$\dot{\hat{y}}\hat{z} \, x(y,z)$' when '$\dot{x}$' is expanded by D26. (Cf. proof of †450; also § 38.)

The relational part V of V is the universal relation — the relation which every element bears to every element. It is the class of all pairs of elements.

†438. $\dot{V} = \dot{x}(\exists y)(\exists z)(y, z \in V . x = y; z)$

Mathematical Logic, Willard Van Orman Quine, Harvard University Press, 1940

I could have reproduced virtually any other page in Quine's 331-page book and it would look pretty much the same. Most of the book now strikes me as incomprehensible, though I know that work of this sort has made valuable contributions to computer science. Computer science is a vibrant and exciting field (in which my own daughter, Nicole, excels).

But it has little to give to the quest for the truths of living.

Many years later, shortly before Quine died, I visited him at the Harvard Faculty Club. I believe he was over ninety years old at the time of my visit. He still had the same warm shy smile. We spoke cordially for a few minutes. I recalled his statement that his career at Harvard had suited him well, and I realized how right he had been about himself.

The conclusion I eventually reached is that the combination of my own youthful ignorance plus philosophy's misguided efforts to become more scientific had made it senseless for me to follow my original plan of pursuing academic philosophy as a career. Academic philosophy had little to teach me or anyone else about how best to live.

This conclusion came as a disagreeable surprise. It upended the plans for my future life that I had cherished throughout my years in military service. Indeed, it evoked the same painful sense of disorientation I had felt in my foster home years. I was face to face with yet another loss.

There was, however, a big difference between the experience of loss in foster homes and the experience of needing to rethink my goals for the future at Harvard. I was no longer a helpless child, dependent on others. I was an autonomous adult, a veteran of the Great War and a fully engaged member of the Harvard community.

I now had a strong sense of agency and independence. It had come as a shock that academic philosophy ignored the quest for how to live. But I had kept faith with this goal.

After weeks of waffling and confusion, I decided to co-major in psychology for my remaining courses because I thought its roots as a discipline were related to philosophy. I had come to believe that some schools of philosophy such as ethics, pragmatism and idealism could not be understood without reference to the psychological convictions of its adherents.

So, instead of focusing exclusively on courses in the Philosophy Department, I applied for a joint degree in philosophy and the new department of Social Relations. Soc Rel, as it was called, had brought together several branches of psychology with other social sciences to form a single unified discipline.

I received my B.A. with high honors, a source of great satisfaction for myself, and especially for my father. His burden of guilt for the breakup of our family had persisted undiminished over the years, and he assumed as a matter of course that I would end up tragically, due to his failure. It was a relief to him that I seemed to be coping and had not been lost to booze, criminality or destitution.

Girls

IN THE FEW REMAINING months of my last semester at Harvard, I devoted much of my time to the pursuit of smart, sexy, funny Radcliffe coeds.

Most of all, I talked.

I talked volcanically from the minute I woke up in the morning until the minute I fell asleep exhausted at night. At that time, there was a Harvard Square restaurant called the Hayes-Bickford that was favored by students. It was a low-priced restaurant chain—a plastic table type of eatery. Almost every afternoon I went there for coffee and talking. I talked with whoever was there. Most of the time I knew the people I talked at. Sometimes I didn't. Sometimes the listeners worked in shifts. I hardly knew the difference.

What did I talk about? Everything. Except for sports, which had ceased to interest me after the Red Sox went into slump mode. No subject was too mundane—or too vast—to escape my commentary, rhapsody, and elaboration. I've been told that at times I talked for four or five hours uninterrupted with hardly a pause to pee or eat a Danish.

Over subsequent decades, the volcanic eruptions of talk burned out, and today more often than not I remain quiet at social gatherings (with rare lapses into loquacity).

But in those few years the release of pent-up energies reached its peak and exploded in an unending flow of speech expressing my wonder at the infinite variety of life experiences. A sense of wonder was one of my major philosophical categories.

When I found a captive audience, especially an attractive coed, I simply could not let go. One day I was having coffee with an adorable student friend, a girl with long blond California-style hair, Muriel Michelova. After an hour or so she got up to leave so she could prepare for her tutorial later that day. I was reluctant to lose her as an audience and I asked her the subject of her tutorial. She said she was supposed to have read Santayana's "Scepticism and Animal Faith," and since she hadn't done so, she wanted to at least skim through it before meeting with her tutor.

"Don't go," I urged her. "I'll give you a quick summary of the Santayana book so you won't get into trouble with your tutor."

"Are you sure?" she asked. "He is pissed at me as it is, and I don't want to make matters worse."

I reassured her and proceeded to a lengthy exposition of what Santayana was trying to convey. Unfortunately, I had not had occasion to actually read the book, but I found the title wonderfully suggestive and laid on Muriel what I thought Santayana would—and should—have said about a theme so pregnant with meaning as animal faith in its encounter with Enlightenment skepticism.

Muriel relaxed. We went on talking until the time came for her tutorial She would later tell all of our friends of her encounter with her tutor. She said he listened to her in a state of stupor, and that his jaw actually hung open—a sight she had heard about but had never before witnessed first-hand.

"That's the most outrageous bullshit I have ever heard," he finally exclaimed in wonderment. "You haven't read a word of the book, have you?" Muriel admitted she had not, and eventually her tutor forgave her, suspecting what had happened. The story, with elaborations, made the rounds, and my smirking friends would ask me to explain Santayana to them.

❧

During my very first summer back from the army in 1946, I managed to get to Provincetown for a number of weekend breaks.

It was there that an appealing medical student from New York, named Alex (for Alexandra), finally took me out of my misery. She couldn't believe that I had served in the army for three years and was still a virgin. Fortunately, she regarded this defect as the symptom of a disorder that any dedicated physician would surely want to cure, and she set about fixing it with enormous dedication.

I couldn't have been more grateful or gratified. And once the summer was over, I shifted my weekend holidays from Cape Cod to the Upper West Side of New York where I spent many splendid weekends in Alex's apartment, until her schedule no longer gave her free weekends. Alex and I drifted apart but I have always cherished my initiation at her "hands."

Once launched, I proved to be an enthusiastic student. Those were the years before the sexual revolution had liberated the nation's campuses. Most of the girls I dated were sexually unresponsive on our first and even second date. But fortunately, the coeds at Harvard were far more cooperative than the young ladies of Dorchester. Patient wooing was definitely encouraged...and rewarded. I devoted much time and dedication to wooing, and I found it deeply rewarding.

"Oh, hello there."

I AM A LOVER of women. Women have always been important in my life. Like many other men, I find failure in love devastating. So in grad school, when I found myself involved with a beautiful, brilliant—and complicated—graduate student, the emotional stakes were high.

She was Canadian. Her name was Mary Mothersill. She was in the philosophy department. I had met her in Willard Van Orman Quine's graduate course, Mathematical Logic 19B. She and I were two of six motley souls who took the course. Even though I was no longer enrolled in the philosophy department, Quine had permitted me to take the graduate course because he knew me from other courses I had taken with him as an undergraduate.

Though she wasn't particularly interested in logic, Mothersill shared my respect for Quine and felt that mastery of logic would balance her interest in the ethical and aesthetic aspects of philosophy. She was fully committed to becoming an outstanding academic philosopher, which she did later in life with great success.

She hung out with three other uber-intellectual Radcliffe grad students whose names I remember to this day: Lenore O'Boyle, Gregor Armstrong (quite female despite her name), and Barbara Jenkins. They were a formidable and intimidating quartet of intellectual women.

In order to be able to spend as much time as possible with Mary, I joined the group as often as I could. They put up with me, though they didn't seem overly fond of men.

After a too-infrequent dinner date, we sometimes would return to her apartment. Each time we did so, I would make tentative advances that didn't get anywhere. Each of those experiences was a downer, leaving me feeling low for days. Then, one night, to my great surprise, she responded to me in a most cooperative, even enthusiastic, fashion.

We had a long tender night together, and at three in the morning I floated back to my own apartment in a state of sheer joy. I hadn't told her how deeply I had fallen for her because I was pretty sure that her feelings didn't match mine and I didn't want to frighten her away. But after that wonderful night together, I was sure that my feelings were reciprocated, and it filled me with happiness.

I awoke the next morning exhilarated and excited. I could hardly wait to see her. After breakfast I walked to Harvard Yard, heading straight for Emerson Hall, the location of the philosophy department where she had a small office. As I approached Emerson I saw her exit the building carrying her familiar green book bag. I walked toward her with a huge foolish grin on my face, ready to embrace her. As we came closer she sidestepped my embrace, paused briefly, and said casually, "Oh, hello there," and walked on.

To say that I was stunned understates the devastating blow of those few casual words. I slowly walked back to my apartment, compulsively repeating: "Oh, hello there."

From time to time I would add a phrase, such as:

"Oh, hello there. So we made love. What's the big deal?" or

"Oh, hello there. You weren't the first and won't be the last," or

"Oh, hello there. Don't get any ideas just because we had a night together," or simply:

"Oh, hello there. Fuck off."

❧

My self-doubts deepened severely after that distressful morning. One of the consequences of unrequited love is a form of self-doubt that psychologists call a "narcissistic injury," a wounded sense of self.

I felt that Mothersill had decided that she would give me a try, and clearly she must have concluded that I had failed. Not only was I disappointed in love, I was also disappointed in myself. Here was the kind of failure I dreaded.

The prospect of seeing her again was simply too painful for me. I couldn't conceive of any outcome other than further rejection. So I decided that I would avoid her and her friends. I had no difficulty in doing so since we belonged to different graduate departments. I tried (unsuccessfully) to put her out of my mind. But I never saw her again.

In later years I learned from friends in New York that she was a highly regarded professor of philosophy at Barnard College and the Graduate Faculty of Arts and Sciences at Columbia University. It wasn't until I started to write this book that I decided to find out more about her. When I googled her, I was saddened to learn that she had died in 2008. I found a long list of articles from her former students, full of fond memories of her.

Here is a quote from one of her friends and former students, Linda Nochlin:

> *Her stories of Canada, of Harvard Graduate School, her family in Victoria, British Columbia were the stuff of myth. Her life seemed mysterious and trans-figured, as did British Columbia when I finally got to visit her and her fam-ily there: the retired British colonels, the white elephant sales at the church, the manicured lawns, the seeming even temper and charming manners of the inhabitants, though Mary explained that the rate of alcoholism and nervous breakdown was high...it seemed as though I were participating in the exotic rituals of a Pacific Island tribe.... It is hard to explain how extraordinary Mary was.*

Another former student and friend, Mary Wiseman, wrote:

> *Although she lived alone, traveled alone, and would have it no other way, she was a good friend, working hard at...seeing things straight and saying them plain.*

The picture that emerges from the variety of remembrances is of a woman with extraordinary intellectual gifts—a good friend to many people, warm but distant, easy to talk to but mysterious, a model of logical clarity but deeply opaque. She lived her entire life as a loner, even to the extent of travelling alone.

Nothing that any of the writers said came as a surprise to me. They depicted their friend as I clearly remember her. But the fact that she had never chosen to share her life with anyone caused me to rethink her withering "Oh, hello there" decades earlier. In retrospect, it probably had not conveyed contemptuous rejection (my conviction at the time) but rather Mothersill's defensive way of maintaining a safe distance from intimacy.

The Mothersill story is just one example of an ingrained pattern. Until I reached late middle age, I had difficulty choosing women who were right for me, and for whom I was equally well-suited. This was probably the most serious consequence of my foster home experience.

Skill in picking a potential mate is a key to the survival of the species. It is a skill acquired unconsciously while growing up. A stable, loving family is probably the ideal environment in which it can develop and flourish.

In my teens (and later as well), I found myself strongly attracted to girls who had experienced a warm family life. My pull toward close-knit family life was stronger in most cases than my attraction to the girls who happened to come from these families.

As another consequence of my foster home experience, I also developed a tendency to overvalue the wrong things and undervalue the right ones. I overvalued high achievement and talent of any sort (musical, artistic, intellectual, high levels of skill in all forms), just as I did with Mary Mothersill. I undervalued warmth and a capacity for intimacy and caring.

I lacked self-confidence, overreacting with gratitude to any and all signs of reciprocity, particularly sexual. This tendency sowed the seeds of future problems.

Mary Mothersill's apparent rejection of my desires for intimacy reinforced my self-doubts about being a person others could love. It undercut my fragile confidence that I could find the intimacy of love with someone with whom I could share unconditional trust.

Deep down I suspected that I was not meant to live a love-centered life and had better not let my expectations rise too high. I should not expect to be accepted as an insider; I was destined to remain on the fringe.

The full impact of the Mothersill incident did not strike until years later. At the time, I was in my early twenties and my energy and animal spirits were irrepressible. I was full of excitement and anticipation about the future. I could hardly wait to find out how my story was going to unfold. It seemed like an amazing adventure, full of unexpected happenings, some bad, but some wondrous.

It was time to woo some new girl friends.

The Worst "Bright Idea" I Ever Had

I WAS DELIGHTED TO discover that there were Radcliffe women who were not aloof, but indeed quite approachable. I was particularly drawn to two—Maritza and Marti—who shared the same Radcliffe dorm.

Maritza was one of the sexiest women I have ever known. She made you understand what the phrase "smoldering sexuality" meant. She was small, rather dark, gorgeously bosomed and demonstrative. When I first met her, she was involved with a good-looking, athletic young man, and when they were together, they couldn't keep their hands off each other.

For reasons I have never understood, the young man subsequently headed off to Alaska. Maritza continued to write to him and even visit him in Alaska, but gradually she warmed up to me—and vice versa. To my great satisfaction, she had no trouble in transferring her demonstrative tendencies.

I also dated Marti. Physically, Marti was the opposite of Maritza. Where Maritza was voluptuous and rounded everywhere, Marti was tall, thin, handsome rather than pretty, with high cheekbones and a classic Nordic look. She was quite striking.

The highlight of my relationship with Marti was two romantic and satisfying nights we spent together in Provincetown, in a small bungalow at the end of a wharf jutting out into the bay. I still remember that the cottage was the rental property of a man with the unforget-table name of Toto Tamborini.

My agreeable dalliances with Maritza and Marti consumed most of my leisure time in my final months at Harvard. Both knew of my plans to go to Paris. Cambridge was not truly home to any of us, and it was assumed that eventually we would all go our separate ways.

After Marti graduated from Radcliffe, she decided to remain in Cambridge instead of going back to her parents' home in Teaneck, New Jersey. Her explanation for not wanting to go home was char-acteristically blunt. She cheerfully announced that she hated her mother and, for that matter, wasn't too keen on her father, who she felt was weak and always knuckling under to her mother.

Marti described her mother as cold, angry, reserved, unloving, demanding, critical, and disapproving. Marti was an only child, and on her fell the full brunt of her mother's disposition.

I had never known anyone who hated his or her mother (or at least admitted to it), and assumed that Marti was exaggerating for the shock effect.

A few months before I was to leave for Paris, Marti received an urgent phone call. Her mother had suffered a stroke, and her father told Marti to get on a train and return home immediately to Teaneck to assist him in caring for her.

Overnight, the bottom had fallen out of Marti's life. Her cool façade dissolved in tears and agony. Her worst nightmare had become reality. She felt trapped and in despair. Her rhetoric about how much she hated her mother took on added intensity. She felt her life had ended.

I sought to console her by saying that her return was likely to be temporary, until her mother recovered. But Marti was inconsolable and certain that she would never escape.

It was then that I came up with my "bright idea."

I said, "Suppose that your mother recovers enough so that you can leave, and you tell them that before she fell ill we had planned for you to join me in Paris."

She said, "They would never buy that unless we were engaged to be married."

It was at that moment that I impulsively blurted out what turned out to be the most disastrous utterance of my life. I said, "So let's tell them we're engaged."

She dismissed the idea as unrealistic and impractical, and went back to "woe-is-me" mode as she started to pack for her return trip to Teaneck hell-on-earth.

Once she had arrived in Teaneck, Marti and I stayed in close touch by phone and letter. Each time I spoke with her, she sounded more depressed, more defeated, more down—even though her mother was making progress in both speech and movement. On one phone call, she said, "Your plan is the only way it can ever work. Do you think you can come to Teaneck and talk to my mother and father?" I reassured her that I could and we made plans for me to do so.

I made a special trip to New Jersey to meet her parents. Their home was small, formal, and exceptionally neat. Her father, whom she resembled, was tall and thin. He worked in New York for a large insurance company. He was cordial and somewhat sentimental, showing me pictures of Marti as she was growing up—to her embarrassment. Her mother did not seem like an ogre. She was smaller and less self-assured than I thought she would be. Of course, she was in a wheelchair and spoke with a slur.

Her father inquired about how I planned to live in Paris. I explained about the GI Bill and my savings, and he seemed satisfied. The word "engagement" never came up. But it hovered unspoken in the background. Before I left, they agreed that if Marti's mother continued to make progress, Marti could join me in Paris in three to four months.

I returned to Cambridge to ready myself for my Paris adventure. In anticipating Marti's coming to Paris, I visualized an extension of our lovely weekend in Toto Tamborini's cottage in Provincetown. Marti would stay with me for a few months until she decided what she wanted to do. I would have done a good deed and saved her from a fate that was grinding her down.

I would enjoy her companionship for a few months in Paris. Then we would go on with our lives, separately.

Ha!

The Rue Servandoni

AS SOON AS MY leave of absence took hold, I took off for Paris, joyful and full of hope for the future.

It was my second visit to the City of Light. I had spent five days in Paris as a soldier in the fall of 1945 while en route to the University of Grenoble in the south of France. Now, I was back in my dream city, Paris, which held a special place in the intellectual life of my generation of Americans.

My first month in Paris was lonely and disappointing. My French friend Rosine had found a furnished room for me to rent. It was a bright, spacious and affordable room on the Avenue de Lamballe in the Sixteenth Arrondissement. The Sixteenth Arrondissement is an upper middle-class family neighborhood, so bourgeois and respectable as to bore a young single American male out of his skull.

I was constantly lonely and ill at ease. The restaurants were expensive and forbiddingly formal. The streets at night were empty except for elegant couples walking their elegant dogs. The stores were daunting for cash-strapped students like myself. I knew no one except Rosine. She spent some time with me every week but had her own busy life to lead.

Every night I would take the autobus to the Left Bank, where the cafés were crowded with young people, including many other Americans. Everyone seemed coupled off, laughing and flirting. The epicenter of the Left Bank was the intersection of the Boulevards Saint-Germain and Saint-Michel. I headed there each night, wandering along the Seine and up and down the two boulevards, lingering over my dinner at one of the less expensive outdoor cafés.

After dinner, I would often stroll by the Deux Magots and the Café Flore, supposed haunts of Jean-Paul Sartre and Simone de Beauvoir, whose ground-breaking feminist book, *The Second Sex*, had recently been published. I kept hoping to catch a glimpse of this celebrated existentialist couple.

During the day I tried to read and write, sometimes in my room, more often at one of the neighborhood cafés. This time, I was not in Paris as a tourist, and though I did some sightseeing and a great deal of walking, I felt I had to focus my time and attention on the writing I had set out to do.

By the end of my fourth week on the Right Bank I decided to move to the Left Bank. I devoted several days to walking up and down the streets looking for a room to rent.

On the third day of my search I found what I was looking for on the Rue Servandoni—a small street in the Sixth Arrondissement that connects the Place Saint-Sulpice and its dark forbidding church with the Jardins de Luxembourg, the magnificent park and gardens that are one of the great public spaces of Paris civility.

My room—a studio apartment—was in a residential hotel with a large courtyard. It was a longish room with a kitchen at one end, a large bed at the other end, and a table, dining chairs, and several comfortable armchairs in the middle of the room. I was to spend my best months in Paris at the Hotel des Principautés Unies, for that was the pretentious name of this most unpretentious of living quarters.

Best of all, a friendly young American, Lyle Joyce, who became a life-long friend, occupied the studio adjoining mine. Lyle was also in Paris on the GI Bill. He had enrolled at the Sorbonne in the same program that I was to join in the spring, working on his doctoral thesis on the writings of Saint Thomas Aquinas.

I soon discovered that Lyle was far more interested in writing poetry than in studying medieval philosophy—and spent considerably more time at it. He came from Spartanburg, South Carolina, and was a graduate of Notre Dame, a devout Catholic who had narrowly missed entering the priesthood. Lyle readily admitted that the appeals of sex and family life had overwhelmed his priestly leanings.

When I was growing up in Boston, Irish Catholics were the enemy. My stereotype of an American Irish Catholic male was of a heavy-drinking, prejudiced, virulent anti-Semitic hooligan. My experience in the army had not weakened this stereotype: I had no close friendships with Irish Catholic soldiers. Here, now, was Lyle, Irish Catholic to the core. Good-natured. Warm. Intelligent. Pleasantly ugly. And totally accepting of my Jewish background, without a smidgen of that Irish anti-Semitic bullying that had posed a daily physical threat when I was growing up in Boston.

Life in Paris was starting to improve. And I was hoping that it would improve even more when Marti was able to join me as her mother recovered.

I hoped that the apartment would not be too small for two people. I was expecting Marti to arrive in a matter of weeks.

On the train from Paris to Le Havre to meet Marti's boat coming from New York, I began to feel apprehensive. Suppose she became claustrophobic in my small quarters on the Rue Servandoni? Suppose she hated Paris? (Marti felt strongly about almost everything, and was usually contrarian in her tastes—despising what others liked and embracing what they rejected.) Most of all, how well would we get along? We barely knew each other: the longest period of time we had spent together was the one weekend in Provincetown.

"Well," I said to myself, "You will soon find out."

I had arrived in Le Havre five hours before her boat docked, and spent a chunk of the waiting time watching a movie at a local theatre. Marti was almost the last one off the boat and I found myself growing increasingly anxious. When she finally got off the boat, her appearance shocked me. She had lost weight and looked like someone emerging from a concentration camp rather than from a luxury liner. Her face was pale and gaunt, and even her smile was grim. She was exhausted and started chain-smoking right away. We both felt self-conscious on the train back to Paris. I apologized in advance for the modesty of my hotel room. But when she saw it, she grumbled that it wasn't as bad as she feared it would be.

When I made a tentative advance toward her, she pulled back, saying she needed time. I immediately stopped, with deepening concern, suspecting (correctly) that it would be some time before she was ready for any form of intimacy. After our Provincetown weekend, we had continued our physical relations, though they were frequently troubled. She would initially respond warmly and enthusiastically—for the first few minutes. Then, more often than not, she would abruptly lose interest, shifting from hot to cold.

I used to refer to this pattern as her Automatic Refrigerating Device. It was as if, in my advances, I inadvertently flipped a switch, turning her from warm to freezing.

I had always assumed that this off-putting response would gradually disappear as we got to know each other better. Never did I imagine that it would worsen and that the switch would mostly be turned to below zero. It was stuck in that position for her first few months in Paris.

Marti had arrived in a state of nervous exhaustion and depression. For weeks, she lacked energy, appetite, interest. It was Paris itself that gradually restored her to normal. She began to take an interest in food shopping. She loved the smells of the cheeses and fruits and fresh vegetables in the open-air markets. She enjoyed buying our lunches of ham and cold cuts in the many small charcuteries on the Rue du Bac. She took a fancy to Gauloises cigarettes, with their pungent odor and taste. She discovered good Armagnac, which became her favorite French brandy. Most of all, she savored the cafés of Saint-Germain-des-Prés, especially the Flore, the most elegant of the three cafés in the square.

She started to enjoy debating theology with Lyle, whom she liked and often invited to dinner. Marti was Episcopalian, brought up in a household with mild anti-Catholic and anti-Semitic leanings, and she enjoyed challenging anyone with strong religious beliefs. Lyle, who had had Jesuit training, took the challenge in good humor and also enjoyed the give and take. No blood was drawn on either side.

Marti was a good cook and began to experiment with *loup de mer* and sole and a particular butcher's excellent veal. She came to feel more and more at home in Paris—more at home, I now think, than anywhere she had ever lived before or since.

Stumbling into Marriage

SEVERAL MONTHS AFTER MARTI arrived in Paris, letters started to come from her parents, asking when the wedding was to take place. At first we ignored them, but as they grew more insistent they began to trouble us, especially me. Every time one of the letters arrived from Teaneck, Marti would go into a funk that lasted for days. (Her funks were never short-lived, and the longer we were together the longer they stretched out.) She started to say, "I guess we are going to have to do it."

I said as little as possible. I found it difficult to tell her that I didn't want to marry her, and even more difficult to say that I did. In retrospect, it is hard for me to believe that I was unable to say what I really felt. Why couldn't I have leveled with her in a straightforward way? Why couldn't I simply have said, "Marti, we told your parents we were going to get married because that was the only way they would have let you go. But at the time we hardly knew each other, and we still don't know each other that well. I don't think we should get married."

It never even occurred to me to say something as simple and honest as that. An inability to be honest and open with each other dogged our relationship and doomed it from the start.

Instead I procrastinated, making the situation worse. I realized that neither of us knew much about happy marriages or family life. She had not come to Paris for love of me; she had come to escape her parents. I had not brought her to Paris for love of her. I barely knew her. If someone had asked me at the time whether there were any women I would like to invite to stay with me in Paris, she would not have been at the top of the list.

I had made an impulsive gesture because she seemed to be in despair, and offering her a helping hand seemed the right thing to do. It drove home the full meaning of the maxim, "No good deed goes unpunished."

As the tone of the parental letters grew more impatient and suspicious, I finally agreed to a wedding date in March of the following year. I felt I was being pressured into a shotgun wedding where ironically the bride was not only not pregnant but had no intention of becoming so. Ever. Marti had made it clear that she didn't want to bear children. She said she was barely able to take care of herself and she thought it inconceivable that she could take responsibility for bringing "another miserable human being into the world."

At that time, my Boston childhood friend, Nat Hentoff, was visiting Paris. I remember confiding my feelings to him. I said that I felt as if I were being pushed down into a dark basement and that as I descended the stairs, the door leading to the basement was ominously locked after me. (Nat listened sympathetically, but made no suggestions.) Every day I grew more anxious and depressed, unable to take any action that would prevent the wedding from occurring.

Inexorably the date in March arrived, and almost eighteen years after my mother's death, Marti and I were married at the Mairie of the Sixth Arrondissement at the Place Saint-Sulpice, less than a year after her arrival in Paris.

My inability to call off my marriage with Marti haunted me for decades. No other event in my life dramatized so vividly the psychological impact of my foster home years. What trapped me was my commitment. Once I had made the commitment to Marti's parents I was hooked, even though she and I both knew that we had no intention of getting married.

During my foster home years my father had made one commitment after another to bring us all back together again. His failure to take these commitments seriously affected me deeply. My foster parents had also made commitments they failed to meet.

At some deep unconscious level, I had come to equate commitments with integrity and with the *menschlichkeit* (male adulthood and maturity) that my mother had worked so hard to install in me. I must have felt that to go back on my commitments would betray her and her memory and my own integrity. I had to live with myself, and I often came to feel that my integrity was the only thing that couldn't be taken away from me.

Over the course of time I was able to get rid of the neurotic elements of my feelings, but the core concept of integrity came to occupy a central place in my philosophy of life.

Shortly after Marti arrived in Paris, I matriculated at the Sorbonne where I sporadically attended lectures on existentialist philosophy, though my attention at the time was mostly focused on playwriting.

I wanted to follow the path that Jean-Paul Sartre had taken. In that quest, the plays of Ibsen were one of the models I studied most closely. They were extremely well crafted, though uniformly depressing. Typically, Ibsen would write about a character whose life was in decline. He would start the play when the decline had already begun, and most of the play's action would center on the further unraveling of the central character's life.

I started to draft several plays following this model. In one of them, my main character was a left-wing ideologue whose personal life was totally at odds with his professed political beliefs, exemplifying a form of "bad faith." It was not difficult to dramatize the hypocrisy and self-deception in which his life was mired, nor to make him come alive as a credible character. But I gave up on the play after drafting the first act, on the sensible grounds that if it depressed even me, the author, it was not likely to attract a willing audience.

I repeated this pattern again and again. I would start a play, write some pages of dialogue, take notes on how the plot was to unfold, and then a few days later toss it all in the wastebasket and start over again.

It was frustrating. But I felt I had to devote time to learning the craft and that writing actual plays was the best way to do so, even though I couldn't seem to gain traction on any one play.

The few years I spent in Paris were probably the least productive of my adult life, in the sense of not having much to show for all the time and effort I expended. I was used to being reasonably productive and in subsequent years I became a workaholic, producing an endless supply of reports, papers, consultations, presentations, analyses, articles, speeches and books. So the lack of productivity in Paris was an anomaly.

It was exacerbated both by stress and illness. The stress came from my unwanted marriage. The illness came from a prolonged case of mono. It struck shortly after Marti and I were married. For months I felt exhausted, short of breath, lacking in energy.

My major physical symptoms were a nagging sore throat and a tendency to get chilled around my chest and shoulders. I had been accustomed to walking around in short sleeve shirts, and now I found myself constantly craving sweaters and scarves. This symptom proved permanent. Almost overnight I shifted from one of those men who never seems to get cold to someone who reaches for a sweater at the first sign of chill. It is the only symptom of the mono that endured.

In retrospect, there may well have been anxiety attacks or depression mixed in with the mono. But the feeling of constant enervation did eventually subside and my energy level returned to normal, though my plays and short stories piled up in various unfinished drafts.

I had expected that after several years in Paris I would have written four or five full-length plays. If so, they would have represented a significant body of work to show for my agonized apprenticeship in a new calling. But I had produced nothing even close to that. And what I did write seemed talent-challenged. I was good at dialogue and character. But my characters seemed wooden and artificial as they spouted ideas at each other. My plots were thin, and my manuscripts lacked the bite of dramatic conflict that makes a play come alive.

Also, I began to question my motivation. I had not been drawn to playwriting because I was committed to the theatre or because so many play ideas were bursting to break out. My motivation was unrelated to the theatre. I had speculated that "plays of ideas" might be a more authentic and imaginative way of doing philosophy than struggling with logical analysis.

But when I sat down to write such plays, I realized that this path to philosophy, while it might work for Sartre, was closed off to me. Sartre's experiences in the French Resistance gave his voice an authenticity that my more limited and parochial experience as a student and soldier lacked.

Not for the first time, a project that seemed to make sense in theory had failed to work in practice, at least for me as a novice.

Life in Paris

ONCE MARTI AND I were married, our lives went on more or less as before. We had been living together anyway, and the simple afternoon civil marriage ceremony was as casual—and about as meaningful—as attending an afternoon concert. In at least one respect, the quality of our lives improved: no longer was the question of our social status as a couple hanging over our heads (this was the beginning of the 1950s). We were now a respectable married couple and we both were determined to make the best of the situation.

That proved a lot easier to do in Paris than it was later in New York because expatriate life was so relaxed and undemanding. And without the constant harassment from Marti's parents, the relationship between Marti and me grew less tense.

The refrigerating device sometimes allowed a warming trend. We spent a lot of time with friends and with travel throughout France, Italy and Spain. We ate well, usually with friends. We laughed a lot, joked a lot, read a lot, talked a lot, and tried every good wine and cheese France had to offer. In short, we succeeded in suspending the reality principle for quite a long time.

I devoted a lot of effort to trying to understand Marti better—without much success. Throughout most of the eight years of our marriage she remained an enigma to me.

She had a strong, willful personality. People always remembered meeting her. You might forget meeting Maritza at a party, but you would not forget Marti. She was quite clothes-conscious and always well dressed. She had a model's figure—tall, slender, narrow hips—and wore clothes well. Mostly she favored tweeds of good quality. Quality was all-important to her. Her ideal was, "Just a few perfect things." Shortly after she arrived in Paris, she splurged on a Burberry double-breasted raincoat and scarf, both of which she wore constantly.

She walked fast, in long strides, and spoke in a somewhat clipped fashion, just short of an upper-class English accent. When she was with other people, she kept a wider than normal physical distance from them. Often her body language seemed to say, "Back off, Buster."

Her pungent expression of her views, often punctuated with obscenities, went naturally with her striking looks. Highly intelligent, even in her most contrarian state of mind, she always presented a coherent point of view. I thought of her mode of speech as "Marti-logic"—sometimes wrongheaded but always cogent.

Contrarianism was her outstanding character trait. She almost always adopted the position contrary to the majority view. She was quick to criticize others. But mostly she turned the criticism against herself. With all her energy, talent, and intelligence, I always assumed that she would find some way to make constructive use of her gifts. But perversely, she put her strong will to work in the opposite direction—to prove that nothing good could ever come of her.

Nonetheless, I cared about her, fretted about her, worried about her. But I never loved her. Both of us were saddled with odd expectations about loving and being loved. She claimed she didn't know what love was, having never met up with it. I, on the other hand, was convinced that I knew what love was, but sadly did not expect to be on the receiving end of it.

I always felt that love had to have a nurturing side to it, and I never felt any nurturing vibes emanating from Marti. I associated nurturing love with marriage, which was why I had been so resistant to marrying Marti, however much I cared for her. Whatever nurturing tendencies she had were too locked within herself to express themselves. She could *accept* nurturance; indeed, she latched onto it. But I don't think she could give it. I craved to be nurtured as well as nurturing.

Once we were actually married, I tried (as Marti did) to make the marriage work. As she grew more at home in Paris, my caring for her grew, making the marriage tolerable even without nurturing love.

As her spirits revived, so did mine. We gradually met other people and formed some lasting friendships, mostly with other Americans, but also with some of Rosine's French friends.

I was particularly taken with a physician friend of Rosine's, a woman named Myriam David. Myriam had been a POW in the same camp as Rosine and had been tortured by the Nazis (a fate that Rosine had avoided). Myriam was unable to speak of this experience. She was ten years older than Rosine and me. Myriam had a gentle humor and a shy but self-confident presence that I found enormously appealing.

Through Rosine I also made friends with a witty and knowledgeable French professor of mathematics, Raphaël Salem, who was married with several young children. I recall the first time the Salems invited us to their apartment for Sunday dinner (a tastier roast veal than I had ever had before). Their apartment on the Rue Léonard-de-Vinci in the Sixteenth Arrondissement (one of Paris's chicest neighborhoods) was vast. It occupied the entire top floor of a very large apartment building and was full of exquisite art and sculpture. Each room displayed an elegance that I associated with royal palace rooms preserved in French museums.

Rosine laughed at the bewildered look on my face as I wondered how a math professor could command such obvious wealth. She explained that before Raphaël had become a professor, he had been a partner in Lazard Frères, the investment-banking firm that subsequently became as active on Wall Street as in Paris.

It was my first exposure to great wealth. I admired it from a distance, but did not envy it. I had never conceived of myself as having, or even aspiring to, wealth of that magnitude. A professorship, yes; a bidder at auctions for French Impressionist masterpieces, no way.

I had met Myriam David and Raphaël Salem before Marti came to Paris and she saw them as my friends, rather than as our mutual friends. But together we did meet a number of expat Americans we both considered friends.

Marti's closest friend in Paris was Dollie Morgan. Dollie was obsessed with the CIA, and on many occasions would volunteer credible reasons why one or another of our friends, including a suspiciously vociferous Marxist, might in fact be a covert CIA agent.

A fashion artist from Philadelphia, Dollie was usually accompanied by her boyfriend, Dick Dale. Dollie was slender and fey and cheerful, always good company in spite of her CIA obsession. (Would that the CIA actually had the capabilities that Dollie ascribed to it!) Dick Dale was far less gregarious. He was a bit of a mystery then, and he has remained so throughout the half-century that I've known him since then.

He came from Arkansas and had been a cameraman for the INS news service in Paris. Before my arrival in Paris, he had quit that position and to my knowledge never again took any pictures.

I don't think he even owned a camera. Instead, he spent his months in Paris fixing an old Citroën car that he had somehow acquired (I doubt that he had actually bought it). By my reckoning, he spent two and a half years in Paris fixing the Citroën, arguably a world's record for puttering with a mechanical object.

In our third year in Paris, Marti and I decided to move out of our one-room studio in the Rue Servandoni into a real apartment—at 76

Rue Notre-Dame-des-Champs. Though only a quarter of a mile away, we had, in effect, moved from bohemia to bourgeois respectability. Marti even decided to look for a job. Luckily, she found a good one as an executive assistant at the offices of the Economic Cooperation Administration in Paris (popularly known as the Marshall Plan, designed to help Europe get back on its feet after the ravages of World War II).

A Respite in the Mountains

IN MY LAST FEW months in Paris, money became a problem. My GI benefits had run out, and we were living on Marti's salary. Neither of us was happy with that arrangement. We both had absorbed the cultural imperative of the times that it was the husband's principal function to provide for the family. Besides, I didn't feel that humankind would be artistically impoverished if I took a break from playwriting in order to make an honest living. So I managed to wheedle a contract assignment for myself from the Economic Cooperation Administration (ECA), where Marti worked.

The contract called for me to locate and interview a number of non-communist labor leaders in several European countries—France, Italy and Greece. At the time, the European labor movement was largely communist-dominated, especially in those three countries. The Marshall Plan's foreign policy experts wanted to sound out some of the non-communist labor leaders to learn how Marshall Plan programs could help to strengthen them *vis-à-vis* the communist trade unions and also to get their assessment of the political situation.

The assignment could not have been very important or they would never have hired a freelance interviewer to do the fieldwork. Chances are that someone in the middle levels of the ECA had suggested doing what French diplomats refer to as *tâter le terrain*—get a feel for the situation on the ground. It was a low-cost, low-risk decision to rent a freelancer to do some interviewing for them.

My motivation in seeking the work had been wholly financial. But once I started my assignment, I realized that it interested me quite apart from my paycheck. I found it hugely stimulating. It gave me my own private window onto the complex politics of Europe. I also liked the idea of representing my country, in however modest a role. And above all, I found myself resonating to the problem-solving challenges that the officials I interviewed were confronting.

I developed great respect for the qualities of the men I interviewed (they were all men). They were struggling to improve the economic security of their members under difficult odds, often fighting their governments, their members' employers and the communist labor unions all at the same time. I sometimes felt that the expensive lunches (with free-flowing wine) that my expense account allowed gave them a rare respite—a chance to relax and unburden themselves to an interested and non-threatening listener.

The officials I interviewed in France and Italy knew that my status was that of a lowly freelance hired hand, and they joked about the amount of wine we consumed on my expense account. But in Greece the situation was far murkier. I couldn't find anyone of influence in the Greek labor movement to interview in Athens.

The local Marshall Plan office assigned two divine young women to me. They told me that the labor leaders I wanted to interview had managed to make themselves scarce, on the assumption that no good could come from such an encounter.

I decided to track down at least a few Greek labor leaders in the remote mountainous parts of the country. The three weeks I spend tracking them down, interviewing them, and reassuring them of my country's good will, accompanied by the two laughing, cheerful, and appealing Greek girls were among the most delightful of my memories of that era.

After I finished my assignment and wrote my report, I felt let down. I had enjoyed the work more than I had anticipated. In the end, the money I received for the assignment was the least of its benefits. Of far greater value was being jolted into realizing that my problem-solving drive was far stronger than any literary urges I may have harbored.

I also realized the importance of interacting with others in the formation of my own thinking. Once I curtailed my own impulse to talk (which was mandatory when I was the interviewer), I became an avid listener. I have always learned more through the ear than through the eye. Others were often better at learning from reading than I was. But I loved all forms of lectures, dialogues, and discussions, and I discovered that I had a knack for pulling together everything I heard into a coherent pattern: a minor but sometimes useful talent.

Nor was it lost on me that in the roughly six *weeks* of my ECA assignment, I had accomplished more than in the preceding six *months*.

"You Will Need a Suit"

WHEN I RETURNED TO France from Greece, I realized that my Paris journey was coming to an end. I had had my respite from academic life. I had experimented with playwriting as a way of doing philosophy. I had used up my GI Bill benefits and I needed to support Marti and myself.

It was time to go home.

Several months before I left Paris for New York, I decided to tell our friends about our plans. Most of them had exiled themselves in Paris for even longer than my three-year sojourn. I knew that my return to the States would be a shock to them, and I was curious about how they would greet the news. (Marti was to remain in Paris until I found a job and a place to live in New York.)

Two or three times a week all of us had dinner together in one of the cheap Vietnamese restaurants near Saint-Germain-des-Prés. On the evening that I planned to announce my impending departure, there was a particularly good turnout—about fourteen of us sat at a long table the restaurant arranged for our group.

After two hours or so, when we finally reached the tasteless-dessert stage of dinner, I stood up and after a brief hesitation said, "I have an announcement to make." The table quieted instantly, because it was such an unusual thing to do. No one remembered anyone else ever having made a formal announcement at dinner.

To my surprise, I found it difficult to start and fumbled about for a while, until I finally heard myself say, "Marti and I have decided to go home. It's been a wonderful three years, but I'm afraid if we don't leave soon, we may never leave, and we don't want to be exiles. Marti will stay here while I find a place to live and get a job. So, I'm planning to take a boat to New York in about two months."

And I sat down. There followed an almost uncanny silence. I suspect that everyone around the table was suddenly and abruptly turned in on themselves, thinking not so much of my departure but of their own situation. My announcement was like a bell tolling for each of them, and in fact all but a few returned back to the States within a year or so after I left Paris.

The silence stretched on for quite a long time, until Bob Gilkey, the most urbane of our group, said in his authoritative way, "Well, then, you will need a suit."

Gilkey was a tall, slightly stooped Philadelphian whom Dollie (of course!) suspected of being with the CIA. He was always ready with a quip or sardonic, cynical observation. But rarely had a retort of his received so boisterous a response. Within minutes, everyone around the table was talking at the same time.

They were busy with the matter of the new suit that all agreed I must purchase forthwith. What kind of suit should it be? What color? Need it be tailor-made, or could I buy it ready-made off the rack? Everyone agreed that the men's French suits of that era were too tight and not right for New York, so where should I buy my new suit?

The group finally reached consensus. I was to make the investment of crossing the Channel and go to London to buy the suit. All acknowledged the effort and expense of doing so, but agreed that the right kind of British suit would at the very least double my commercial value in the New York job market. (Inevitably, someone cited the familiar slogan that the formula for success in New York was to "think Yiddish, dress British.")

Though there was universal agreement around the table that the suit would double my value, lots of disagreement prevailed about the precise number to be doubled. Here again, the worldly Gilkey led the discussion. Unhesitatingly, he pronounced that without the suit, there was no way I could earn more than $3,500 a year, not a handsome salary for an expensive city like New York. (At the time, the cost of living was far higher in New York than in Paris.)

This meant that with the suit, I should be able to earn $7,000 a year (more than $60,000 in today's dollars), and that would be ample even for New York City. None of us was in a position to challenge Gilkey's economics, so it was settled. I would head off to London in the next few weeks, check out the less aristocratic men's tailors on Savile Row, buy myself a reasonably expensive suit (ideally off the rack, since this would save time and money) and thus armored, be prepared to do battle in the New York job market.

There were a few skeptics among my friends who doubted my strength of character. It was agreed that with the suit, I must *promise* to hold out for the full $7,000 a year, and not cravenly accept five or six thousand, which some of my friends were sure would happen. So it was settled. I took an oath that once properly suited, I would not accept less than $7,000 a year.

The dinner, and the era, came to an end.

Return to Reality

THE FOLLOWING WEEK, I crossed the channel to London, went directly to Savile Row and found exactly the right suit. Fortunately, it was not extravagantly expensive.

Pleased with this show of resolve I returned to Paris in a positive frame of mind. Despite my troubled marriage and lack of visible productivity in Paris, I thought of my three years there as a glorious experience. I had actually learned a lot about playwriting and other forms of narrative writing such as short stories and novels. I had recovered a sense of balance and perspective that I had started to lose at Harvard. I had made lots of new friends, traveled throughout Europe, and developed a deep appreciation of French life and culture. And I had come to a self-understanding that has persisted ever since: I am quite comfortable as an outsider in the world of thought and ideas as a seeker of philosophical truth, even without a lot of formal credentials.

In April 1952, the boat from Le Havre to New York took five days to cross the Atlantic, leaving me plenty of time to think about the future. I have always thought about the future. I have always lived in the future. The future has always been more real for me than the present.

It became clear to me that I had to resolve my troubled relationship with academic philosophy in one way or the other. Others had found ways to resolve it. My Paris friend Lyle Joyce, whose older brother ran Notre Dame University and who was himself a doctoral student in philosophy at the Sorbonne, had no trouble ignoring the prevailing fashions in philosophy. Like his brother, his orientation led him to Jacques Maritain and other Catholic philosophers who simply dismissed contemporary Anglo-American philosophy out of hand.

My background, training and orientation did not permit me to follow this form of resolution because I had no prior commitment to Catholic theology or any other formal doctrine, including Judaism.

Living for three years in the hotbed of French existentialism on Paris's Left Bank, I might have turned in that direction. On a personal level, I found the thinking and writings of the existentialists of that period profoundly appealing. They dealt with themes of existence, good faith, betrayal, and the existential freedom to shape one's own destiny—themes to which I deeply resonated.

At the same time, however, I sensed something alien for me personally about these themes. Their haunting subtext—and political/cultural context—was the craven fall of France to the Germans, the Nazi occupation, the French Resistance, and the overarching influence of the French revolution and its consequences.

These events were seared into the souls of the French people and dominated their writings. They were extraordinary—and *existential*—experiences. But they belonged to the French thinkers of that era, not to my quintessentially American experience. It was their world, not mine. I decided that while I would continue to look to existentialism for personal guidance, I would seek out a more American-based core of beliefs as my overall philosophical framework.

By the end of my Paris sojourn, I had made the provisional decision to pursue the kind of philosophy that interested me, but without pursuing an academic career. Throughout its three thousand-year history, Western philosophy has never been completely confined to the academy. There have always been non-academic philosophers, like Spinoza, who ground lenses for a living, and Peirce, who made his living working for the United States Geodetic Survey.

My hope was that I, like Spinoza and Peirce and Sartre and Nietzsche, would become a "philosopher without portfolio": that is, a freelance philosopher. Like their poet-compatriots, freelance philosophers do not usually make a good living, but they do exist and they do make valuable contributions. I knew that I would not be well paid for my efforts. But I could at least continue the quest that had haunted me almost from childhood. I had grown up in poverty and it didn't frighten me.

At the end of my three-year Paris stay my mindset was that of someone reaching the end of a long vacation when post-vacation reality stubbornly begins to intrude itself. I had a lot on my mind— what to do about a troubled marriage, how to support a wife as well as myself, and how to honor my commitment to keep plugging away at philosophy even though I no longer saw it as a paid vocation.

These were powerful obstacles. On the other hand, I now had an expensive suit.

My Job Search

FORTUNATELY, I HAD FRIENDS in New York, though most of my friends lived in or around Boston. But my old roommate and life-long friend, John Stern, had recently married and he and his new wife, Marina, a lovely Venetian-born artist, lived in a splendid apartment on the Upper East Side of Manhattan.

Unlike most of my friends, John had a wealthy father. After trying freelance journalism for a few years, he had reluctantly caved in to family pressures and joined his father's Wall Street firm as a broker. John and Marina put me up while I searched for an apartment and a job.

I found what I thought was an agreeable apartment on East Seventy-Sixth Street between Third and Second Avenue—three rooms and a large outdoor patio. It was handy to the Lexington Avenue subway. It was far less posh than Park Avenue, Madison Avenue, and Fifth Avenue to the west of it, but with our savings, we could afford the rent for the four months that I had allocated to finding a job. Both Third Avenue and Second Avenue were full of people at night, making my evening walks stimulating.

But while an apartment was easy to find, a job was not. The Harvard Club offered a job counseling service where well-established Harvard grads gave guidance to newer graduates. A television executive gave me some scripts to edit. I was paid for my work, though I don't believe my edits were ever used.

Several times a week I went on job interviews, a somewhat ambiguous undertaking since I didn't have a clear idea what kind of job I was looking for. The closest I came to a realistic description of the job I wanted reflected a work experience I had had while still in graduate school at Harvard after the war.

At that time, I had realized that if I were to take a leave of absence from Harvard to live in Paris, I would need to save some money to pay for the expense of the trip and hopefully for a taste of Parisian life. I was lucky to find the ideal part-time job at Harvard that didn't interfere with my graduate studies but actually advanced them. One of my psychology professors had been invited by the MIT administration to conduct a study of MIT students who were returning vets like myself. The administration was concerned because so many of their former-soldier students were having difficulty adapting to civilian life at MIT. Their problems ranged from poor grades to suicides, with lots of dropouts and nervous breakdowns. The administration asked my professor to recommend any actions MIT might take to reduce tensions for these students.

My professor assembled a small team of professionals and included me as a member of the team, on the premise that as a veteran as well as a grad student, I would have shared experiences with the MIT students.

And indeed, I found it easy to interview (and to empathize with) these disgruntled MIT students. I had also had problems returning to student life after military service abroad. In my interviews, some veterans admitted that they had serious problems adapting to student life, and all of them bridled at university rules that they characterized as written for eighteen-year-old adolescents. After years of military experience, not being allowed to have girls in your room and other such constraints seemed "ridiculous" in their eyes. Loneliness, isolation, and lack of direction were constant themes.

Our team leader reported these findings to MIT's top executives. To their credit, they took immediate action. They discarded the outmoded parietal rules for the veterans, dropped other *in loco parentis* constraints, hired a member of our team as a counselor, and instituted dances and other social events where students could meet one another and, more to the point, their female counterparts from Simmons, Wellesley, Radcliffe, and other women's colleges in the area.

I found the work we had done, and MIT's response to it, admirable. Our team had applied professional skills to a real-world problem. We had uncovered a flaw in the system, identified it, and teased out its implications for remedial action. The institution had responded immediately and constructively—no defensiveness, no denial, no cover-your-ass resistance.[7]

That experience gave me a model that was uppermost in my mind as I was looking for a job in New York. It implied that institutions have a fiduciary relationship with their constituents heavily dependent on trust (a stewardship obligation). Both the institution and those it purportedly serves—in the case of MIT, its students— needed to insure the continuing vitality of that relationship.

As I looked for a job in New York, I also recalled my stint interviewing Greek labor leaders, which had had much in common with my MIT experience. In both instances, institutions needed to confront problems with their key stakeholders. In both instances, learning to see problems from the stakeholders' perspective proved vital in suggesting solutions. Surely, I thought, this sort of work serves a valuable social function.

Looking back at my experiences in Greece and at MIT, I concluded that my best chance of finding a satisfying job was to offer my

---

7   Recounted in my book *Wicked Problems, Workable Solutions: Lessons from a Public Life* (New York: Rowman and Littlefield, 2015), 41–46.

services as an analyst of how institutions might become more responsive to the needs, wants, and expectations of those they served—the government in response to voters, colleges in response to students, newspapers in response to their readers, unions in response to their members, companies in response to their employees and customers.

Today, this concept is a familiar one. But in the early 1950s when I started my job hunt it mostly elicited a blank stare when I described it. Still, the concept did provide me with some guidance and unity. Not so incidentally, though the stewardship concept was amorphous at the time, it is a fairly good characterization of the work I would undertake for the next half century.

My First Full-Time Job

WITHOUT A CLEAR IDEA of where to find a position of this sort, I didn't land a lot of promising job interviews. And those I did get rarely went far enough to invite a serious discussion of salary. In virtually every interview, the interviewer would ask, "What sort of work do you think you are best equipped to do?" I would give my vague answer, receive the blank stare, be told untruthfully that I would hear from them, and be dismissed back to the canyons of New York.

There was one exception to this pattern. The interviewers at advertising agencies nodded receptively when I answered their inevitable question about my qualifications. They were used to well-educated young people who were articulate but lacked clarity about their own qualifications. I was offered several trainee jobs in copy writing at derisory salaries, which I turned down because neither the work nor the money was appealing.

Finally, I received a serious job offer. It came from the research department of the J. Walter Thompson ad agency. I later learned that the person who offered me a position was well known and respected in the ad agency world. Her name was Herta Herzog. She was, I believe, Austrian by birth, a war refugee.

Her interview focused neither on me nor her nor the agency. Unlike all the other interviewers, she immediately launched into the specific problems she was wrestling with. From the start, she homed in on issues of ad strategy that were uppermost on her work agenda.

She wanted to know how I would address a range of problems of concern to her.

At the end of the interview, she offered me a job. I found the prospect of working with this obviously gifted woman quite appealing. I asked how much the job paid. She said her budget permitted her to pay no more than $5,000 a year.

So, here it was. The Crunch. The situation that my unworldly expatriate friends in Paris had anticipated had actually arrived—very much in the form they had expected. I was anxious to find a job, and was not making much headway in doing so. Finally I had an offer, but it fell significantly below the $7,000 threshold we all agreed the suit was worth. And I was on the spot: my impulse was to accept. I was sure my Paris friends all expected me to yield and if I had, it would not have troubled them for an instant. But it would have troubled me.

I told Herta that I was not able, for practical reasons, to accept any job that paid under $7,000 a year. She was sympathetic and said she would speak to Don Armstrong, the head of the research department, to see if they could make an exception to company policy.

Later in the week she phoned and said that while both she and Don wanted me, they were constrained by company policy and could not increase their offer. So, with expressions of regret on both sides, it was back to the sidewalks.

I discovered that I felt a sense of relief (as well as anxiety because I was rapidly eating through my savings). I had not caved to temptation. And while I respected Herta Herzog and Don Armstrong, I really did not feel comfortable working for an ad agency: it seemed like a betrayal of the Harvard philosophy department. Maybe Harvard's philosophers weren't able to capture the true nature of reality, but they were wary of spin of any sort, and I shared that wariness. I still do.

A few weeks later an industrial design firm, Nowland & Schladermundt, agreed to meet my $7,000-a-year requirement. Roger Nowland, the head of the firm, explained that he and his partners knew very little about the people who used the products they designed. He said that for his male engineers, a refrigerator was a repository for beer and ice cubes surrounded by useless space, and that they (along with the entire design field) insisted on designing ovens that caused the housewives who used them to get a backache every time they had to stoop down to reach inside.

So, he said, he had invented a concept he called "pre-design research." Instead of designing products for users whose needs were unknown, he had the revolutionary idea of asking actual and potential users about their use patterns and needs for products like automobiles, refrigerators, washing machines, cameras, projectors, watches, and adding machines—the products the firm was currently designing.

Nowland asked me what I would do if his firm were invited to design a new station wagon. What questions would I ask, what information would I be looking for, what advice would I give the firm's designers?

I answered that I had no experience either with station wagons or market research, but that I had driven a jeep in the army for two years and I spoke about the questions I would ask myself if someone were designing a new jeep for me. My answers appeared to satisfy him—especially, I think, my ignorance of traditional market research.

"Can you do the job the way it should be done?" he asked. I answered that I thought I could.

He took me outside his office and explained that he and his partner had the only closed offices and that I would work alongside everyone else in the open, with the same kind of high stool and drawing table that served as workstations for the architects and designers.

When I offered no resistance, he asked: "When can you come to work?"[8]

I started my job the next week. Nowland hadn't fussed about my salary demands. He never did fuss about money—as long as the firm was doing well.

I found it uncomfortable to work on a stool and drawing table with lots of people around me, but it didn't bother me much. I was given a huge amount of work to do in my first few weeks and I plunged into it with enthusiasm.

I was to work for Roger Nowland's industrial design firm for the next six years. Twice in that six-year time span, I shifted from full-time to part-time, with significant consequences.

Nowland was my first and only boss. He was, by and large, a good boss, but I didn't like working under any boss, and never did so again after I left his employ.

8　This event is also recounted in *Wicked Problems*, 47.

Marti Rejoins Me in New York

NOW THAT I HAD found a job, I was free to focus on Marti's imminent return. I couldn't have been more ambivalent about it. Part of me wanted her to come to New York, and part of me dreaded what would happen if and when she did.

We had parted with tension and sorrow. It felt more like a permanent goodbye than an *au revoir*. Her letters from Paris were stiff and full of information about our mutual friend, Bill Charmatz.

Charmatz was a large hulking man who drew skinny—and charming—cartoons and fashion illustrations. He and Marti enjoyed each other's company, and I began to suspect that they were enjoying each other a bit too much.

Later, after she did return to the States, we never discussed what she had done—or felt—during the four months of our separation. That was not surprising, because we were only rarely able to talk honestly about any aspect of our relationship. From a number of her comments, I got the impression that she had hated the prospect of coming back to the States, especially to New York because it was so close to her parents in Teaneck.

She may or may not have had an affair with Charmatz. Probably not. Any sexual relationship would have been too overwhelming for her to manage. But I think she passionately wanted to stay in Paris and was pulled back to the States by the sort of generalized guilt that her parents had constantly manipulated to control her. So I think she returned for all the wrong reasons. Guilt. Anger. Despair. Duty. Resentment. Fear.

While waiting for her to come to New York, I tried to push aside my anxieties so that I could concentrate on my job search and on fixing up the apartment I had rented on East Seventy-Sixth Street. I may have consciously stifled my concerns, but they found a way to express themselves psychosomatically.

Toward the end of the few months of waiting for Marti, I remember having dinner with a friend from Harvard, Natasha Karpovich, at her apartment on Second Avenue in New York's Lower East Side. Natasha was the daughter of a professor of Russian history at Harvard who himself had been a member of the Kerensky government in Russia before Lenin and Stalin deposed it.

I genuinely liked Natasha and her acerbic wit and easy-going manner. We were not romantically involved but were good friends.

When I showed up for dinner, Natasha exclaimed, "What is the matter with you?" My right shoulder was hunched over in pain, my throat hurt, I had a headache and indigestion and I seemed distracted. She said, "You are a mess. You have every psychosomatic ailment in the book. What is going on?"

I shared with her some of my ambivalence about the Marti situation, in particular Marti's flat refusal to have children. She listened thoughtfully. She knew Marti and knew how high-maintenance she was. She was sympathetic, but she didn't offer any views of her own.

Later I learned that she felt that our marriage was a disaster waiting to happen, but at the time she decided she would mind her own business and say nothing. Natasha had a horror of interfering in the lives of others (nor did she want anyone poking into her own life).

I'm sorry she didn't open up and share her honest doubts about the wisdom of Marti coming back from Paris. In retrospect, I lost the best possible opportunity to break off the relationship at a time and in a manner that would have done the least damage to both of us.

I believe Marti would have been vastly relieved if I had suggested that she stay in Europe instead of coming to New York. Both of us sensed that once the marriage lost the vacation-like context it had in Paris, it was destined to hit a storm.

I had not confronted this reality while we lived in Paris. Once I had agreed to the marriage, I had made up my mind to make a go of it. I have always taken commitments very seriously. In later years I came to regard my inability to refuse to marry Marti as a sign of being whipped about by forces I did not fully understand and over which I had little control.

Now, however, for better or worse, Marti was my wife and about to join me in our New York apartment. I had come back to the States to get ready for her return. I had found us a place to live and a job with a satisfactory income. I was lonely. I had resisted seeing other women because I was a married man. I was eager for us to get on with our lives, and I pushed aside all my doubts about the marriage in my determination to accept it and make the best of it.

Once Marti did come to New York it did not take long for the storm to hit. She arrived angry and disheartened. As soon as she walked through the door of the new apartment, she announced that she hated it, she hated the tony neighborhood in which it was located, and she didn't particularly like the terrace that for me had been the apartment's chief attraction.

She immediately announced that we should move to a place with lower rent in some other part of New York. She said the terrace would get too sooty from all the traffic and air pollution, and that my image of our enjoying cozy dinners sitting on the terrace was impractical. She was right about the soot and the high rent, but her reaction hit me like a brick to the head. It was not an auspicious start to our new life in New York.

We did move within a few months. I had not yet signed a lease, and we were obliged either to make a two-year commitment or move, so we moved far away from the wealthy enclave in the Upper East Side to the other end of the income scale.

We found a fourth-floor walk-up on Mulberry Street in Manhattan's Little Italy, close to the Bowery and the Lower East Side. This was decades before the Bowery became gentrified, and at the time its streets were crowded with drunks, bums, panhandlers, and druggies.

We sublet the apartment from a blind man for twenty-eight dollars a month. By way of comparison, I paid thirty-five dollars a month to garage my car. I had not planned to put the car in a garage, but after I found my tires slashed for the third time when I left the car parked on the street overnight, I got the message and rented garage space.

In the year or so that we lived on Mulberry Street, we heard gunfire a number of times and once, leaving early for work, I tripped over an apparent corpse on my way to the subway. Mulberry Street was full of mysterious "clubs"—storefronts full of working-age men at all times of the day or night with no apparent activity visible to the casual observer. But the neighborhood was surprisingly safe for residents like ourselves, even if we weren't Italian. It was a "protected" neighborhood. Anyone caught breaking into an apartment ran a greater risk of ending up dead on the street than of being caught by the police.

Marti vastly preferred Mulberry Street to the Upper East Side. She had a streak of reverse snobbery. For her, the Upper East Side apartment was the equivalent of Paris's snooty Right Bank, and Little Italy came somewhat closer to the more plebeian Left Bank.

In our first few weeks in the Mulberry Street sublet, she furiously painted all the rooms in the apartment stark white and furnished it with monkish simplicity. She was proud of her work and eager to show it to me when I came home from my job at night for dinner. At dinner, we rarely talked much about my job, which she held in mild disdain. I think she found it déclassé, a bit too close for comfort to her father's lower middle-class job at the insurance company.

She still smoked two packs of cigarettes a day, but switched from Gauloises to Camels—her major concession to swapping the United States for France. Usually when I came home from work she would have several strong gin martinis or scotches while I nursed one weak martini (the gin made me thirsty and sleepy). Our conversations were superficial and a bit strained.

On weekends, we spent time with friends, reading the Sunday *New York Times* (she devoted hours to the crossword puzzle), going to the movies, and eating at local restaurants where the food, mostly Southern Italian, was far heavier and less digestible than the Vietnamese food in Paris's inexpensive restaurants. The Automatic Refrigerating Device was switched on again. Most of the time, Marti seemed so tense that I felt she was constantly on the verge of exploding.

One night she did. We were walking back from a movie. We had stopped at the liquor store to buy a bottle of scotch. She was carrying it. As we climbed up the third floor of the walk-up, the bag slipped out of her hand and broke on the staircase. "FUCK! FUCK! FUCK!" she exploded, kicking the bag and the broken bottle down the stairs as she stomped up to the apartment. She had been drinking and, as usual when she drank, she was in a foul mood.

I lived in horror of those kinds of explosions. They came too close to expressing my own frustration. I had had a similar outburst of temper while we were still living on Seventy-Sixth Street. One night, I got so angry that I swept the dinner dishes off the table, breaking them all. Afterwards, I was ashamed of my flash of violence. Marti confided to our mutual friend Dollie that she had actually been pleased by my show of temper, because it showed strength.

I, however, associated violence with weakness and lack of control. I utterly rejected the violence of my youth that had gotten me into so much trouble. Marti's meltdown on the steps had a devastating effect on me. I hated it. And I resented her for doing it.

Taking Refuge in Work

LIKE SO MANY MEN of that era with unhappy marriages, I took refuge in my job. I didn't know much about the products the firm designed, but I soon realized that serving as a bridge between the people who bought and used the products and the people who designed them was no simple matter. People often don't know what design features in a product will work best for them. They get used to a particular product design and adapt themselves to it, just as I was adapting myself to working at an architect's drawing table.

I found the work absorbing, and gave it my full effort.

A number of the firm's clients became devotees of pre-design research—Roger Nowland's valuable innovation. It grew so popular that it began to create tensions in the firm. Clients began to say, "We don't need your design service but we would like to buy your consumer research."

The work of my small three-person unit within the firm soon became a profit center in its own right, and eventually grew into the firm's main money-maker.

I found the work technically challenging. I learned that it wasn't as easy as I had assumed to find out what sort of adding machine or camera or washing machine or automobile would appeal to the consumer's demands, where considerations of function, quality, price, esthetics, and status were all jumbled together and markets were bewilderingly diverse. But Roger Nowland gave me complete freedom and support, sometimes risking the firm's reputation.

For the next three years, I devoted all of my energies to implementing Roger Nowland's concept of pre-design research.

But I grew dissatisfied. Gadgets and products have never held much interest for me. Even today, I drive a beat-up fifteen-year old Toyota, wear unfashionable clothes and cheap watches, and drink moderately priced wines. I have never been a very classy consumer.

Total immersion in the world of consumerism was making me miserable. I yearned to return to the world of ideas rather than the world of products. My exposure to world-class thinkers at Harvard and the Sorbonne had powerfully reconfirmed this propensity.

I didn't know how to escape the trap I had built for myself. I had to continue to make a living. I had to support Marti and myself. She had supported me briefly in our last few months in Paris, and neither of us found that arrangement acceptable. I spent countless nights awake in bed trying to figure out a way that I could devote myself to philosophy and earn a living at the same time.

Then, one day, an offbeat opportunity presented itself and I grabbed it. In 1954 and 1955, we were living in Greenwich Village. In that era, there was no IKEA selling do-it-yourself inexpensive furniture—the kind of furniture that the inhabitants of Greenwich Village desperately needed.

With the help of a few friends, I opened a store to meet the need. The store, called the "Door Store," was an instant success, and eventually grew into a national chain.[9]

After the new store had been in business for a few months, I realized that I could not successfully juggle two such demanding work commitments. So I asked Roger Nowland if I could go on a three-day-a-week work schedule for a reduced salary.

---

9   For more on the origins of the Door Store, see *Wicked Problems*, 50–52.

During this same period, the firm had moved from its convenient location in midtown Manhattan to Greenwich, Connecticut, where Roger had purchased the old estate of Henry Luce, the founder of Time, Inc. The Greenwich estate was a beautiful and restful place, more like a campus than an office. Most importantly, from Roger's point of view, it was a great real estate investment for him personally, and an equally great personal convenience since he lived just a few miles away in neighboring New Canaan.

But for the younger staff members who lived in Manhattan it was a huge nuisance. It meant we had to commute in reverse every day. It wasn't a bad drive since I was driving against the traffic. But, from my point of view, it had all the disadvantages of commuting and none of the advantages.

In making the move, Roger had also saddled the firm with a higher break-even point. To meet its fixed expenses and payroll, we now had to bring in net revenues of at least $50,000 a month (a piddling sum today, but a sizeable burden for a small firm in the 1950s). I think Roger was pleased to save 40 percent of my salary, and he was confident that I would not shirk my responsibilities. (I did not.)

With the move away from Manhattan, fewer potential clients were visiting the firm and its revenues were gradually falling below the break-even point. But at that time, my responsibilities were confined to seeing that the firm's work was done well. I was not involved in the financial side of the business.

Approximately a year after the Door Store opened, and eight months into my three-day-a-week schedule for the firm, Roger called me into his office. I was very apprehensive about the meeting. I knew the firm's situation had deteriorated and I was afraid Roger was either going to cut my salary or force me to choose between the firm and the Door Store.

Typically, without small talk, he got right to the point. He said, "Dan, I know you are trying to develop your retail business, but I'm not sure I understand why. You never expressed any interest in the business end of things in our firm. What is motivating you?"

I explained to him that what I really wanted was some free time—just a few days a week—to be able to devote myself to philosophy and that I was building a business that I could sell in order to buy myself that time.

He smiled wanly at my naïveté: "And of course you now have less time for what you want to do than before you started your new business. It sounds to me like someone who jumps into the water to keep from getting wet in the rain."

I acknowledged that it sometimes felt that way to me too.

He said, "I am prepared to offer you a plan that has a much better chance of accomplishing your goal." He had apparently given the matter thought beforehand.

I felt a wave of relief. Roger, the engineer and problem-solver, was being true to his character in seeking a positive way to resolve a tricky issue.

He said, "I'll keep it simple. I think you have a gift for our kind of work. The clients always ask for you, and Bob Hills [the firm's salesman] likes to take you with him on sales calls. He says you help him close the deal. Since you went on your three-day-a-week schedule, you haven't been going on calls with him. We can't go on much longer with a $50,000-a-month breakeven and $35,000 in revenues." (I hadn't realized that things were that bad.) "So, here is what I propose. If you give up your retail venture [he talked that way] and instead give us 100 percent of your time and 200 percent of your commitment to help us dig out of the hole we are in, as soon as our volume of business gets above our breakeven, say more than $60,000 a month, you can go back to three days a week. But instead of earning 60 percent of your salary as you now do, we will pay you as if you were working full-time. That guarantees you the few days a week you are looking for, without the burden of having to run another business."

I was astonished. I never thought he would go for a strategy of that sort. It was an offer I couldn't refuse, and didn't. Also, I was enormously relieved. I had much more confidence in my ability to help the firm acquire more business than in managing the Door Store with its picky special orders that consumed every waking minute.

Over the next month, I turned over the store to my Paris friends, Dick Dale and his new wife Annie, and wished them luck with the arduous but promising new business. I then met with Bob Hills (the firm's salesman) and planned a series of calls we would make together in the Midwest.

I threw myself into the new effort. Roger thought it would take at least a year to meet our goal, but seven months later, we were well above the $60,000 a month level of revenue. I was a bit fearful that he would ask for more time or set some new condition. But I had nothing to fear. He was overjoyed, and he seemed genuinely pleased with the deal we had made.

My Philosophy "Sabbatical"

THIS TIME, INSTEAD OF managing the Door Store, I had four days of the week to read, study, take notes, and plan out strategies for writing about philosophy. I began to think of this period as my "philosophy sabbatical."

The lifestyle suited my temperament marvelously well. It relaxed as well as stimulated me. The opportunity to concentrate on ideas quietly and purposefully was balm to the spirit. Marti said it made me easier to live with, and I found the frustrations of our troubled marriage easier to absorb when I felt comfortable with the other parts of my life.

This opportunity to slow down to a less frenetic pace and take stock of my life could not have come at a more opportune time. Before Roger made his offer, I was down on myself and anxious about the future. I was bogged down in a failed marriage. I had been wearing myself to exhaustion juggling two jobs. And I was not doing the philosophical work I craved.

I remember having some questions about my continuing interest in philosophy. I couldn't help wondering what it was that made me persist in the quixotic quest to make sense out of philosophy and to understand why it had gone so badly astray. Why did I care so much about contributing to a conversation I had long abandoned? I knew enough about academia to realize that an outsider like myself would carry zero credibility.

Why was I continuing to gnaw on the old bone?

Yet, after each wave of self-questioning, I came back to the realization that I had deliberately chosen the lonely path of the non-professional philosopher and had no genuine regrets about the decision. I had been pursuing a particular line of thought since I was eighteen years old, as a result of my encounter with philosophy as a freshman at Harvard. Having chosen that path, I certainly would not abandon it because I had encountered some bumps and detours.

I ultimately resolved this dilemma by taking an active rather than passive posture towards philosophy. It was now possible to contemplate the previously unthinkable: I would write a book about philosophy. You don't have to be a professor of philosophy to write a philosophy book. (The only drawback is that if you are not part of the circle of insiders who write for each other, it may be difficult to get your book published and widely read.)

I resolved that if I did succeed in writing one or more philosophy books, I should not expect the sort of success that comes with large readership and royalty checks. Instead relying on an *external* audience, I would shape my own standards. I resolved not to write anything that smacked of amateurishness. I didn't know whether I could live up to this austere resolve and whether it was realistic. But I did know that I felt strongly about it, and that it was an important part of my identity.

Over the years, I have come to feel that this decision was one of the sounder ones I've made in a life pockmarked with mistakes. Shaping high standards and keeping faith with them has proven a highly effective method for maintaining self-respect when external validation has been slow in coming.

I then had to confront the question of what to write about. I didn't feel qualified to write scholarly books on philosophy, nor did I have a yen to do so.

I wanted to write about why philosophy had taken the wrong turn and how to get it back on the right path. But after making a number of attempts to tackle that question in its full breadth, I realized that I needed to scale down my ambition and focus on an aspect of philosophy that would have some practical relevance. Then as now, my mind gravitated toward pragmatic problem solving.

If philosophy had grown dysfunctional, it must inevitably be creating all sorts of practical problems. Where, I asked myself, was philosophy creating the sorts of practical problems that I was most qualified to solve?

I was wrestling with this perplexing question when circumstances once again turned my life upside down.

Screwed

AFTER SEVEN MONTHS, ROGER Nowland brought our three-day workweek arrangement to an abrupt end. I was obliged to cut my ponderings short and put my work in philosophy back in the closet.

It was a disheartening setback.

Though not directly involved in the finances of the firm, I was aware that Roger's product design business had slowed. I didn't think the slowdown would undermine our arrangement until Roger spelled it out for me. He seemed genuinely distressed that business conditions no longer permitted him to keep his commitment. He said he had learned something he had not realized before.

Our salesman, Bob Hills, had never required much help when he was selling product design work. He understood it well enough to deal with the concerns of prospective clients. But he didn't have the same feel for consumer research. Roger explained that the essence of selling professional services was not persuasion but anxiety reduction. In those days, companies didn't typically resort to consumer research unless they were experiencing problems that made them anxious.

"Because you know how to do the research," Roger said, "You are able to reduce the client's anxiety."

"By transferring it to myself," I said gloomily.

"Exactly," Roger said. "And once that happens, Bob can move in and close the deal. The two of you are a great team. You can't do what he can, which is to open doors and woo clients. But he can't do what you apparently do quite well, which is to communicate that you understand the client's problem and know how to solve it, thereby reducing his anxiety."

Roger went on to say that he knew I preferred the present arrangement to more money and a promotion, but that he no longer had a choice. He said he would almost double my salary and make me a Vice President, but I would have to help him "pull the firm's chestnuts out of the fire." And that, he added, would take a full-time commitment and then some. The alternative, he observed dryly, might well be that we would all be out of a job.

Then he apologized—something I had never heard him do before. I realized how difficult it must have been for him, a man of enormous pride, to go back on his word. And I sensed that his analysis of the sales problem was correct. Bob Hills was a hard working, effective, and impressive salesman. But it was not his job to master the firm's research methods, and without a firm grasp on how to solve puzzling marketing problems, he could not reduce the client's anxiety level.

It was a revelation to me that when it came to professional services, anxiety reduction rather than persuasion was the surest way to win new clients.

I saw no alternative to accepting Roger's offer. I pushed my books and notes aside and went back to full-time work with the firm. Bob Hills and I were once again a team, and as Roger had predicted, the combination of the two of us succeeded in reestablishing a strong base of business in less than a year.

It took me a long time to realize what a serious setback this development was for my own personal goals. In the first few months of my return to full-time work, I was too occupied with the task at hand to take in the full meaning of the change.

Roger Nowland's inability to maintain our three-day-a-week arrangement threw the project I had launched for myself badly off course. Once the firm's fortunes had been revived, I began to experience a gnawing emptiness—a growing sense of shame and disappointment.

For as long as I can remember, I've taken the metaphor of "life as a journey" literally. I've found the journey exciting in and of itself, but I've always focused on its destination. This is not what most people mean by life as a journey, but that is what it meant to me.

It was during my three-year sojourn in Paris that my self-confidence began to falter. Marriage to Marti was a serious setback to love. A trunk full of unfinished plays that would remain closed forever was a serious setback to work. And I had no idea of how I would ever be able to contribute to the world of thought—my most powerful aspiration.

In my Paris stay, I was still in my twenties; I felt I had time to experiment with my life. But I was in my thirties when I made the three-day-a-week Nowland arrangement. I took it as a sign that my life's journey was finally back on track. When the arrangement fell apart, I knew that the journey had taken a radically different turn.

I knew I had been sidetracked—not by Roger, whom I liked and trusted, but by the vicissitudes of life whose power I consistently underestimated.

PART THREE

STRUGGLING TO TURN MY LIFE AROUND

Facing Up to the Mess

I BEGAN TO FEEL once again, as in my childhood, that circumstances had seized control of my life. As a child, there wasn't much I could do about unwelcome changes. But now, as a functioning adult in my thirties, I knew that unless I took charge of my own fate, I would be repeating the sad story of my father's passive acceptance of circumstances, an acceptance that had taken a huge toll on his own life and the lives of his children.

The collapse of the arrangement with Nowland, for which I had voluntarily surrendered my ownership of the Door Store, meant that I had now bumped up against an impasse in virtually all of my life goals.

I knew that finding a way out of the dead end of my marriage would, at best, be deeply troubling and push me to the limits of my being.

I knew also that I would have to make fundamental changes in my work life and that these might prove risky.

I knew that I had confined myself to a narrow private life, while my quest for meaning required that I shift, at least partly, toward public life.

And I knew that my relationship to philosophy—my main source of meaning—had grown complex and confusing and that I would have to clarify it, at least for myself.

None of these setbacks was a cause for despair. I never felt that the situation had grown desperate and that all was lost. I didn't feel

I was "hitting bottom" or anything as dramatic as that. I was simply astonished that the future suddenly looked so bleak. I had given myself permission to experiment and to act on impulse. I had had confidence that I would make the right life decisions on my own.

But I hadn't.

It wasn't supposed to work out the way it did.

When I left Harvard for Paris, it felt like a well-earned temporary break. I never imagined it would turn into a series of uncontrollable events pushing me into dead ends in the most important aspects of living.

In retrospect, I had badly underestimated the power of circumstances and overestimated my ability to control them. Initially, when I made the decision to leave Harvard, I didn't realize that I was abandoning a secure career path. No one had forced me to move to Paris; I made the decision to leave Harvard as a responsible adult. No one had obliged me to invite Marti, with all her problems, to join me there. After I returned from Paris to the United States, no one had coerced me into having her rejoin me in New York even though I knew that our marriage was a mistake.

My self-conception was totally at odds with the day-to-day reality of my life. I thought of myself as a loving, caring family man. But the reality was that I was locked into a loveless, childless marriage.

I had been blessed with a remarkable education in how societies function, but I was stuck in a minor job in the bowels of the business world.

I had a self-image of being groomed for the exciting role of public intellectual, while in reality I was cut off from all aspects of public life except how consumers behave.

My major ambition was to make a genuine contribution to the world of thought, but if my current life trends continued, I was likely to end up as a pathetic amateur in matters philosophical.

I knew that without major changes, my life's quest for meaning would become an anticlimactic failure. I was determined not to let this happen.

At the time, I had no idea of how long and how much time and effort it would take to turn my life around.

As an outsider, I also knew that if I were to fix my own personal problems, I would also need to develop a better grasp of the forces at play in the larger society. How did my own life fit with the norms and expectations of our rapidly changing American culture?

Every generation faces distinctive tradeoffs and predicaments. For my generation—the World War II generation now passing from the scene—the cultural norms and tradeoffs that oriented our lives were starkly clear: work hard, live by the rules, secure a good education, get married, have children, sacrifice for them, find a job that provides a good living, and thrive.

We had no bewildering plethora of alternative life styles to confuse and disorient us, no insuperable obstacles to getting ahead if we came from a poor family, no sense that the deck was stacked against us. For vets like myself, the GI Bill was an incredible gift, making college and graduate school possible without requiring us to assume crippling loans or work part-time.

The tradeoffs were equally clear-cut. In exchange for a stable lifestyle, our generation was required to sacrifice much that was precious to us, such as life choices that best suited our autonomy, self-expressiveness, a sense of intimacy, and creativity. We gave up choice for stability.

In sharp contrast, in today's American culture there is no paucity of lifestyle choices and few constraints on self-expressiveness. Current generations—baby boomers, generation X, generation Y, millennials—confront very different predicaments. Their challenge is not a conformist culture that stifles self-expressiveness. Instead, they face obstacles such as the growing rigidity of today's social class hierarchy, especially for those hoping to move out of poverty to middle- and upper-class income levels.

Americans are much freer today than they were in my generation to select the life choices that are best for them—provided, of course, that they know *what* is best. Actually, many Americans do not know what life choices would permit them to flourish, for a reason that is surprisingly obscure.

Today, the major obstacle to making the right life choices is *an erosion of social norms in the larger culture.* As Americans have become freer to make their own life choices, the authority of our cultural institutions has shrunk. Social norms have weakened: the family isn't as influential as it used to be, nor is the church or the school or the job or the media or older mentors. As we've grown more individualistic, we find ourselves relying mainly on ourselves. There are fewer well-trodden paths, more uncharted territory.

Curiously, we do not seem troubled by this lack of cultural support. We feel fully competent to make our own life decisions, and indeed, we welcome the new freedom to do so. We bravely state that we want the freedom to make our own mistakes. And in many ways we are right to cherish this freedom. The expansion of cultural tolerance and individual freedom in American culture is truly remarkable and rightly cherished.

But we shouldn't be complacent about the dangers that come with the freedom to make our own mistakes without strong cultural retaliation. The main reason for complacency is our assumption that we will have the freedom to correct whatever mistakes we make in a timely fashion and without undue dislocation in our lives.

Unfortunately, for most people this assumption is simply incorrect. It underestimates the power of circumstance once one abandons the well-trodden path, and it overestimates the degree of control people have over their own lives and fortunes. All too often, making the wrong life choices can lead to disastrous consequences: aloneness, dead-end jobs or joblessness, estrangement from loved ones, addiction, failed marriages and other relationships, homelessness, emptiness, despair, depression, ill-health, poverty, stagnation, anger, resentment, rage, and more. The damage can be quite serious and is often irrevocable.

What kinds of mistakes are people most likely to make when cultural norms have lost much of their potency? Here are some of the most common ones:

- Making serious commitments too casually, without being prepared to accept the consequences.
- Failing to take responsibility for others, without being prepared to accept the consequences.
- Assuming that cultural norms are stronger than they really are (for example, splurging on elaborate weddings that lead to marriages that last for a year or two).
- Having children without strong support systems, such as a responsible spouse, family support, and community support.
- Exaggerating one's ability to manage drinking, drugs, careless driving, and other indulgences that can quickly grow out of control.
- Failure to control anger and rage.
- Dithering over what jobs, careers, or lifestyles to commit to.
- Indulging in self-pity instead of coping with one's problems.
- Unwarranted fearlessness about assuming heavy burdens of debt, such as large student loans, credit card debt, unaffordable mortgages, etc.

What, if anything, can people do to fix problems that their own wrong choices may have created? Don't expect much help from the larger culture. Indeed, we owe our greater personal freedom to the very fact that cultural norms and imperatives have grown weaker and more flexible. For better or worse, we are on our own.

Applying Philosophy to Life

IF WE CANNOT RELY on our culture to guide us to the right life choices, where shall we turn for guidance?

Here is where philosophy comes to our rescue. Without a well-honed philosophical perspective, we are at the mercy of whatever cultural norms happen to dominate at the moment.

With the right sort of philosophical perspective—and a strong sense of agency—we can fix our life mistakes, even the deeply existential ones.

I began to reflect seriously on why I had made so many misjudgments and what I might do to correct them. Inevitably my thoughts turned back to my childhood and my reactions to my father. I had always felt that my father had let life ride roughshod over him and that he had, in my judgment, been far too fatalistic.

I had reacted against his fatalism. Adopting a proactive stance, I had blithely assumed that if, instead of his passive acceptance of circumstance, I was willing to seize the initiative, I would be able to shape my own destiny.

I had started out with far greater privileges and advantages than my dad. I was native-born, not an immigrant. I spoke English fluently and had enjoyed a first-class education. I felt comfortable with people I didn't know. I didn't feel that any doors were closed to me, and I felt that my life path was a matter of my own choice.

Unlike my father's situation, the obstacles in my path were of my own making. I came to the sobering conclusion that there must be something seriously error-prone in my own thinking and decision-making. How else could I be left approaching middle age in such a fucked-up situation?

Here was I, a man who prided himself on his problem-solving ability, facing a wide range of dead ends without a practical plan for finding a way around any of them. Worse yet, I had no idea of what kind of error-prone thinking had led me into these dead ends.

So many things were out of whack in my life that it was confusing to know where to begin. The realization that I had made a number of bad decisions obliged me to start with myself. Once I realized how blinkered my thinking had become, I began to feel it was urgent to change my way of understanding my own life—not a comfortable, confidence-boosting task to accept or execute.

As I spent night after restless night agonizing over what was wrong and how to fix it, I gradually came to several conclusions that were uncomfortable for me to accept but that I felt were correct.

One of my most discouraging convictions was the sense that I had not used my head properly. Despite my devotion to philosophy, I had failed to think philosophically about my own life.

This assertion may sound strange, even laughable. No one these days looks to philosophy for a strategy for living and a way of solving personal problems. But I had dedicated enormous effort to understanding philosophy, and yet I had failed to apply its lessons to my own personal affairs.

I had now reached a crisis in my life, and I knew that I needed to think about it philosophically or lose control. I asked myself an obvious question that hadn't occurred to me in earlier periods of my life. If philosophy was such an indispensable aspect of life, how could it help me solve the problems that were dragging me towards failure? Could philosophy reveal some genuinely practical ways for me to resolve my own personal issues?

I was surprised when I discovered that the answer was "yes." Philosophy might not solve all of life's problems, but it could definitely alleviate some of the most urgent ones.

Why was I so convinced that thinking philosophically would help me find my way back on track with my life? Because philosophy is the only way of thinking that provides the breadth of perspective needed to achieve a modicum of control over one's life. Philosophy asks questions such as:

- What is truly important in life?
- What can you control and what can't you control?
- How does life really work?
- What is the nature of things?
- What is the human condition?

Many philosophical thinkers have addressed these questions. Their work has become my constant companion, and I read and reread their iconic books. In particular, apart from the existentialists, I find inspiration for sound philosophical thinking in the writings of Alfred North Whitehead and Isaiah Berlin on the history of ideas, the pungent reflections of Hannah Arendt, and the provocative thinking of Jürgen Habermas, Richard Rorty, Martha Nussbaum and Charles Taylor—all respected philosophers, though not all in the mainstream of the Western tradition of philosophy.

Three practical uses for philosophy make it possible to counter the distortions of our culture when it becomes dysfunctional, as it has in the present era of our history.

Philosophy insists that we never lose sight of the whole. This is its first counterbalance to contemporary culture. The necessary specialization and reductionism of science have become the enemy of keeping the whole in sight at all times. I believe that Freud's scientific commitment to reducing human behavior to Newtonian-like laws of motion caused him to lose sight of the whole person as a social being.

I think that today's cognitive scientists are so fixated on locating the processes of the brain that they lose sight of people's practical issues. Many of the professionals I encounter in my day-to-day life—business executives, lawyers, accountants, doctors, professors, bankers—have trouble keeping their own specialized frameworks from distorting their overview of life.

The second application of philosophy that makes it a counterbalance to a dysfunctional culture is its focus on distinguishing what is truly important in life from what is less important. The most familiar of life's traps are often misleading cultural cues that cause you to lose sight of what is truly important to you and those you love.

The third practical use of philosophy is to help individuals develop a better understanding of the flaws in our cognitive processes. Cognitive scientists like Daniel Kahneman have learned that our ways of seeing the world are inherently distorted and subject to systematic error. The distortions include: leaping to false conclusions, falsely attributing causality to events, mistaking the part for the whole, and other mistakes of cognitive judgment.

It is the function of philosophical critique to identify and correct these twisted judgments.

A Head Makeover

A SECOND, VERY DIFFERENT conclusion I reached during this period of agonizing self-examination was that I ought to seek professional help in coming to grips with emotional problems rooted in my unstable childhood.

In my graduate studies at Harvard I had immersed myself in studying psychological therapies. Psychoanalytic therapy was our major focus. There were lots of things wrong with psychoanalysis and in later years they caused psychoanalysis to lose its credibility and high standing. But psychoanalysis had a particular appeal to me because it was grounded on an important truth.

It is a truth foreshadowed in the discoveries of Freud, and it is currently to be found in the work of Daniel Kahneman. More than a century before cognitive psychologist Kahneman won the Nobel Prize in Economics for his experiments showing just how error-prone the human mind is, Freud had discovered that aspects of our mental and emotional life essential to our well-being are not accessible to consciousness without therapeutic intervention.[10]

Today's cognitive theories are just beginning to catch up with Freud's great insight. Contrary to the idealist belief of the Enlightenment that we are rational creatures and that logic and reasoning will bring us to the truth, scientific research shows us that our minds are inherently error-prone.

---

10 *Wicked Problems,* 26.

If our perceptions tend to be distorted and if we are not even conscious of the mistakes we make, then rational thinking is a much more feeble decision-making tool than Western culture has assumed.

The core truth that lies at the heart of psychoanalysis, a truth of vast significance, is that our conscious minds block our own understanding of our most crippling problems, and these problems are then repressed into unconsciousness. For more than a century, psychoanalysis has been groping to discover the most effective ways we can bring these problems into consciousness and find practical solutions to them.

In light of this understanding, I concluded that I was a prime candidate for psychoanalysis. I had fallen into a full-blown psychological neurosis. The best definition of neurosis is: "the experience of being whipped about by dimly understood forces over which you have little or no control." Jung pithily summed up the challenge of neurosis: "Unless you make the unconscious conscious, it will direct your life and you will call it fate."[11]

I was a reasonably intact person with a well-functioning ego who had placed much too much confidence on my own rational thinking, and as a consequence, I had made a series of bad decisions. I had assumed that my conscious mind was capable of grasping my own motivations, strengths, and vulnerabilities, even the unconscious ones. I now knew enough to realize that I couldn't rely on my conscious reasoning power to penetrate to the core of what had gone wrong in my life, and so I might benefit from professional help.

I settled on a highly recommended psychoanalyst, Dr. S. Dr. S was a pleasant and intelligent woman in her fifties. She was a classic Freudian who was sparse in her interpretations, reluctant to give

---

11   Quoted in Rachel Cusk, "Alexandra Fuller's 'Leaving Before the Rains Come,'" *New York Times Sunday Book Review*, January 18, 2015.

advice, and off-puttingly silent throughout most of the two years I devoted to psychoanalysis. Integrating her rare interpretations with my own, I want to try to sketch out a rough picture of the neurosis that so bewildered me.

Dr. S theorized that my strong empathy with Marti's plight when she was trapped at home by her mother's illness made it just about impossible for me not to come to her rescue. I think Dr. S was right about the empathy—an unconscious process that exerts a powerful influence without being fully understood.

I experienced a constant anxiety in all the years Marti and I were together. Marti would often seem pale and listless, especially after a period of tension between us. Dr. S pointed out the connection between her pallor (and my frequent complaint about how anxious it made me) and my mother's pallor in the weeks preceding her death.

In the years with Marti, my childhood anxieties would sometimes flare up and become intense. They would then subside, but they never went away completely. They were always ready to take over. I became anxious when we had had an unresolved argument. I became anxious when I grew strongly assertive or edged toward loss of temper and violence. I became anxious when I felt trapped in the relationship without any clear way to escape from it.

Dr. S interpreted my inability to leave Marti as due to multiple causes. She felt that my reaction to my father's broken promises made it difficult for me to go back on my own commitments, especially the serious commitment of marriage. She felt that my empathy and identification with Marti made it difficult for me to abandon her and thereby repeat my own traumatic abandonment caused by my mother's death.

Most of all, she pointed to the tremendous burden of guilt I felt about the possibility that Marti might take her own life. This latter interpretation rang particularly true because Marti had on occasion threatened to do so. The heaviness of the guilt constantly weighed on me.

The therapy revealed that the origins of the neurosis that haunted my marriage to Marti came from a series of traumatic experiences in my youth that had piled up one on top of the other, each one reinforcing the others while leaving its own lasting impact.

The first traumatic experience took place in the few months before my mother's death. I have always realized that my mother's death had had a profound impact on my life. The loss was abrupt and total, with devastating consequences. Her death was the defining event of my youth. But it wasn't until I began with Dr. S that I came to realize how traumatic the few months preceding her death had been.

The weeks before she died were the bleakest period of my young life. My mother's lack of responsiveness, along with her pallor and listlessness, created wave upon wave of anxiety in me. Since I didn't realize she was ill, I saw her reactions as a withdrawal of love that my misbehavior had brought about. I felt that her non-responsiveness must be due to something I had done. It took many years for me to realize that her withdrawal was due to her illness, not my misbehavior.

The second trauma was my mother's totally unexpected death. It took all of us, especially my father, by complete surprise. No one knew or even suspected how gravely ill she was. The bottomless hole her death left in my life gave all the other traumatic experiences an intensity they would not have had if she had recovered from her illness. It left me feeling lonely, abandoned, guilt-ridden, anxious, and believing myself partly responsible for her death.

The third traumatic event was one Dr. S emphasized. She believed that my father's inability to support us and keep us together in the period following Ma's death had left me resentful and angry. Her view was that I resolved to be, in effect, my own father, determined to avoid being victimized by life.

I did not reject her judgment, but it struck me then and still does as highly theoretical, because I have never felt any conscious anger at my father. On the contrary, I continued to feel deep affection and love for him throughout all the years that followed, up to his peaceful death at age eighty-seven. The only negative feeling I recall was disappointment when he was unable to keep his promises, which happened many times. As a consequence, I developed the opposite tendency—a virtual inability to break any commitments that I make.

The fourth and longest period of trauma stretched out over the years of living in foster homes. The years with foster parents had left me with a hunger for belonging. I yearned to feel like a full member of the family rather than an outsider. Every encounter I had with other people's family warmth evoked an aching envy and an almost desperate need to be accepted.

The final trauma—and it was a doozy—was being kicked out of the Friedman foster home after I threw a heavy bookend at the Friedman's older daughter, Devorah. Thereafter, I came to mistrust the violence in myself and kept it under tight control. I felt intense anxiety whenever it threatened to break out.

Looking back on Dr. S's interpretations, my feelings are mixed. I think she was right to help me relive the traumas of my youth and thereby come to see them in a new light. But I also think she was prone to over-psychologizing. For example, during my therapy, she kept picking away at my interest in philosophy. At many sessions, she would repeatedly ask me why it meant so much to me. I angrily resented her probing ("resistance" is the label she gave my resentment).

I feared that she was trying to "explain away" the thing that gave me comfort and solace. Presumably, if she could reveal the "neurotic roots" of this interest in philosophy, it could then be discarded onto the junk heap of my life as just another expression of childhood angst.

Dr. S's traditional Freudianism helped me in a number of ways, but we never did penetrate to the insight that philosophy had become my way of understanding the upheavals that had turned my life upside down.

My attachment to philosophy may have had its roots in childhood bewilderment, but it had evolved into my way of coping with life—a way that worked better for me than becoming overly psychological or simply going with the flow.

A Shift in Perspective

GOING TO THE PSYCHOANALYTIC repair shop to get my head re-aligned was a humbling experience. It made me aware that one of my main coping skills—thinking things through logically—was far less effective than I had believed.

In my psychoanalysis, Dr. S placed her main emphasis on unconscious conflicts and motivations. It is true that understanding your own unconscious assumptions can explain some aspects of life, especially those that run counter to your own conscious wishes and intentions. But I have come to suspect that there is something profoundly distorting about an exclusively psychological framework. Psychologizing people's ways of being is almost inevitably reductionist.

After a lifetime of conducting psychological studies, I have concluded that most are radically incomplete. It is all too easy to identify someone with his or her neurosis, thereby missing the rich complexity of life: we are more than the sum of our motivations and neuroses.

I don't mean to devalue psychological understanding. The search for such understanding has occupied a considerable part of my own life. But as I've learned to think philosophically, I've come to understand the limitations of an exclusively psychological perspective. To act effectively in the world, either on your own behalf or that of others, you need two resources in addition to psychological acumen. You need ethical centeredness and you need a repertoire of practical coping skills.

ॐ

My own ethical centeredness is an important part of my heritage from my mother—Ma's constant admonition that her son become a *mensch*. The code of honor reflected in the concept of being a mensch has exerted a powerful influence on my life.

There are many ways of defining *menschlichkeit*, but they all include:

- Standing on one's own two feet
- Caring for others
- Accepting and fulfilling one's responsibilities to others
- Being trustworthy and reliable—someone others can depend upon
- Acting with courage
- Showing leadership
- Acting in good faith

Framing the issue philosophically, I believe that my ethical aspirations are best expressed by the concept of *stewardship*. Stewardship incorporates within itself many of the connotations of being a mensch, such as caring, taking responsibility for others, and safeguarding the interests and concerns of others, whether individuals or institutions.

My part-time jobs after the war brought the centrality of stewardship into practical focus for me. The first was learning how MIT as a university could best carry out its stewardship responsibilities to its students. The second was learning how European union leaders could best serve their stewardship function, both for their members and for the cause of democracy. Both assignments contained the core elements of the kind of work I highly valued. Both sought to strengthen the stewardship bond between institutions and those they serve.

I trace my high regard for the ethic of stewardship back to my experience as a child and teenager of having some positive models of stewardship to shape my ideals. Mrs. Ellis, my fourth grade teacher, came to personify the virtue that I would later learn to call stewardship. She embraced an ethic of care, kindness, and concern as part of her calling as a teacher. The same was true of Ms. Luftman, the welfare agency caseworker, who regarded it as part of her calling to extend kindness and consideration to me and others.

My foster parent Mrs. Smith performed her responsibilities with the same sort of unfailing kindness. She wasn't a real mother to me, and sometimes that hurt. As a fourteen year old, I didn't distinguish clearly between the role of paid foster parent and biological parent. But in later years, I recognized—and was deeply grateful for—her care.

My English instructor in my first year at Harvard, the poet John Berryman, also adopted a strong stewardship stance towards those he taught in his small class of style-challenged freshmen. And so did Captain John Hartshorne, my army commander and friend.

Practical skills for coping with the world, as well as ethics, are grounded in the first five years of life. It is then that a child develops the self-confidence of those who as infants and little children are loved and accepted unconditionally.

I had the good fortune to enjoy a lot of emotional security in those all-important first five years of life, so that even though I bumped up against many mishaps later, I was armed with the core security I needed to struggle, to cope, to survive, and in many ways to flourish.

Psychologists refer to these as "ego strengths," but they can also be judged as traits of character. For example, in trying so hard for so long to make the marriage with Marti work, neurotic anxiety was admittedly a factor. But so was strength of commitment to promises

I had made, as well as a refusal to give up if there was any chance, however slim, of finding some sort of solution. In other words, my virtues and my weaknesses reinforced each other in locking me into the marriage for so long.

During the stress-ridden foster-home period of my life I was also busy building coping skills. Indeed, I depended on them to prevent myself from becoming a victim of circumstances. Some of them weren't praiseworthy. But they helped me survive, and while I'm not proud of them I'm not ashamed of them either.

For example, even at that young age I was engaged in a struggle against the seductions of victimhood and self-pity. These are powerful forces, often underestimated in the impact they have on people's lives.

There has to be a strong reason why self-pity takes up permanent residence in so many people. Wallowing in victimhood allows you to blame everyone but yourself for your problems. It stimulates satisfying feelings of self-justification and righteous indignation. Like sitting in the corner and sucking your thumb, it relieves you from having to engage reality in hand-to-hand combat. You simply declare yourself out of the battle because an unjust and rotten world has stacked the odds against you.

In her novel *Foreign Affairs*, Alison Lurie visualizes self-pity as Fido, a shabby white dog who accompanies her main character everywhere she goes. Fido grows and shrinks. Sometimes he is huge, sometimes he is small. But he is always present.

In those foster home years, I struggled to resolve the conflict between self-pity and self-help. Fortunately for me, the self-help side prevailed. If the foster homes wouldn't take care of me, I would take care of myself. If Pa could not afford to support me, I would find a way to do it myself (and eventually to support him as well). If my foster parents wanted to exile me, I would call Miss Luftman and exile them instead.

If they didn't want to hear the truth about how I felt, I would keep my feelings to myself or, if necessary, lie about them. If Devorah wanted to manipulate me by playing on my vulnerabilities, I would build stronger defenses against losing my temper.

Here is where the basic trust and self-confidence established in my first years of life kicked in. The powerful impulse to prevail (the source of virtues such as self-reliance, independence, and pride as well as vices such as willfulness and hubris) swept away the consolations of self-pity.

One of my other coping skills was a state of readiness I came to think of as my action mode. When trouble arose, I would make an abrupt transition from an inattentive state to an intensely vigilant one. My shoulders would tense up and tighten, and I would immediately start to work out plans for action. After a while, I would grow more reflective and dig down for a deeper understanding of the problem. But my initial reaction was a strong form of the primitive flight-or-fight response.

Nor was shoulder-tightening my only physical response. I would concentrate my attention. The adrenalin would flow. I refused to be distracted. I was poised for action and usually took it.

Being so action-prone, I was obliged to develop a strong sense of what psychologists call "means–ends realism"—a pragmatic ability to make judgments about the likely consequences of one's actions. For action-prone types like myself, not having sound means–ends realism is a formula for trouble.

Another form of coping that had its roots in those years is a socially reprehensible skill that I have come to think of as "low cunning." When Ma was still alive, I had been used to blurting out whatever I felt, however indiscreet and tactless. The worst consequence of my thoughtlessness was my mother's chasing me around the house, determined to give me a hearty swat on the tush. It was a game I relished because I was able to gain her undivided attention, with no real harm to either body or spirit.

In the foster homes, however, all forms of spontaneity, especially those that involved criticism, expressions of independence, anger, petulance, or disobedience had nothing but negative consequences. So I gradually learned to curb my outspokenness and to dissemble my feelings.

I developed a persona that revealed as little as possible about my feelings and myself. And I began to find unobtrusive ways of doing what I wanted to do. For example, when Miss Luftman visited the foster homes, the foster parents did not like me to speak to her privately. So I would quietly leave the house before she did and wait outside for her.

When I was living with the Friedmans, I found it oppressive to eat dinner while Uncle Jack monitored how many pieces of bread I ate. I gradually found ways to snatch something to eat before or after he had his dinner.

Knowing how much Aunt Rose fed on constant expressions of gratitude, and how much they meant to her, I would force myself to repeat how grateful my sister and I were for everything she was doing for us. This was not out-and-out hypocrisy, because I did feel gratitude. But I would have preferred to express it on apt occasions, rather than chant it ritualistically.

Breaking Up

AFTER MARTI KICKED THE broken bottle of scotch down the stairs on Mulberry Street, I decided that I'd had it with the blind man's twenty-eight-dollar-a-month fourth floor walk-up, with its chaste white walls and its quietly menacing neighborhood. I insisted that we move, which we did, to a more comfortable apartment on Waverly Place, overlooking Washington Square, in the heart of Greenwich Village.

The move helped a bit but did not end the bad vibes between an unhappy, tense Marti who felt exiled and rootless, and me—dissatisfied, restless, and constantly on the lookout for a way out of this trap of my own making.

I was growing ever less tolerant of the cold war that characterized our marriage. From the time Marti had come to New York from Paris, through the moves from the Upper East Side to Little Italy to Greenwich Village, to opening the Door Store and then turning it over to new owners, to my seven-month fling with studying and writing about philosophy four days a week, to my return to a full-time commitment at Nowland & Company—throughout that entire span of time, Marti had nursed her anger and resentment and depression. Our relationship had grown distant, formal, and polite, punctuated by outbursts of anger, sometimes from her, sometimes from me.

I never understood what she did with her time. She didn't want a paying job. She didn't want to do volunteer work or go back to school or try her hand at something creative that might prove personally satisfying. Despite her striking appearance, high intelligence, and strong will, she steadfastly embraced the negative. The grim depression and low self-esteem that caused her to fear defeat as inevitable created a paralysis of will that left both of us in a state of exhausted frustration.

My own reaction was, I suppose, a form of denial. I took refuge in work, because I didn't know what else to do. Every once in a while, when the tension grew too intense for me, I would try to break through to her. More than once I said to her with great bitterness, "I just don't understand why you want to live with someone you hate and resent."

She would then deny that I was the object of her anger and resentment. For a few days after these angry confrontations, we would both try to recreate the warmer ambience of Paris. But it never lasted, and soon we would be back to a strained, formal politeness. The physical distance between us may have been measurable in inches or a few feet, but the emotional distance seemed like light years.

The worst period of our relationship came soon after we had moved yet again, this time to a larger, more expensive apartment on West Twelfth Street. I thought fixing it up might give Marti something to do. But that didn't happen. The movers moved our books, furniture, the few pieces of art we had purchased, and our other belongings into the large sunny living room in the new apartment.

Over the first weekend after the move, we unpacked just enough to fix up the kitchen, dining room and bedroom. When I left for work after the weekend, I assumed that Marti would unpack some of the books and other things so that we could use the living room and have access to the things we needed. But when I came home that night she said that she had been too tired to unpack.

The rest of the week came and went and she had not unpacked any of the boxes cluttering up the living room. I would come home in the weeks that followed, each night hoping for and expecting some symbolic gesture in making our new apartment livable. But nothing would be touched. I could, of course, have accepted the situation and unpacked the boxes myself. But I didn't. I didn't want to. The untouched boxes became a battle of wills. They symbolized the paralysis in our relationship.

We lived in that apartment for a year and a half and never once sat in the living room because it was too full of boxes.

After months of living with the untouched moving boxes and the rising tension, I finally faced the reality that the time had come to go our separate ways. In exposing myself to psychoanalytic therapy, I felt I had taken the first step towards digging my way out of the hole I had dug for myself. It was now time to take the next step. I needed to find a way to extricate Marti and me from the paralysis and stagnation that had overtaken us. The prospect filled me with dread.

I knew I would have to take the initiative. Marti was too depressed to take any initiative on her own.

I began to speak to her about separating—conversations that proved incredibly painful. She felt I was rejecting her for reasons she was powerless to prevent. She felt bitter, alone, and abandoned. She said she didn't know what she would do with her life, and she felt desolately alone.

Several times I started to leave but she would persuade me to stay "just a little while" and talk it over. I would do so, and then be unable to leave. After a brief truce, the tension and formality between us would reassert itself.

One night I screwed up the courage to leave without talking it over. As I left, she asked me where I was going so late at night. I told her I was going to sleep at Nat Hentoff's place. A few hours later, after I had gone to sleep, she called and said she was in a panic. She had tried to take her own life by sticking her head in the oven. I put my clothes on and dashed back to Twelfth Street. Our apartment stank with the smell of gas, even with the windows open. I stayed the night and the next night and the one after that and the weeks that followed.

Nothing had changed.

My fear was that if I left again, she might try another suicide attempt and it might succeed.

Months passed. I began to spend time with other women, particularly with Jasmine, an attractive research assistant in the Nowland office. We would often have lunch or dinner together. And one night, we made love.

Instead of going through the motions as if she were carrying out a routine household chore, she responded in a manner I had not experienced for years—loving, passionate, enthusiastic. Even more wondrous still, Jasmine subtly managed to convey the message that she would be quite receptive to more of the same. And I found more of the same irresistible.

Eventually, I confided in Jasmine, sharing my fears and my now desperate need to separate from Marti. She suggested that I call Marti's friend, Barb, to ask her if she would stay with Marti when I left so that Marti would not have to undergo the ordeal alone. It was a practical, sensible idea. I arranged to meet with Barb, who after some initial hesitation agreed to stay with Marti for as long as necessary.

One morning, several weeks after meeting with Marti's friend, I packed a suitcase, left it in the trunk of my car, and in the early evening called to tell Marti I was not coming home and that Barb would soon be arriving. I did not tell her where I was going.

I checked into a cheerless room at the Harvard Club where I would live for the next few weeks in a constant state of misery and anxiety. Barb knew where I was if she felt she had to reach me.

A marriage that should never have taken place had dragged out for eight years, the last five of them in unrelieved tension. It was now finally moving toward dissolution and resolution.

Several months later we were formally divorced.

My relationship with Marti had deep roots. It was a caring and empathic bond with a woman caught up in conflicts that threatened her innermost self, her very being. In later life, Marti and I came to have a more cordial relationship, and I was pleased that I was able to be helpful to her financially (over and above the alimony I paid each month).

I did so voluntarily because her means of support were so meager, but also out of concern for her. It is true that she was difficult to live with, but if I had been stronger at the time, I might have saved both of us unnecessary suffering.

In later years, she was dismissive of our married years together. In a letter to me some years ago, she wrote, "those years were a mistake for both of us (pathetically young and inexperienced) and a waste of time for both."

My attachment to Marti during that period was my most important relationship. And yet the relationship was the opposite of what I was seeking. It lacked genuine intimacy, warmth, security, love, and mutual nurturance.

Lacking these all-important qualities of a love relationship, what were the forces that held us together for so many years? That even decades after we were divorced made me willing to continue to support her beyond my legal obligations?

When I had invited her to come to Paris, she was really hurting. I had cared for her and wanted to do everything I could to alleviate the pain. I had seen her as a fellow sufferer, and I believe she was.

During our marriage, I had abandoned my aspiration to find the kind of love with her that I craved. I thought it was unattainable—available to others, perhaps, but not to me. My attachment to her was based on identifying with her as someone who, like myself, had given up on love but craved caring. I enjoyed her company. Her astringent wit was clever and vehement, and it made me smile. I respected her armor of self-protection, having put on similar armor myself. I valued the touch of class she had developed for herself. I admired her acute intelligence. I liked her looks, those of a classic Nordic beauty. And I cared for her.

I learned that the kind of relationship we had was not tantamount to a real marriage. A sort of friendship, yes. A true love-grounded marriage, no. My bond with her was closer to a stewardship bond than a love one. I learned the hard way that without abiding and steadfast love, you cannot do for another what I had hoped to do for her and for us together.

Marti needed salvation. If I had loved her enough, I conceivably might have met that need. But it couldn't be done without a vast amount of love. And I was not able to give her that love (nor was she able to give it to me). I began to learn some rudimentary lessons about love.

They were negative lessons, to be sure. But they were lessons. Gradually, over the ensuing years, I learned some positive lessons about love. And I am still learning.

The Next Big Step

AS I MENTIONED, IN the final months of my marriage to Marti, I had begun an affair with a co-worker. Jasmine was in charge of production at the Nowland firm. In the pre-computer age, it was she who translated our hand scribbles into impeccable professional typed proposals and reports.

She was probably the most reliable person in the company. Often working under great pressure, she unfailingly did whatever was needed to meet the client's time deadlines. Whenever someone wanted to make sure that something would get done well under pressure, he would say, "Give it to Jasmine."

As we grew more intimate, I learned more about her life. She had gone to work immediately after graduating from high school at age seventeen, so for half of her life she had been supporting herself and helping to support her family. Her parents had immigrated as adults to the United States from Armenia to escape the Turkish massacres.

After an arduous five-year trek across Europe, her parents finally settled in New York City's Washington Heights with their four children. Jasmine explained that her parents never called her Jasmine. They always called her "Hassie" (a diminutive of her Armenian name Hasmieg, which translates as "Jasmine" in English). While I continued to refer to her as Jasmine at the office, I shifted to calling her Hassie when we were alone.

At the time of our affair, her siblings were all married and all of them had children. She was the only unmarried one in the family, and it weighed heavily on her and on her parents. They were a large close-knit family for whom marriage and children were what life is all about. Hassie wanted above all to be a mother, and at thirty-four she couldn't wait much longer. Nor did she relish being "an old maid." Marriage and family were by far her preferred destiny.

Hassie told me that she had recently broken off a long-distance, five-year affair with a Swiss businessman and that she was just about ready to accept the "old maid" identity that her family now assumed would be her fate. She was, she said, aware that her biological clock was ticking ominously and she herself had begun to fear that she would never have children—the sharpest regret of her life. She loved children and was constantly fussing over and buying things for her nieces and nephews.

She spoke far more feelingly and poignantly about the prospect of missing out on being a mother than missing out on being a wife. She and her mother were exceptionally close. She was more ambivalent about her father, a man with strong dogmatic views who had been a tyrant with the children while they were growing up.

She gave me a book to read, Margaret Housepian Dobkin's *Houseful of Love*, adding that the author was a family friend and that the book presented a faithful picture of Armenian family life. It made a deep impression on me. It evoked an extraordinary warmth and closeness. It described just the sort of supportive and loving family life I had longed for after my mother died.

As Hassie and I grew closer, I was amazed at how different her life outlook was from Marti's. She was hopeful and optimistic and willing to take risks. She was positive and supportive. And she actually enjoyed our physical intimacy, wanting to prolong it, not get it over with as quickly as possible. I was eager to be with someone who wasn't negativistic and depressed all the time.

I asked Hassie if she would marry me if and when I was able to extricate myself from my debilitating marriage. She said she needed some time to think about it. She took a week's vacation and went to Saint Martin in the Caribbean to think it over.

When she returned, she said yes, she would marry me once my divorce was final. She was tired of working. She wanted to be a home-maker, and she knew that I would be able to make enough money to permit us to live with comfort and economic security without her having to keep her demanding job. She also knew that my religion would not create conflicts with her own. Hassie's family faith was Methodist—the Protestant minority among Armenians. Though I was Jewish, I have always had a strong aversion to sectarianism in all of its forms. Hassie knew that I would be content to have our children (if we were lucky enough to have them) brought up in both faiths—something we both wanted.

Hassie and I were married in the fall of 1958 in her family's small Armenian Protestant church on East Thirty-Fourth Street in New York. Our marriage got off to a good start. We moved into an airy and comfortable apartment on New York's Upper East Side.

Hassie busied herself with decorating the new apartment. She hugely enjoyed doing so and was good at it. She also enjoyed shop-ping for food and learning to cook new dishes. She constantly went out of her way to make life comfortable and agreeable for the two of us.

We spent a lot of time with her family. I liked all of them. But I soon discovered that I liked them more as individuals than as a unit. This came as a surprise to me. I thought that I had wanted to belong to a large, loving family like Hassie's. Her family reminded me of the family of the first girl I fell in love with—Evelyn Davidoff and her warm, welcoming family who opened their living room to all of Evelyn's friends.

What I failed to realize was that Hassie's family were so close knit and so committed to their ethnicity (all three of Hassie's siblings had married Armenians) that however welcoming they were, I would always be the *odar*, the non-Armenian outsider.

Ironically, instead of recreating the family of my childhood, I had inadvertently recreated the foster home situation of my youth where I never was, nor could ever become, a real member of the family.

I also finally realized that the idea of belonging to a large close-knit family appealed to me far more than the actuality. I suppose that those who actually spent their formative years as part of a large family might want to recreate it in their adult years. But for those like myself who had not grown up with such a family, the hidden negative side came as a disagreeable surprise. Beneath the surface, jealousies and resentments grew in lush abundance. Ancient grievances somehow never lost their sting.

I found the small inconveniences of family togetherness both funny and frustrating. For example, Hassie's family had a beach house on Long Island's North Shore. The house was located about two miles from the beach, too far to walk while schlepping mountains of beach paraphernalia. Since all the siblings had their own cars, the sensible thing would have been for each couple to go to the beach separately with their own kids as different parts of the extended family got ready. But no, that would have violated the unwritten family code.

For reasons that were never made explicit, the entire family must all go and all return together as an indivisible unit, which meant waiting until the last child finished the last pee while everyone else stood around shuffling from foot to foot. It was, of course, humorous in concept. But for an impatient type like myself, it seemed senseless to wait until it was so late that, once we arrived at the beach, we would immediately have to start preparing for the collective trip back.

Our marriage was old-fashioned in the sense that we were always respectful of one another. Always. Unfailingly. But there was more formality to our marriage than suited me. Hassie was accustomed to formality in marriage. Her parents were formal with each other and locked into the tradition of sharply different roles for husbands and wives.

In the early months of our marriage, Hassie focused on getting pregnant as quickly as possible, an exercise in which I participated eagerly. A year and a half later our beloved daughter, Nicole, was born. But we were never able to have more children. Hassie subsequently suffered through five miscarriages until the doctor warned her that she had to stop trying.

Engaging in Public Life

BEING OBLIGED TO RETURN to full-time work at Nowland made me realize that I was moving further and further away from my goal. Doing a successful job at a business research firm was certainly nothing to be ashamed of. On the contrary, I found the work interesting and absorbing. But it was not the direction I wanted my life to take.

I knew that most men of my generation had been obliged to leave behind their hopes of creative self-expression in the interests of making a living to support their families. But I was unwilling to abandon my life goal of thinking philosophically and applying that thinking to the larger society. One way of doing that would be to become what is called a public intellectual—a person whose musings about public life reflect serious thought.

In my years moving in intellectual circles in New York, I had formed personal friendships with a number of well-known public intellectuals, whom I greatly respected as well as embraced as friends. They included Irving Howe, the left-leaning literary critic whose writings were always lucid and stimulating; Irving Kristol, a right-leaning political thinker (and former lefty) whose views were quite influential and always expressed trenchantly; Richard Hofstadter, an insightful and elegant historian; Robert Heilbroner, a popular economist whose Harvard PhD thesis became a best seller and sold four million copies; the former journalist and famous sociologist, Daniel Bell, a thinker of large thoughts; and William Barrett, a literary editor and philosopher who subsequently became my coauthor of my first book, *Ego and Instinct*.

All were distinguished thinkers and writers. I suspected that my writing skills were not as impressive as theirs. But I didn't feel inferior to them in range and depth of thought. Given the opportunity, I felt, I could demonstrate that my philosophical thinking led to useful perspectives about our society and times. But I knew I couldn't achieve this goal if all my energies were devoted to business research. To find the time and occasion to write about the state of our society from a philosophical perspective, I needed an operating base that would give me more freedom and flexibility than my current job allowed.

I gave some thought to rejoining the academic world, where I would have the freedom I needed. This was tempting, but I knew that Hassie hated the idea and might have felt compelled to go back into the work force if my income fell much lower than it was.

Up to this stage of my life, my personal philosophy had a strong inward focus. Rising out of my youthful years of wandering from one foster home to another, its original purpose had been to reconstruct an inner compass that would give my life the sort of stability and firm grounding I had enjoyed when my mother was alive and my family intact.

This defensive philosophy of my youth had proven invaluable. Apart from some troubled love relationships, I had been able to cope with life reasonably well, without experiencing the kinds of failure my father feared as a consequence of our family breakdown.

Now, as I was approaching forty and part of a stable family, I became self-confident enough to be less preoccupied with myself and more concerned with the larger culture and society.

It was a society with which I had been able to cope, but I nonetheless felt that that it was flawed in a serious way. I felt a need to understand what the flaw might be and how it might be addressed. I was eager to broaden my self-preoccupied philosophy of life to embrace the larger society.

I developed a thesis that over the course of years became ever more self-evident. I had come to feel that our culture was evolving in a lopsided fashion with too much emphasis on self-satisfaction and self-fulfillment, and too little emphasis on communal ethical values.

The evolution of the highly successful investment bank, Goldman Sachs, is a particularly vivid example of the transition. I had a direct encounter with Goldman's top executives in the 1980s, when Trinity Church in lower Manhattan—New York's oldest and wealthiest Episcopal Church—invited me to conduct a series of dialogues among leading Wall Street executives on the subject of corporate social responsibility.

In chairing these dialogues at the church, I came to know and respect the top echelon of Goldman Sachs partners. Among all the Wall Street representatives in the dialogues, Goldman's executives held the firmest conviction that their financial transactions had to be conducted within a sturdy ethical framework of stewardship.

Unlike some of the other Wall Street dialogue participants, they correctly understood Adam Smith's seminal insight that the invisible hand of the market works to everyone's advantage when, and only when, it is guided by a human instinct that Smith called "moral sympathy"—an inborn empathy that predisposes us to do well by others as well as by our individual self-interest. It is what I mean by an ethic of stewardship.

It is mindboggling to reconcile this admiring image of Goldman Sachs with *Rolling Stone's* characterization of Goldman as "a great vampire squid wrapped around the face of humanity" sucking out its blood. Journalist Matt Taibbi wrote this famous line in 2009, after the Securities and Exchange Commission charged Goldman with civil fraud in deceiving its clients by actively pushing them to buy deals designed to lose money. The SEC claimed that Goldman had withheld key information from the buyers about how these deals were deliberately constructed to fail.[12]

How in the world can one square Goldman's trading practices and conflicts of interest with the ethical stance its executives had so eloquently represented years earlier in my Trinity Church dialogues? The impression I have of the company as it now exists under the leadership of its CEO, Lloyd Blankfein, is that the firm's profitability has come to exercise total priority over its stewardship obligations, indeed, ahead of any and all other considerations.

In his Congressional testimony, Blankfein vigorously defended the firm's actions. His defense rang an all-too-familiar bell. Goldman didn't break the law, he stated, and therefore could not have done anything wrong. The clients who bought the tainted mortgage-backed securities, he said, were not helpless and naïve widows and orphans. They were "sophisticated investors" responsible for doing their own due diligence.

Blankfein's argument was commonplace. I encountered it frequently in my work with business companies and non-profits. The chasm between Blankfein's narrow, self-justifying mindset and the communal ethic of his predecessors is vast. If our culture is obsessed with individuals satisfying their own needs, limited solely by considerations of legality, the society at large will inevitably degenerate into a Hobbesian struggle of each against all.

The Goldman executives of the pre-Blankfein era whom I knew from the Trinity dialogues were hardly grand statesmen. They were members of the establishment, full of old-boy snobbery and privilege. But they represented an ethic of noblesse oblige and stewardship.

---

12 Matt Taibbi, "The Great American Bubble Machine," *Rolling Stone*, July 9–23, 2009.

They cared about others as well as themselves. They cared for the well being of the larger society that had brought them such good fortune. They cared for the city that supported them. Above all, they cared for their clients, out of an ethic of enlightened self-interest. They knew that trust and reputation were their strongest assets, and that it would be self-destructive to jeopardize those assets.

The values of noblesse oblige, stewardship and enlightened self-interest are expressions of caring. They transcend the self and connect the self to the larger world of people and things beyond the self.

My guess is that this ethic still holds credibility for some Goldman executives. I fervently hope that they will find their way back to their older tradition of caring for the larger community as well as for their own narrow financial interests: that they will return to the capitalism of enlightened (rather than unenlightened) self-interest.[13]

---

13   Portions of this chapter appear in *Wicked Problems*, 35 –38.

Launching My Own Firm

THE DECISION TO START my own research firm was not easy and came after much reflection and many troubled nights. I was confident that I could make a go of it financially—my projects at Nowland were well received and often successfully implemented. I was also sure I could find projects that would give me a fresh angle of vision into the larger society.

If I owned my own firm, I would be free to seek out the kind of research that might be less profitable than product planning and marketing but more productive of insight into how our society's ethos and culture work—an important aspect of social philosophy. I would also be in a position to carve out time for study and for writing a book that explored my thoughts about philosophy, which I hoped to do as soon as possible.

At the same time, the arguments against making this leap were compelling. At the time (1958), the economy was in recession, and the unemployment rate was high. Ordinarily, a recession would be the least propitious time to open a new business research firm: the first costs that companies cut are for these kinds of services.

Moreover, I was hardly in a promising position to start a new business. Though I was making a moderately good living at Nowland, I needed a stable income for alimony to Marti and, I hoped, for furnishing a new household for myself.

As a Nowland employee, I did not have an independent reputation. I had published very little during those years and was unknown outside the small circle of the firm's clients. I did have close ties to a number of Nowland clients, but it would have been unethical for me to try to woo them away. The company was having a hard time in the recession and the loss of key clients might have been a fatal blow. I did not want to start a new life with that kind of a burden on my conscience.

Over and above these compelling practical obstacles, there were other less tangible reasons to hesitate. I liked and respected Roger Nowland. I knew that he was not to blame for reneging on his part of the bargain that had induced me to give up ownership of the Door Store in exchange for time to write. Indeed, I had no burning itch to start a business of my own. I was comfortable and well positioned at Nowland.

All in all, it seemed impractical for me to leave a secure job to strike out on my own. But nonetheless I felt compelled to do so because the job at Nowland lacked the opportunity I craved to make a contribution to the world of thought and to exercise stewardship.

I devoted an inordinate amount of time to agonizing over what to name the new firm. Should I give it my own name? If the firm did engage in newsworthy projects I wanted to link them to my name to strengthen my claim to being a public intellectual.

Also, putting my name on the firm would give me a certain amount of personal security, especially if I decided to seriously pursue philosophy. Devoting my time to writing philosophy might displease my colleagues in the new firm, but they would find it difficult to push me out if the firm carried my name.

On the business side, however, I assumed my name would be a definite disadvantage. I was sure that it would be a turnoff for conservative corporations more comfortable with ethnically-neutral names like Nowland and McKinsey and Gallup. (This assumption, to my amazement, turned out to be mostly wrong. Many conservative companies looking for an outsider point of view felt reassured that they would find it in a firm with such a blatantly outsider-ish name as Daniel Yankelovich.)

In any event, I took a chance and named the new firm Daniel Yankelovich, Inc. Just before Hassie and I were married, I quit my job at Nowland and rented a small office near Grand Central Station. I had a sign painted with my name to put on the door of my new office. It was a huge relief not to have to commute from Manhattan to Greenwich every morning and evening. By subway I could make it from my apartment to my new office in thirty minutes.

A Welcome Change

THE LIFE CHANGES I managed to bring about in those early years of my marriage to Hassie made a huge difference to my morale and well-being. They dramatically transformed my life for the better.

Within a brief few years, I had undergone a makeover for my head. I had set up a normal household and fathered a lovely and deeply cherished daughter. And I had founded my own firm offering a broad range of business consulting and research services.

In a stroke of great good luck, in its first months of operation the new firm secured a large client, the Swiss Watch Federation, representing all the major Swiss watch companies. The Federation remained a good and faithful client for our firm for many years.

And the new firm also quickly won other clients. Indeed, I was amazed and gratified by how readily our firm gained acceptance and client confidence. Within our first few years we were overwhelmed with assignments from major corporations, mostly from the Midwest—Dow Chemical, Ford, General Mills, Schlitz Brewing—but also from the East Coast, including General Electric and IBM.

In retrospect, I attribute at least part of the firm's success to my graduate training in psychology and philosophy, as well as my experience at Nowland. My psychological orientation tuned us into the authentic voice of the consumer, enabling clients to see their products and services as their customers saw them. It also equipped me with techniques for measuring what was most important to consumers and for simplifying the cacophony of customer voices to be heeded.

For example, for the Swiss watch industry we were able to simplify the watch market into three large categories of watch buyers: people whose watch held a sentimental or prestige value as a piece of jewelry; people who cared primarily about the quality of their watch in terms of accuracy, durability, and precision, and people simply looking for the least expensive watch that could give them the time of day. We showed how the various brands fit into these customer-value categories, which watch features, branding methods, and retail outlets consumers favored, and how the Swiss might compete better against Timex and other non-Swiss brands that had recently entered the market.

While my background in psychology helped us to emphasize the perspective of the customer, my background in philosophy led me to take a holistic approach to our clients' problems. A philosophical skill I have come to value highly is the ability to see the larger picture, however vaguely, as distinct from the perspective of one or another area of specialization.

Every field of specialization comes with its own built-in framework. You cannot detach them from each other. The more you immerse yourself in a specialized field, the more difficult it is for you to see the larger context. This is one of the reasons that technicians, computer experts, economists, accountants, and other gifted specialists sometimes appear parochial. Their frameworks are so compelling that they have trouble transcending them. A world of knowledge consisting primarily of what experts and specialists know is a nightmare of confusion for those who seek a broader perspective.

Specialization is a must in today's society. But specialization by itself is not enough. The more you specialize, the more you need a counterbalancing capacity for taking a broader view of how the world works.

This is where philosophy comes in. Not philosophy in the sense of a technical body of knowledge and reasoning, to which only an argumentative few analytic philosophers have access. But philosophy in the sense of a mode of thought that any reasonably intelligent person can learn, just as he or she might acquire any other cognitive skill.

If breadth is needed—and our greatest challenges do require considerable breadth of perspective—every specialist should, ideally, receive training in philosophy. Also, there should be plenty of room in academia, business, politics, finance, and the professions for people with a philosophical bent who may not be at home in academic philosophy.

These were extraordinarily busy years. I worked all the time, weekends as well as weekdays, nights as well as days. But the work was constantly interesting and challenging.

My new marriage lent a great deal of emotional stability to my life. Hassie appreciated not having to work for a living and was grateful that the new firm's success provided us with financial as well as emotional stability. I plunged enthusiastically into the hard work needed to make the new firm grow.

Initially, most of our projects were fairly conventional marketing projects. We explored every nook and cranny of buyer behavior: how Americans shop, cook, eat, drink, dress, drive, decorate, tend their children and their bowels, diet, save, shave, read, watch television, and wash their cars.

I initially subordinated my own personal ambitions to the firm's marketing projects, especially after we added new staff members whose jobs depended on stability of income. But after the first few years, we had a large enough inventory of business that it became possible for me to seek out assignments that I found interesting for their own sake and not just for the revenue they produced.

As owner of the company, I was now free to roam beyond the sphere of marketing to search for projects with broader scope. Once the firm was solidly established I pursued the kind of social and political projects that permitted me to stake my claim as a public intellectual.

The first of these assignments—and it was a significant one—was an invitation from *LIFE* magazine to conduct a series of lengthy and searching interviews with voters to gain a better understanding of what qualities and characteristics voters desired in an "ideal" president.

Our voter study took place in the early months of 1960, before the Republican or Democratic conventions had chosen their presidential candidates for the election that John Kennedy ultimately won by a squeak.

In our interviews, we probed voter attitudes toward seven potential candidates, including Republicans Richard Nixon and Nelson Rockefeller and Democrats Adlai Stevenson and John Kennedy.

Our research showed that eight months before the election, those who favored Richard Nixon's candidacy held an image of him as:

- "A good family man."
- "Someone who has made his own way in the world and did not just have things handed to him."
- "Someone who can get opposing groups together and work out agreements."
- "A man who has the knowledge and understanding necessary for handling foreign affairs.

Voters who didn't like him saw him as:

- "A cold person—no real warmth or feeling for people."
- "Someone who doesn't come out and say what he means. You can't tell what he really believes."

- "A man who is after the presidency for what he himself can get out of it rather than for the good he can do for the country."

Those who favored John Kennedy saw him as:

- "A man who will stand up and fight for what he believes is right."
- "Strong-minded and not easily influenced by other people."
- "Someone who won't be swayed by his political party or his church. He will put the welfare of all the people above these loyalties."

Kennedy's one major negative was:

- "He's not presidential timber yet. He hasn't had the right kind of experience."

Adlai Stevenson was lauded for his superior intelligence but criticized for a lack of forcefulness and for the fact that he had been twice defeated as a presidential candidate. Those who favored Nelson Rockefeller saw him as "a fresh, sincere and dedicated political voice." Those who rejected him did so primarily because they saw him as a person of immense wealth who couldn't be expected to "sympathize with people like us." Sensitivity to his wealth caused people to attribute many of his actions to snobbery.

In the LIFE piece, based on our research, I reported that there were:

Five qualities that Americans demand in an ideal President. It is striking that not one is connected with a party label or party record. In fact, these requirements add up to a personality contest rather than a contest over specific issues or platforms:

- *A man of conviction who is willing to fight for his principles but who is able, by conciliation and compromise, to avoid such a fight.*
- *A man who is above partisan considerations.*
- *A man with the common touch.*

- *A vigorous, decisive man who can make up his mind, get things done and not be pushed around by other governments—especially the Soviet Union.*
- *A man with experience in foreign affairs.*

Voters in that era did not want their president beholden to his party, to any one section of the country, or to any particular bloc of voters. They demanded that the president be nonpartisan in a moral sense, determined to advance the good of the country as a whole.

When we asked voters what qualities were *least* desirable in a president, voters put excessive personal ambition first by a wide margin. Other bad qualities were partisanship, opportunism, immaturity, insincerity, weakness of character, inexperience, ineffectiveness, aloofness, and physical unattractiveness.[14]

It was clear that despite his inexperience, especially in foreign affairs, John Kennedy came closer to the voters' ideal than any of the other candidates.

LIFE published our study as the cover story of its March 21, 1960 edition, and it received a huge amount of attention. (At the time LIFE was at the peak of its popularity and prestige.) As the author of the study, I had my first experience on the public stage.

I was delighted with the publicity the piece in LIFE generated for the firm and the personal attention I received. It reinforced my appetite for occupying a public intellectual role.

A number of my friends—Bell, Hofstadter, Heilbroner, Howe, Kristol, Barrett—-had carved out niches for themselves as successful public intellectuals. I aspired to being invited, like them, to interpret the important issues of the day.

Shortly thereafter, a different kind of opportunity to occupy the public intellectual role presented itself, and I grabbed it with

---

14 Dan Yankelovich, "The Ideal President," *LIFE*, March 21, 1960.

enthusiasm. In the early 1960s, Marshall McLuhan, the Canadian philosopher of communications and public intellectual, made the cryptic pronouncement that "the medium is the message." This assertion stirred a huge amount of controversy. McLuhan devoted years of books and lectures to elaborating this famous statement.

McLuhan was calling attention to the provocative theory that the same message would convey different meanings depending on its context. McLuhan's slogan struck a responsive chord because it seemed intuitively true, though at that time there was scant credible empirical evidence to support it.

This was a period of intense competition between print media and television, as well as among the vast array of magazines that competed for readership and advertising. Some forms of media reacted to the McLuhan thesis as a threat, and others saw it as a potential competitive advantage.

Several magazines and the television network NBC invited our firm to explore what value, if any, the media context added to their content. Our research for *Business Week* won an award for demonstrating that, for many business readers, the *Business Week* context gave extra gravitas to the ads appearing in the magazine.

Another media client gave us an ideal assignment with no direct commercial purpose. One of *Fortune's* most thoughtful editors, Charles Silberman, was eager to contribute to our generalized pool of knowledge about the workings of the media. Silberman wanted to test the McLuhan hypothesis by learning how the same story influenced people when conveyed in print or by television.

Several months before receiving this assignment from Silberman, I had set up a new communications laboratory in a town in New Jersey close to New York City. We called it our "Communications Clinic." It was a facility for bringing together small groups of people for the purpose of testing out various forms of communication.

We designed four experiments to learn more about the relative impact of television vs. print. For each experiment, we convened matched samples of people. One group was exposed to a story or stimulus in print form, while the other was exposed to the same story or stimulus via television. Each group was subsequently tested for what they remembered and how they experienced the stimulus.

The experiment I remember most clearly involved stories about the voyage of the SS *Triton* in 1960—the first nuclear-powered submarine to execute a submerged circumnavigation of the earth ("Operation Sandblast"). The *Triton* adventure was covered both in *LIFE* magazine and also on television on Pathé News. We first screened out people who had either read the magazine or seen the Pathé News story. We then exposed each of two matched samples of people to either the print or television story, followed by extensive interviews and tests of their reactions to the story.

The differences in responses were striking. Empathy for the crew, as well as for their families (who had been left completely uninformed throughout the voyage), was much greater in those exposed to the magazine story. The television watchers' reaction was more detached and impersonal.

Also, people who read the story in its magazine format retained a more vivid memory of details of the crew's experience but were vague about the overall narrative. Those exposed to the television version had a clearer feel for the purpose of the *Triton* journey but had a hard time remembering many of the specifics.

There were other differences as well. I came away with the sense that television communicated directly with the non-conscious aspects of cognition while print elicited the more conscious and detached aspects.

Our client was pleased with the results, but also a bit frustrated because of the lack of a clear application for it.

I admit that I found this sort of research more appealing and interesting than our marketing research. Its scope was broader and more compelling in its contribution to our understanding of the way things work. It was also a better fit with my own background in philosophy and the social sciences.

Our firm's success in carrying out these quasi-public assignments encouraged me to seek more of the same, something I was constrained from doing while I was working for Roger Nowland's design firm.

An Instructive Failure

SSEVERAL YEARS LATER, IN 1965, I established a nonprofit organization in Cambridge, Massachusetts, called the Cambridge Center for Behavioral Science Research. It was designed as an inter-university research facility for the larger Boston area that would bring together the two worlds of academic and applied social science research.

At the time, President Lyndon Johnson had launched his Great Society and War on Poverty programs. He explicitly encouraged support for research-based programs to combat delinquency, mental illness, drug addition, urban blight, poor housing and other problems associated with poverty.

The Johnson administration assigned our firm an eleven-city project. Its purpose was to evaluate the effects of the government's Community Action Programs (CAPs), which provided services to people in poverty and asked low-income people and communities to play a major role in implementing the program. This self-help dimension of the CAPs distinguished Johnson's War on Poverty from earlier anti-poverty efforts.

I was eager to work with universities in the Boston area to shed light on how well these self-help programs were working, what obstacles stood in their way, and how lessons learned from successful programs could be applied to cities with differing political and economic contexts.

In January 1966, I presented a long paper titled "Program Research: Research to Solve Social Problems" to a staff conference of the psychiatry department of the Tufts–New England Medical Center. At the time, I was collaborating with the Tufts psychiatry department on another government-sponsored project and had established a cordial working relationship with its members.

In my paper I spelled out the differences between academic and non-academic research practices, with special reference to the role of survey research, one of our firm's main research tools. I elaborated on how our firm's highly experienced researchers had developed supplemental research tools to make more efficient use of survey methods in the quest to find effective interventions to solve troublesome problems.

Our eight stage process, called *Program Research*, carried the research process all the way from generating initial hypotheses, through screening, testing, and quantifying them, to developing possible modes of intervention and then testing and refining them. I applied this process to our joint project of finding and testing ways to intervene in a local Boston-area housing project, Columbia Point, which housed a large number of families in deep poverty. The Columbia Point housing project had, in effect, become a warehouse for single mothers who were unable to cope with the burdens of childcare, self-care, and earning a living.

Many of the women had lost their sense of agency to such an extent that they seemed unable to help themselves even when they were offered a helping hand. (We always knew when the women in our typing pool were working on the interviews with Columbia Point mothers. Tears would be running down their cheeks, and they would be making comments like "Oh my God, isn't that awful?" and "How could things get so terrible?")

The female Columbia Point residents with more intact egos were able to take advantage of the government's programs, with encouraging results.

Unfortunately, the Cambridge Center for Behavioral Science Research never really took hold. I've often looked back and asked why this might have been. After all, the national political climate in the 1960s was far more encouraging and supportive of such an effort than it is today. The Johnson administration was full of enthusiasm for social science initiatives and generous with its financial support. The public was not yet polarized along party lines and was eager to spread the benefits of economic growth so that more Americans could enter the middle class.

The major reason for the failure was, I believe, on the academic side. The culture of academic social science research was far more resistant to change than I had assumed it would be. The specialization culture was almost as strong then as it is now. And the preference for individual, as distinct from team, research exerted a powerful appeal on the faculty. Faculty individualism was as strong a force then as it is now. Senior faculty members were determined to devote their time and research to their own interests and projects.

Unfortunately, these interests rarely coincided with the nation's most urgent problems. It was naïve of me to assume that merely because I had learned some useful things about the methodology of researching large populations, I could motivate academics to abandon their comfort zone.

A Unique Opportunity

IN THE MID-SIXTIES, MY two main goals were to take care of my family and to carve out a role for myself as a public intellectual as a way to express what I was learning philosophically. I scrambled furiously to find assignments that engaged issues of core social values involving the larger culture.

In 1965, I hit the jackpot! I was invited to dig into the causes of the student unrest exploding on college campuses all over the country, from Columbia University on the East Coast to Berkeley on the West.

One of our clients, the Institute of Life Insurance (ILI), was anxious to learn whether the campus rebellion expressed transitory political protest linked to the Vietnam War or whether it represented something deeper culturally—a challenge to our society's traditional ethical values like sacrifice for others, living for the future, postponing personal gratification, and other values essential to the vitality of the life insurance business.

What was most gratifying to me personally was our client's reason for granting this intriguing assignment to our firm: the Institute explicitly stated that we had won the assignment because of my standing as a public intellectual! It was a victory that had taken many years to achieve, and it did wonders for my self-confidence.

It made me feel less guilty about how badly I had messed up my life in my younger years.

Eventually, this project led to our firm carrying out a series of annual surveys on how America's social values were being transformed—initially on college campuses and then in the society at large.

My initial research identified a "forerunner" minority of college students who had indeed begun to question some of their parents' core Protestant ethic values. Generally, these students came from the nation's most affluent families. Most of them took their privileged positions for granted.

They had concluded that their fathers' nose-to-the-grindstone way of life and their mothers' sacrifice of self for the family didn't make sense in the emerging affluence of the time. They acknowledged that sacrifice for the family was obligatory when circumstances required it. But if it proved economically unnecessary, why sacrifice something as important as one's own self-expressive needs?

Forerunner student attitudes spread with incredible speed beyond the nation's campuses, influencing more than 80 percent of all adult Americans by the late 1970s.

To be sure, the distribution was not universal, and among the 80 percent, a majority was highly selective in picking and choosing among the new values it found most congenial. But nonetheless the transformation in social values was extraordinarily sweeping in its scope.

The vast cultural changes of our present era (including multiculturalism, gay marriage, women's rights, reduced social conformity, weakened ethical norms, new forms of self-expressiveness and the preoccupation with self and health) can only be understood in the context of how the revolution in social values that incubated on the nation's campuses in the 1960s has subsequently taken possession of American culture.

Indeed, the era confronts us with one of the sharpest discontinuities in our history as a culture. Observers have attached a variety of names to the changes. Journalist Tom Wolfe famously labeled the period as the "me generation." More academically, Ron Inglehart referred to the new values as "post-materialist" and documented their spread from the United States to other industrialized democracies. The label that I (and others) prefer for the new ethos is expressive individualism.

It is not a crisp sound bite, but it has the virtue of precision: the changes in values revolve around the twin issues of what role "expressiveness" and "individualism" play in people's lives. The new ethos gives priority to the expressive side of life even at the expense of economic benefits. By the end of the seventies, the majority of Americans had come to believe that everyone should have the opportunity to develop his or her own inner potential for self-expression.

A belief in individualism is, of course, as old as the nation itself. But prior to the 1960s, American individualism focused mainly on the political domain—freedom to speak our minds, to pursue our own religious beliefs, to live where we chose to live. In the 1950s we were a nation of political individualists but social conformists. The 1960s ushered in a radical extension of individualism, broadening it from the political domain to personal life styles.

By the 1990s the ethos of expressive individualism had grown into a national preoccupation, becoming ever more extreme with the passage of time and showing no signs of abating. Even though this ethos was developed in economic good times, it has persisted under more troubled economic conditions. It has come to dominate our culture to an extraordinary degree, playing havoc with our moral norms.

My research had deeply impressed me with the power of the culture to transform the lives and values of individuals and institutions. This realization led to an existential shift in my personal philosophy. I began to place less weight on the ability of the self to control one's destiny and more on the power of culture to channel human nature in one direction or another.

I came to appreciate the insights of William James and the existential philosophers that even in a world shaped by powerful forces over which you have little control, your own will endows you with a powerful sense of agency.

I began to make explicit some of the principles that had come to constitute my personal philosophy.

- Focusing on the integral nature of the whole and never losing sight of it, rather than regarding it merely as the sum of its parts.
- Setting explicit value priorities for ones self.
- Developing the skill and the will to live by the priorities you have chosen.
- Acknowledging your obligations to the larger society.
- Making explicit the frameworks underlying your philosophy rather than leaving them tacit.
- Deploying the tool of "critique" to identify crooked thinking and distortions in thought.
- Living the examined life.
- Bringing an ethic of stewardship to bear on judging both individual lives and entire civilizations.

Becoming an Insider's Outsider

AFTER I TURNED FORTY, I became less anxious. I had a comfortable home life, lots of friends, and few financial worries. My marriage was fairly serene, and my lovely daughter was blooming.

I worked constantly and enjoyed most of it. I liked, trusted, and respected my coworkers. Morale at our firm was high and, year after year, we were growing steadily in size and reputation.

In the late 1960s, I broadened the ownership of the firm, in recognition of the fact that its success was largely due to the efforts of my two partners, Florence Skelly and Arthur White. We changed the name of the firm to Yankelovich, Skelly and White, dividing the ownership into roughly equal parts. Both Florence and Arthur were friends as well as business associates and both gave me extraordinary moral support in my efforts to become a public intellectual. They felt that it enhanced the reputation of the firm, and they were willing to carry the lion's share of management responsibilities for the firm while I was engaged in writing and other non-business activities.

For the first time since childhood, I came to feel less like an outsider, and I basked in the novel warmth of being accepted by others. The role of public intellectual felt surprisingly comfortable: it seemed made to order for people like myself who had positioned themselves on the fringes of society, but who nonetheless wanted to participate in the life of their times. I kept finding new ways to connect myself with the action.

In my professional life, for years I had wanted to be accepted as a member of the Council of Foreign Relations, whose headquarters on New York's Upper East Side I passed on my daily walk to work. I eventually did gain membership and I soon found myself writing articles for its journal, *Foreign Affairs*. After a few years I was even invited to serve on its membership committee, a true insider assignment.

Surely, the mark of the real insider is the license to judge all eager applicants and turn down most of them. Not surprisingly, I wasn't invited to serve a second term because I violated the unwritten rule of the Committee by voting to accept too many applicants, especially women.

I gradually discovered that I was most at home in the role of an *outsider insider*. Here is an example of what I mean. In the 1970s, Columbia University had launched a series of scholarly ethnic study programs, one of which was its Armenian Studies Program. I was startled to be invited to become its chairman.

The true basis for the invitation soon became clear. The program was ridden with internal Armenian political factions. Its members recognized that they needed an *odar* to preside over it—an outsider not enmeshed in ancient Armenian feuds. Being married to an Armenian woman made me enough of an insider to be considered for the post; being Jewish and uninvolved with Armenian politics made me the perfect *odar* for the job.

Becoming chairman of the Armenian Studies program at Columbia was one of many improbable roles I've played in my life. I thoroughly enjoyed it, and I think I did it successfully. It exemplified the role of bridging between worlds that I discovered best suited my temperament. Over time, the desire to be accepted as an insider morphed into a feeling of satisfaction in understanding, and empathizing with, disparate points of view as an outsider.

The most arduous "outsider" effort I made in those years was the book I wrote with NYU professor of philosophy William Barrett: *Ego and Instinct: The Psychoanalytic View of Human Nature—Revised.* The book is a critique of psychoanalysis and the philosophical framework that underlies its theory and practice.

It took a lot of chutzpah to write a book about a profession so specialized that its practitioners were required to earn a medical degree before completing five additional years of psychoanalytic training. I gave the chutzpah full freedom to roam: Why stop at Armenian Studies? Why not plow ahead and tell psychoanalysis how to do its job?

At first glance, these raids into disparate fields (like Armenian Studies and psychoanalysis) may seem random and lacking in respect for other people's turf. But in reality they were not. Each effort was a serious and respectful one, with its own rationale, and even with a useful result. My life experience had taught me to regard conventional boundaries as artificial; indeed, it had taught me that in pursuit of a major goal it was often necessary to poach deliberately on other people's territory.

Digging into psychoanalysis was important to pursuing a goal precious to me—a goal I had pursued my entire life. At twenty-one, fresh out of the army, my ambition had been to return to Harvard to pursue studies that would eventually lead to my becoming a professor of philosophy.

By the time I entered graduate school, however, I had become disillusioned with academic philosophy. In graduate school I mainly studied psychology and other social sciences. My hope was that these would give me a better perspective on "genuine" philosophy—philosophy that gives insight into how to live life both as an individual and as a society.

At the time, I was surprised that there were so many different branches of psychology and that they all had fierce quarrels with one another. In that era, the dominant goal in most branches of psychology was, as in philosophy, to become exemplars of scientific inquiry on the model of physics and chemistry.

It seemed to me that this ambition was distorting their focus and undermining their effectiveness. Senior scholars like psychologist Sigmund Koch reinforced my suspicions. Koch concluded his seven-volume study of psychology with a damning judgment. He had become convinced, he said, that the shining success of the older sciences had seduced psychology in destructive ways. Psychology, in his judgment, had put its commitment to science ahead of its commitment to understanding people.

The deeper I delved into psychology the more convinced I became that the quarrels among its various branches could be directly traced to their differing philosophical frameworks. Clinical psychology, my own field of specialization, had a radically different philosophical framework from other branches of psychology such as behaviorism, experimental psychology, or existential psychology. When I attended the Sorbonne, the teachings of Merlau-Ponty and other existential philosophers powerfully reinforced this conviction.

I was obliged to push my pursuit of philosophy into the background when I returned to the United States from Paris in the interest of making a living and straightening out my domestic life. But I never abandoned my determination to demonstrate that philosophy had genuine practical value and wasn't just an exhausted scholarly relic.

My psychology studies convinced me that there was a way to demonstrate that philosophy could have practical value. If faulty philosophical frameworks were undermining psychology's effectiveness, why not target one important branch of psychology and demonstrate how fixing its philosophical plumbing could enhance its effectiveness?

The branch of psychology that most needed its plumbing repaired was clearly psychoanalysis. Its flawed philosophical framework was an accidental consequence of Freud's formal training as a physiologist committed to upholding the rigid scientific standards of his era.

Even when he shifted his attention from physiology to people's emotional problems, Freud held fast to his formal scientific beliefs, which were largely Newtonian and mechanistic. His formal theories always sought to reduce human experience to abstract concepts of a balance of forces. Human energies were reduced to what he called "cathexes." The individual personality was divided into three basic forces: ego, id, and superego.

It is a tribute to Freud that as a therapist he didn't let his scientific theoretical obsessions get in the way of helping people with their neuroses. He called his case histories his "short stories" to distinguish them from "real science." Over a period of decades, the gap between abstract theory and practice in psychoanalysis became ever more unbridgeable.

Barrett and I came to think of this gap as a "philosophical neurosis"—a conflict at the heart of psychoanalysis that was preventing it from achieving its goals. We savored the irony that psychoanalysis was itself suffering from an internal neurotic conflict. We conceived of our book as a way of helping it cure itself.

Since then I have written a dozen or so books, but I have never worked as hard or given as much of myself as I did to writing *Ego and Instinct*.

Was it worth the effort?

I think it proved to be. To my agreeable surprise, I subsequently learned that psychoanalytic institutes throughout the nation had used the book for training young therapists. The San Diego

Psychoanalytic Institute, for example, assigned one chapter of the book each week to candidates in its advanced training program.

For me personally, this acceptance of *Ego and Instinct* was reassurance that my lonely quest in search of practical goals for philosophy was real, and not just my personal fantasy.

Other Chutzpah-Filled Adventures

MY COLLABORATION WITH MY coauthor William Barrett whetted my desire to reestablish my ties with the world of higher education. I began to teach part-time. I gave some courses and supervised students who were writing their PhD theses in the graduate psychology department of NYU.

At NYU I coauthored a book, *Work, Productivity and Job Satisfaction*, with a leading scholar of industrial psychology, Professor Raymond Katzell. The book, funded by the National Science Foundation, was a search for evidence-based research on whether it was feasible to improve job satisfaction and worker productivity at the same time. Developing evidence-based research to support solutions for important issues of national policy was, and continues to be, the major theme of my research.

A few years later, I was awarded a research professorship in the graduate faculty of the New School for Social Research. In my student years at Harvard, I had discovered that I loved attending the large lectures given by popular scholars. I now discovered that I equally enjoyed giving these sorts of lectures.

At the New School I co-taught several psychology courses with Dr. Nancy Wexler, an insightful and friendly woman of infinite charm and grace. We became close friends. At the time, she was fearful about getting married or even closely attached. She had a family history of the dread and deadly Huntington's disease—a progressive genetic brain disorder. It had killed her mother at an early age, and it constantly hovered in the background as an existential threat to Nancy's life. She lived with the fear that it might strike her at any time, and she rejected the prospect of anyone else becoming a victim of her suffering.

Her father, a psychoanalyst in Los Angeles, had set up a foundation to study Huntington's disease and to search for ways to conquer it. In later years, as her chances of developing the disease diminished, Nancy gave up psychology to join her father in devoting herself to researching the causes of and potential cures for Huntington's assault on mind and body. It is my impression that her research has proven quite productive and promising.

Nancy finally reached a stage of life when she felt safe enough from the scourge of the Huntington horror to marry, and she has become contentedly hitched. She was one of a number of women friends with whom I was lucky enough to establish close platonic relations. These constitute some of the warmest and most satisfying experiences of my life.

The *New York Times* was one of our firm's favorite consulting clients. One of our assignments for the *Times* involved interviewing the paper's writers when they went on strike. We were impressed by the pride these writers took in the newspaper even in the heat of the strike. They knew they were part of a world-class institution. Our interviews proved helpful to management, so much so that when several years later the *Times* decided to enter the political polling field, they invited us to do their polling for them.

After testing our polling in the New York governor's race (without publishing the results), the newspaper went national with a series of surveys on important issues such as how the increasing pace of stagflation was affecting average Americans. To our great satisfaction, they named their surveys the *New York Times*/Yankelovich Poll.

More than any other project the firm had ever undertaken, the *New York Times*/Yankelovich Poll spread the firm's reputation throughout the country. Even though it was only a tiny part of our firm's work, it was the part most exposed to public scrutiny.

I was sorry to see this project come to an end after a number of years. It did so when CBS News offered to replace us as the polling partner at half the cost to the *New York Times* while expanding the poll's reach. This was an offer the *Times* couldn't refuse, and the poll became the *New York Times*/CBS poll.

After losing the *New York Times* to competition from CBS, we kept our hand in the polling business by partnering with *TIME* magazine on what became known as the *TIME*/Yankelovich poll.

During this same mid-seventies period, I also partnered with Cyrus Vance (who later became Secretary of State in the Carter administration), in establishing a not-for-profit think tank we named the Public Agenda.

Vance was a friend with whom I lunched regularly. We mostly talked politics. I shared Vance's frustration at the fact that the candidates for the 1976 Presidential election were focused on trivial issues irrelevant to the public's concerns.

We decided to raise enough money from our friends and ourselves to cover the costs of conducting a series of in-depth interviews with the public and with policy experts. Our interviews would identify what issues were likely to have the greatest impact on the forthcoming election.

We agreed that I would conduct and analyze the interviews and that Vance would set up the organization and convey the results of our research to both the Republican and the Democratic candidates.

Both of us took our commitments seriously. We scrounged about $100,000 from people we knew, and each of us contributed $5,000. Vance's law firm set up a non-profit organization to manage the funding and to insure that we avoided any direct political engagement. Vance felt it was of paramount importance that we avoid any hint of partisanship. So we agreed we would make no recommendations from our research but simply share with the candidates how Americans were thinking about the issues that most directly affected their lives.

The interviews helped us to identify three electoral issues of vital concern to voters: the stresses caused by the rising tide of inflation and unemployment, our bitter Cold War struggle with the Soviet Union, and the troubling issue of how to assure strong moral leadership from our government.

I recruited some professional friends and colleagues who volunteered their help in analyzing the interviews and drafting three reports, one on each of the three issues.[15]

Our original intent was to make the Public Agenda a one-off effort and close it down after the election. But its work was so well received that, with the encouragement of the Ford Foundation and others, we decided to keep the Public Agenda alive for a "just a few more years." (Those "few more years" kept on going: in the spring of 2015, Public Agenda celebrated its fortieth anniversary.)

One purpose of the Public Agenda's work is to narrow the gap between expert elites and the general public. Our elites give lip service to the importance of heeding the public voice, but in practice, they ignore it.

Experts and the public bring very different frameworks to understanding national issues. The public's framework is mainly a matter

---

15 For a detailed description of the "Moral Leadership in Government" report, see *Wicked Problems* 116–17.

of values. Expert elites like to *claim* that their frameworks rest on a firm factual basis, but they often overlook or obscure their own values.

The Public Agenda frames key issues so that the public's viewpoint can exercise some influence in shaping policies of concern to the nation. The current focus of the Public Agenda is less on elections than on problems of year-round concern to the public. Its continuing purpose is to frame and research these urgent issues in ways that permit policy makers to respond to them intelligently. Much of Public Agenda's work focuses on how to improve the life chances of Americans through enhanced educational opportunities.

In those years, I also became involved with the Aspen Institute. The Institute organized a wide variety of intellectual seminars and music concerts in Aspen, Colorado. Its president was a high-energy impresario named Joe Slater. Joe and I became good friends, and I became a fixture at many of Aspen's seminars.

One of the Aspen seminars was devoted to a comparative examination of work and work practices in Western nations. I teamed up with two other members of the seminar: Sidney Harman, the founder and CEO of Harman Industries (which specialized in manufacturing sound systems), and Per Gyllenhammer, the CEO of Volvo in Sweden. Together the three of us headed a team to carry out a comparative study of work conditions and worker attitudes in a number of Western industrialized nations.

One day, out of the blue, I got a call from Paul Austin, then CEO of Coca-Cola. He asked me if I would introduce him to John D. Rockefeller III. At first, I thought someone was playing a joke on me. It seemed inconceivable that Austin would try to get to Rockefeller though me.

Logically, though, it made sense. My firm did a lot of consumer research for Coca-Cola. I was doing annual youth surveys for the John D. Rockefeller III Fund. Rockefeller had written a preface to my book reporting the survey findings, and I sometimes accompanied him on his fund-raising visits to New York companies. Psychologically, however, I found it difficult to visualize myself as the kind of Establishment insider who could get John Rockefeller on the phone.

Another event in those middle-aged years made me realize that I had improbably and against all odds made it into the ranks of the Establishment. Shortly after my fiftieth birthday, I received an invitation from Louis Cabot to join an elk hunt on his company's ranch in Colorado. When I came home from work and told Hassie, she thought I was joking, and she laughed immoderately at the image of me hunting elks in the Colorado mountains.

When I showed her the invitation, she said: "You aren't going, are you?"

"I wouldn't miss it for anything", I said, "How in the world can a poor boy from Boston turn down an invitation from the Cabots!?" And I recited for her the verse well known to all Bostonians:

> I come from the city of Boston,
> The home of the bean and the cod,
> Where the Lowells speak only to the Cabots,
> And the Cabots speak only to God.

"What will you do if you actually shoot an elk?" she asked in horror.
I told her not to worry, that nothing could be more unlikely.

I was one of the very few guests to arrive at the Cabot camp without his own private plane. Carrying a rifle on the hunt, I was relieved to hear, was not expected of everyone, especially when I was told that any elks I happened to shoot would be frozen in large chunks for storage and then shipped to me.

To my relief, some of the other guests were also content to accompany the hunters, without rifles and in separate jeeps, in the hope of spotting one of the great elks. We did spot a few, but I was thankful that no elks were actually killed.

Poker was the main activity at night. If I had known about the poker in advance I would have taken more money with me. But I had brought only a few hundred dollars, and camp etiquette forbade borrowing. (This was before the era of the ATM.) I had played a lot of poker in the army, and was eager to get into the game even though the stakes were far higher than I had ever encountered before.

As soon as I began to play I realized that I was way out of my league. To this day, I recall with embarrassment the comment made to me by one of the other players, Bill Hewlett, who along with David Packard, had founded Hewlett-Packard. Referring to my reluctance to drop out even when I didn't have a promising hand, he said, "Dan, this is not a wedding. You don't have to dance every dance."

As it turned out, I danced very few dances because I quickly lost all my money the first night of play.

When I came back to New York, Hassie was relieved both by the fact that UPS would not be depositing hundreds of pounds of frozen elk at our door and that I had lacked the foresight to take more money with me.

I relished the idea of having been included by the quintessential insider, Louis Cabot, even though the setting was so improbable. A constant theme of my life story found expression in the elk hunt at the Cabot ranch. It was my lifelong quest for *acceptance*. As a foster child, I had always found myself on the outside, never fully accepted. I craved to feel like an insider, and to be treated as one.

In the Jewish neighborhood of my childhood, big shots were referred to as *machers*—a Yiddish word for someone who can make things happen. Later we referred to them in more refined terms such as "movers and shakers" or "elites" or "people of influence" or some such phrase suggestive of high standing in society. And, *mirabile dictu* (as we used to say in the Boston Latin School), here was I, included among the *machers* who came with their private planes to hunt elk and to shape the fate of nations.

Some years later, in 1988, Sidney Harman and I, with the help of my friend, the gifted and warm-hearted professor of philosophy John Immerwahr, coauthored a book titled *Starting with the People*. The book examined and compared public attitudes on a number of important issues, such as the nuclear arms race, relations with the Soviet Union, and trade and economic competitiveness with Japan.

How, we asked, could the American public develop shared frameworks on issues such as these that evoked a severe clash of values, especially when these clashes were partially hidden from view?

At the time, I felt that it was a thoughtful and insightful book, but in all of these subsequent years, I have never encountered a single person who has admitted to reading it. Reviewing it in retrospect, I find it somewhat abstract but very much on target. The kinds of problems it elaborates and the need to find common ground between the experts and the public on these problems are both even more valid today than when we wrote the book so many years ago.

Over the past half century I have been writing one book after another. Many of them have gone unread. But I think that *Starting with the People* may well enjoy the dubious distinction of being the most unread of them all.

Writing books is such hard work that it is discouraging when they go unread. But I have learned, to my agreeable surprise, that if you persist long enough, and keep writing and framing your ideas in differing contexts, those ideas gradually get through, here and there, to thoughtful individuals. These admirable souls spread the word, amplifying your ideas in ways that do affect the dominant climate of opinion.

Over the years, a handful of ideas that I have sought to promulgate through books, articles, speeches, and actions have, I now realize, begun to catch on. Among these ideas, I include:

- The extent to which experts and specialists have sidelined the American public from decision-making on issues essential to the public's well-being.
- The way that expert opinion, even though it may be more knowledgeable than the public's value orientation, is a deeply flawed guide to the public interest.
- The folly of seeing the media's mission as dumping tons of information on the public, which does nothing to enhance the public's understanding of how to solve urgent issues.
- The important distinction between raw opinion and thoughtful public judgment, and useful methods for converting one into the other.
- The centrality of public judgment to the healthy functioning of democracy.
- How certain forms of structured dialogue can help to shape public judgment.
- The social sciences' false distinction between basic and applied research, and the need for the social sciences to devote more energy and commitment to solving the nation's most urgent problems.
- Practical uses for philosophy that are essential to maintaining the well-being of our institutions and shaping the goals of the individual in today's specialized world.

The Shah and I

MY ENCOUNTER WITH THE Shah of Iran was one of the most unexpected events of my life. Like the elk hunt at the Cabot ranch, it was yet another sign that I had inadvertently slipped into the ranks of the Establishment.

One night in early 1977, I received a phone call from a man who introduced himself as Simcha Dinitz, Israel's ambassador to the United States. I had seen him on television and knew who he was, but I had never met him before.

He asked me if I would be willing to come to Israel with him on the following Sunday to meet with officials of the Israeli government, who wanted to speak to me about a possible assignment. He said he realized that it was asking a lot but he was confident that when I heard the full story I would realize that the mission was important enough to warrant the imposition on my time.

I had never been to Israel. I couldn't imagine what conceivable use I could be to the Israeli government. But I unhesitatingly accepted his invitation. Whatever it was, it was sure to prove interesting. I leapt at the chance to go to Israel without having to do so as a tourist. So I packed my bags, cancelled my meetings for the first few days of the following week and arranged to meet Dinitz, who would be travelling with me.

We arrived in Tel Aviv on a Sunday night and were driven to the old part of Jerusalem. We stopped at a house lit up from the outside. It was strangely beautiful: all the other houses nearby were dark and

257

quiet; the outline of the house was architecturally symmetrical and graceful like an old Parisian mansion. I was told that it was the home of General Yigal Allon, one of Israel's military heroes and its foreign minister.

We were escorted into the living room to meet General Allon and three other men. I remember only one of the three, a tall lanky Israeli named Shlomo Argov, Israel's Minister of Information at the time.

They didn't waste much time on small talk. General Allon said, "I'm sure you're curious about why we schlepped you across the ocean in the middle of the night to talk with us, and we thank you for making the trip without needing to know a lot of specifics."

I allowed that I was indeed curious, but also honored at the opportunity to meet with them on something that was clearly important to them. He said, "It *is* important," and asked Argov to elaborate.

In his raspy Oxford-accented voice, Argov explained that Israel was totally dependent on Iran for its supply of oil, and that the Shah of Iran was threatening to shut down the supply. The reason for the Shah's displeasure, Argov said, was the bad press the Shah was receiving from the leading media in the United States. The American press accused Iran's secret police, the SAVAK, of torturing political dissidents and of engaging in a useless arms race.

I nodded my head in agreement; I'd read the press coverage. But why was the Shah pissed at the Israelis? When Argov saw that his statement was not self-explanatory, he said wearily, "Of course, the Shah assumes that your major media, like the *New York Times* and CBS, are owned by Jews and that Israel controls them. The Shah tells us, 'Just make them stop criticizing me.'"

I asked, "Can't you convince him that you don't control them?"

"That is our dilemma," Argov said, "In many ways it is very useful for us to have the Shah believe we have more influence than we do. We certainly don't want him to know that we have no influence at all. But in this case, it's not good for us that he believes we can get the

American media to stop accusing him of so many self-aggrandizing things."

I agreed they had a problem, and just as I was wondering where I fit in, Argov said, "That's where you come into the picture. We offered the Shah a solution of sorts. We told him that we were willing to sponsor a probing study of the American media to find out why the media hold such negative views about him and what might get them to change their minds. We would like you to conduct such a study and report it directly to the Shah."

He explained that he knew that my research firm had close ties to both the *New York Times* and CBS, and that we did a lot of work with related media. He said that if I personally conducted and reported on the results of the study to the Shah, it would have credibility with the Iranians.

When I remained discreetly silent, he said, as if he were a mind reader, "We know it may not be the most effective strategy, but at least it buys us valuable time."

Now that made sense to me. It would take months to do a thorough study of the sources of American media attitudes toward Iran and the Shah, and who knows what might happen in the interim. I would have to try to make it a good long interim.

I agreed to do what the Israelis wanted me to do.

I hadn't realized that I would have to make repeated trips to Tehran over the following months so that I could work closely with officials in the Iranian government. On these visits, I was given a luxurious suite at Tehran's leading hotel for foreign visitors.

My Iranian hosts could not have been friendlier or more hospitable, and I was invited to one or another of their homes every night I stayed in Tehran. The dinners were invariably served buffet style, and my otherwise punctilious Iranian hosts, who were in all other respects models of decorum, were quite aggressive in their attack on the buffet table, stopping just short of shoving me aside so that they could get to the food. It was an odd cultural quirk that I have never forgotten.

On my trips to Tehran I also made friends with Israel's unofficial ambassador to Iran, an intelligent and perceptive man whose name I've forgotten. I will call him Ira. Ira told me that he was so unofficial that his very existence was denied. When a British reporter sitting close to him at a press conference had said to the Shah, "We are reliably informed that Israel has an ambassador to Iran living here," the Shah looked the reporter in the eyes and asked menacingly, "Are you calling me a liar?" (It was Ira who warned the CIA weeks in advance that the Shah was about to be deposed. The CIA ignored his warning.)

When the final report was ready, I arranged to meet my Israeli contact, Argov, in Tehran so that we could both go to the palace to present the report to the Shah. He explained that he would not be allowed to participate in the presentation but would park himself in the official waiting room while I met with the Shah.

Just before entering the palace, he placed his hand on my shoulder and said, "Dan, pause for just a moment."

"Why?" I asked.

I had been concentrating on my presentation, and I couldn't imagine why he wanted me to pause.

He said, "I don't know whether or not you realize it, but this is an historic occasion. It may be the first time in 2,500 years that two Jews have walked through the front door of the Palace of the Persians."

Argov, whose family had lived in Palestine for at least five generations before the founding of the Israeli state, had a deep sense of history. His statement, uttered in a stage whisper, made a profound impression on me, and it made me even more nervous about my presentation. (Argov had a tragic fate in store for him. Years later, when serving as Israeli's ambassador to Great Britain, he suffered severe brain damage from a would-be assassin's bullet.)

Inside the palace, a high government official I had met briefly before, a courtly and somewhat elderly man named Mr. Alam, greeted us. He was Iran's Minister of State, reported to be a close personal confidant of the Shah and his wife, the Shahbanu. Alam said he would take me to the Shah and accompany Argov to a room where he could wait comfortably for my return. Several other high officials of the government were loitering outside the Shah's office, and Mr. Alam introduced me to each one of them. I heard one of the officials mutter to me in English, "Good luck."

He and I entered the Shah's office. It was an immense suite of rooms gorgeously carpeted in Persian rugs. Alam introduced me to the Shah and disappeared. The Shah was quite courteous, and much more casually dressed than I was, in a tweed sports jacket and non-matching pants.

What does one say when introduced to the Shah of Iran? I said, "You have a lovely office."

He replied, "Yes. I spend a lot of time here so I like it to be comfortable."

He waved me to a seat, sat in an armchair facing me and gestured for me to make my report. I handed him a thick document and said I would summarize its highlights. I told him that the American media had a number of informants inside Iran, some highly placed, who had backed up their assertions of SAVAK torture with persuasive documentation. He brushed aside this point and several others that I recounted.

Nothing I was reporting seemed to bother him particularly, until I got to the media's criticism of Iran's purchase of jet planes to strengthen its air force.

"Do they know why I need those planes, given the balance of power with the Arab nations?" he asked.

I hesitated and then as I had done many times in touchy situations with clients, adopted my most impartial tone of voice and said quietly, "They don't accept your official explanation. They think you are buying the planes for your personal aggrandizement."

His face grew red. He rose from his chair, took the heavy report I had given him, and threw it violently to the floor. He then turned and stalked out of the office, slamming the door behind him.

That was the end of my presentation. I was crestfallen when I met Argov later in the waiting room. I told him what happened. He said I was lucky to be leaving the palace in one piece, but he otherwise seemed nonplussed. From Israel's point of view, the Shah's anger had no doubt been deflected onto the American media and away from Israel. So Israel was content with the outcome. The Israelis had bought an invaluable five months to arrange for alternative sources of oil while the Shah's attention had turned elsewhere. And the officials I had met were pleased that I had escaped unharmed.

Argov said he had been sure that I would be unharmed, but he was nonetheless relieved to see me. He did not share my distress at leaving a disgruntled client.

❧

I assumed that this was the end of my involvement with the Shah's government, but several months later I received a call from Mr. Alam, asking me to meet him in Nice, in the south of France. Once again, I couldn't resist. I couldn't imagine the reason for the meeting.

I met him at a hotel in Nice. He told me that his request to see me was completely unofficial, something he was doing on his own initiative. He said he knew that I had a personal relationship with Cyrus Vance, who was then Carter's Secretary of State. He asked me if I would go to Washington to see Vance and to ask him what Iran had to do to be taken off of the State Department's list of nations that endorse torture. He said that torture in Iran was a thing of the past, and that Iran wanted to remove the stigma of being associated with the other nations on the list.

I said I would be pleased to convey his message to Vance. I also asked him why he wanted to use me, a person without official standing, as a back channel, when Iran had direct access to our state department. He said he was old-fashioned and liked to do things through personal relationships. I liked and respected him, and I remembered having been told that he was a close personal confidant to the Shah.

Shortly after I got back to New York, I called and requested an appointment with Vance. I was pleased to see him. We had not met since he had moved to Washington as Secretary of State. He was sitting in a rocking chair, nursing a bad back.

As soon as I relayed Alam's question, he asked me, "Does the Shah know about this?" I said I didn't think so because Alam had gone to such pains to tell me that he was doing it unofficially on his own. Vance then went on to tell me that he would be pleased to expedite Iran's removal from the list of nations who support torture, *if* indeed torture in Iran was really a thing of the past. He would personally see to it that conversations were held with that objective in mind.

I later learned that the Shah had not known about Alam's initiative. When he found out, he removed Alam, his closest advisor for decades, from his government. The Shah did not abide others taking the initiative.

PART FOUR

AN UNEXPECTED TURN

My Life Turns Upside Down

WHEN I WAS IN my late fifties, a momentous—and highly improbable—event shook up my life. I fell into a genuine love relationship. Out of the blue! No forewarning! No mental prep!

In my past many random events had caught me by surprise. But they were mostly negative. I had learned to mistrust the random side of life. This time, however, a random event brought me joy and a new perspective on living.

Like most people, I associate love with youth. In books that describe the traditional seasons of a man's life, love generally belongs to the early adult years (one's twenties and thirties). Yet it wasn't until my late fifties that I had the kind of experience with love that many men have decades earlier in their lives. The last thing I expected as I approached age sixty was a love affair that would turn my life upside down.

I had long ago reconciled myself to missing out on the kind of romantic love that obsesses our culture. I had benefited from a more practical kind of married love based on clear husband-and-wife roles. And I was deeply grateful for it. It gave me a stable home, a beloved daughter, and a caring wife. It provided stability and comfort. But it was not the love story I had imagined for myself when I was a young man.

My marriage with Hassie had worked well from the outset, and it had endured for three decades. It was in most respects a sound traditional marriage. A clear and sharp division of roles prevailed. The husband (me) was the sole breadwinner, supporting the family and working to improve its standard of living. Having babies, caring for them, and managing the home was the province of the wife.

Both of us adhered strictly to these roles. Hassie carried out her wife-and-mother role with unfailing grace and fidelity. She was an excellent cook, enjoyed furnishing our apartment, which she did with good taste, and willingly entertained our many friends. Above all, she was a loving, adoring mother who regarded our daughter Nicole as the fulfillment of her destiny.

We were always mutually respectful. We were a bit formal with each other, courteous and polite. I was all too conscious of the sharp contrast between her demonstrative love for Nicole, and her more reserved attitude towards me. My comforting marriage was ambiguous on the matter of mutual love.

We rarely used the language of love. After we were married, I don't remember either of us stating a simple "I love you" to the other. Before we were married, she had had to take a week's vacation to decide to accept my marriage proposal. Being married, having children, and conducting the traditional role of wife with dignity and fidelity were important to her life; love was another matter. My own disastrous first marriage to Marti had left my dread of being "unlovable" intact—at both the conscious and unconscious level.

Throughout my married life with Hassie, I felt like an outsider marrying into a tribe whose rituals were unfamiliar to me, but who all knew a great deal more about marriage and family than I did. Hassie had a large and extended family with whom she was more comfortable than with my friends.

They were all churchgoing Methodists, very ethnically Armenian in their identities. I never detected even a smidgen of anti-Semitism in their relationship with me, though I was clearly the *odar* in the family. They were all intensely child- and family-oriented, and when Nicole was born they showered her with gifts and attention and pride. The great regret of my wife's life after Nicole was born was that she was unable to give birth to more children.

As I approached my sixtieth birthday, I realized that I had become a less anxious person. With wider public recognition and acceptance, I had also grown more self-confident.

Amidst all the meetings, conferences, speeches, and lectures, I had begun to pay attention to the many attractive women I encountered. I noted (with mixed feelings) that I was growing more susceptible to their appeal. And I grew concerned that I might jeopardize my marriage if any one of several casual relationships developed into an affair.

With Nicole away at school and with my immersion in work, Hassie and I found ourselves drifting apart.

But the event that finally separated us was not linked to any of the women I knew at the time. The relationship that threatened our marriage came from an unexpected—and unlikely—source. Indeed, it developed so slowly and unobtrusively that I wasn't fully aware of what was happening until it had happened.

In early January of 1983, just after my fifty-eighth birthday, I found myself delivering a series of lectures on the Irvine campus of the University of California. Several years earlier, UC Irvine had instituted what they called a "Distinguished Lecturer" series. The lecturers—professionals from various fields—were invited to spend a few weeks on campus with faculty and students to share their insights and experience.

My friend, Judge Shirley Hufstedler, had been invited to participate in the series a year earlier. She found the experience rewarding, and she urged me to accept. I did so, without any realization that it would transform my life.

Arriving at Irvine, exhausted from our trip from New York, Hassie and I were met at the airport by a tall, slender, leggy Californian with long blond hair, wearing brief white shorts and sporting a spectacular smile. She introduced herself as Mary—the graduate student who had been assigned to be our guide and driver. She said she would take us to the house reserved for official visitors, and would drive us around Irvine for the first few days of our stay. Once we were familiar with the terrain, we would be provided with a rental car for the remainder of our two-week stay.

As Mary drove me from meeting to meeting around the vast Irvine campus, she told me that she had volunteered to be my driver and guide. She said that she had just received her MA in Social Ecology, and was planning to come to New York in about a month's time. She had read my book *New Rules* as one of her course assignments. She was hoping a make a career doing the sort of research I had conducted for the book, and she thought I might be able to give her some hints about job possibilities in New York City.

I said I would try to help.

I added that with my lousy sense of direction I would inevitably get lost if I had to drive a rental car around Irvine's bewildering maze of streets. I said, "If you are willing to squire me around to my lectures and meetings for the two weeks of my visit, I will give you a running tutorial on the New York job scene and all the booby traps and pitfalls you should avoid."

"That would be wonderful," she said enthusiastically. And so, every weekday for the next two weeks, Mary drove me to my various destinations. Sometimes there would be an hour or two between appointments or lectures, and during those intervals, I would talk to her about the differences between social research as taught in universities and social research designed to solve real world problems.

I shared with her my experience in working in the social research field in New York and described the idiosyncrasies of potential employers. I didn't downplay the difficulties she was likely to encounter. I told her a bit about the Public Agenda, and said I might be able to put in a good word for her there if she couldn't find a job elsewhere.

Diligently, she took notes and asked many probing questions. I felt I was living up to my side of the bargain; I didn't want to take advantage of her generous willingness to spend so much of her time driving me around without her getting some practical benefit from it.

I learned that the long blond hair and leggy look notwithstanding, she was not a native Californian. Indeed, she came from the opposite end of the country—from the small town of Fulton in upstate New York. Her full name was Mary M. Komarnicki, and her mother and father were second-generation Americans of Polish origin.

Mary was the youngest of four children, with an eight-year gap separating her from her closest sibling. All members of the family were practicing Catholics and regular churchgoers. All four siblings attended parochial schools and Catholic colleges. She had graduated from Saint Bonaventure, a small, liberal Catholic college near Buffalo in upstate New York.

Her years at Bonaventure had been a peak experience for her. To earn tuition, she had worked as secretary to Bonaventure's philosophy department. The chairman of the department, Richard Reilly, and his wife had welcomed her into their family as well as into her job. She also had built warm relationships with her fellow students and with other faculty. Her theology courses had transformed her Catholicism, making it more compatible with science without undermining her faith, which remained steadfast.

After graduating from "Saint Bonnie," as she called it, she had searched for a graduate school that combined high quality with low tuition. At that time, the prestigious University of California system offered very low tuition to out of-state students. So once she gained admission to UC Irvine, she packed her bags and drove her Dad's old gas-guzzler Pontiac across the country to California and UC Irvine. She told me that she had devoted two and a half years of hard work, drudgery and loneliness to getting her MA with honors in the University's new department of Social Ecology.

The highlight of her undergraduate years at Bonaventure had been her romance with her classmate Michael—a friendship that had blossomed into a love affair. Indeed, before she left Saint Bonnie for California, Michael had given her a ring and they had become engaged. Part of her loneliness at Irvine came from the fact that she was engaged to a man three thousand miles away—a reality that badly crimped her social life at Irvine. She had resisted seeing other suitors because she was engaged. But it turned out that Michael had had no qualms about seeing other women.

Michael had found a job at an advertising agency in New York City. He had then fallen in love with one of the women at work. Shortly before Mary was to join him in New York, he had called her, told her his news, broken off the engagement, hung up the phone, and thereafter refused to take her calls.

That refusal was particularly painful to her. She admitted that she had a visceral need to vent her feelings. She wasn't able to keep them bottled up without becoming overwhelmed. The break with Michael had been completely unexpected. She felt that her whole life was coming apart. Not being able to talk it all out with Michael was agony for her.

Sitting in the Pontiac beside her, I was surprised by how deeply her pain distressed me. I hardly knew her. I was a stranger, married, with a daughter just two years younger than Mary. That conversation in the car got to me. I had a strong desire to hold her. I quickly pushed it aside as inappropriate.

She collected herself and apologized for being so personal and emotional. I thanked her for being willing to share her feelings with someone close to her Dad's age. I squeezed her hand and went off to deliver my lecture.

From Walking to Mentoring to Loving

SHORTLY AFTER I HAD returned to New York from my Irvine assignment, I got a call from Mary to tell me she had driven herself cross continent again, this time from California to New York. She was now settled on Long Island at the home of her cousin, Antonia (Toni). I was impressed with the independence of spirit it took for her to drive herself across the full length of the continent in a rickety old jalopy.

When I had lunch with her about a week later, I was surprised to find her dispirited. Cousin Toni had welcomed her warmly, she said; she was comfortable staying with her and was excited to find herself living in the Big Apple. But her breakup with Michael continued to obsess her, especially since she had to keep her anger and frustration bottled up. She said she didn't know Toni well enough to lean on her emotionally, and the only other New Yorkers she knew were Michael's friends.

Mary and I gradually fell into the habit of seeing one another every few weeks. She would come into Manhattan from Long Island for job interviews, and after she completed her interviews, I would take a break from work and walk with her, often stopping for coffee. Sometimes she would walk me home. Both my office and my apartment were close to Central Park. When she walked me home, we would always take the longer route through the tree-lined pathways of Central Park, pausing to rest on a bench and talk when the weather permitted.

For more than a year our relationship remained extremely casual—essentially a walking relationship. She was preoccupied with finding a job and with brooding over the loss of her first love. I was preoccupied with my firm's research work and my non-profit projects for the Public Agenda, the Aspen Institute, and the Kettering Foundation. I knew she was lonely and that I was one of the very few people she knew in New York. I enjoyed her company. She was vivacious, warm-hearted, and interested in everything.

I got to know her a lot better on these walks. She answered all my questions about her family, her life at Irvine and before that at Bonaventure, her future plans, and her often-stormy relationship with Michael.

Apart from Michael, she talked mostly about her family. She admitted to feeling closer to her dad than to her mother. She said that she resembled her father physically. Like her, he was tall and slim. She talked about him glowingly. Clearly, they had a strong emotional bond. Mary's attitude toward her mother was more ambivalent. She said that her mother was a non-stop talker and complainer, prone to extended bouts of depression.

Mary greatly admired her sister, Kathy. Kathy was a genuine beauty, with boys constantly sniffing around her. Mary felt awkward and naïve compared to her big sister. Mary's brother, Paul, was closer in age to Kathy. Another brother, Stevan, had died when Mary was thirteen. Mary, as the youngest child, was sure that she had been unintended, an accident born into a strict Catholic family that didn't believe in birth control.

❧

About a year after Mary came to New York, our casual walking relationship evolved into a closer mentoring relationship. Two changes in circumstance brought about the shift.

One was my help to her in finding a job. Her job search had not gone well, and it was getting her down. At the time, the research department at the Public Agenda needed a junior analyst for qualitative research, a job for which Mary was quite well-suited and trained. I set up an appointment for her, and to her great delight, the Public Agenda hired her.

The second change was Mary's success in finding an excellent low-rent apartment on West Ninety-Fifth Street on New York's Upper West Side. Suddenly, she found her life's prospects much changed for the better. After a frustrating year, she had landed both a good job and a place of her own in New York. Also, the passage of time and extensive venting (in a notebook I bought for her for that purpose) had helped her to stop obsessing about Michael. She was excited about building a new life—succeeding at her new job, finding new friends, and forming new relationships.

On our walks she started to turn to me for advice about her job and even about the best way for her to conduct her new relationships with young men of her own generation. She had no hesitation using me as a sounding board. She was determined to avoid repeating the Michael disaster. I felt that as someone who had also suffered in love relationships, I might be helpful to her. Our relationship changed from casual walks to a closer mentoring one.

Up to then, physical contact between us had been confined to an affectionate hug when we parted company. But that began to change after I visited her in her new apartment. One weekend morning I arrived at her apartment unannounced, bearing coffee and Danish pastries. She was surprised to see me, and also embarrassed. Technically, as chairman of the Public Agenda, I was her boss, and the visit struck her as inappropriate. Naïvely, I hadn't seen it in that light. I didn't interfere in the day-to-day operations of the Public Agenda and therefore didn't think of myself as her boss.

But I was also self-conscious about the visit, for a different reason—I was a married man visiting an attractive unmarried younger woman. So that morning we had our coffee and Danish pastries in an uncomfortable self-conscious state of mind. But my awkward—and uninvited—visit nonetheless proved to be a turning point. My next visit was by explicit invitation. I soon found myself promoted to "friend-with-privileges" status.

We continued to relate to each other in this fashion for another year. Almost three years passed. I was very attracted to Mary. But I kept my feelings in check for obvious reasons: the stability of my marriage, and the enormity of the age gap (more than thirty-three years) between Mary and me. I have never been attracted to younger women simply because they are younger. Actually, I find the division between the generations difficult to bridge and am most comfortable with people of my own generation.

Yet a strong desire for a more intimate relationship bubbled up in me. I assumed that the enormity of our age gap would provide us with a foolproof safety valve against threats either to my marriage or to Mary's marital prospects.

I would have the joy of an intimate affair with a young woman I had come to cherish. And she would eventually find a young man to marry and to father her babies. She had an intense yearning to start raising a family.

I would not stand in her way; on the contrary, I would encourage her and hopefully send her off with my blessings to an appropriate Catholic hunk her own age to raise as many babies as she wanted. I would be left with a warm and glowing memory to comfort me in my old age.

Why doesn't life ever abide by the scenarios we plan for ourselves?

The Safety Valve Fails

SAMUEL JOHNSON WROTE THAT the prospect of hanging concentrates the mind. I suspect that approaching one's sixtieth birthday concentrates the mind in the same way. Symbolically, for most of us age sixty signifies the beginning of the end. For someone like me who had always lived in the future rather than in the present moment, my sixties meant that there wasn't much future left.

My relationship with Mary had slowly evolved into a full-blown love affair. For decades, I had pushed down my yearning for intimacy—a powerful desire to nurture and be nurtured. For the first time since my mother's death more than a half-century earlier, I found the love and caring I so desired in this beautiful young woman. Given the age difference, it was natural for me to nurture her. But to my surprise, the nurturing was reciprocal despite the age gap. Nurturing the man she loved was inherent to Mary's nature and womanhood.

I fully understood why I had come to love her. Why she loved me was harder for me to grasp. I chalked it up to her loneliness, to the rebound from Michael, to gratitude for my help. I knew that these were transient feelings. So I harbored no illusions about the future; I simply assumed that there would not be a future for us together. I was convinced that our affair was one of those lucky happenings that occur almost randomly, adding a momentary touch of grace and tenderness to life.

But Mary treated our age gap differently. Its significance was one of the very few things we argued about. She insisted that I exaggerated it out of all proportion. I argued that our thirty-three-year age disparity was unbridgeable. As a young woman with her life's joys ahead of her, the last thing she needed was an old fart like myself holding her back. I urged that we enjoy our wonderful interlude together, without kidding ourselves. I was sure that it couldn't be anything but an interlude.

We kept going over the same ground without settling anything. The disagreement didn't affect our relationship, which kept growing closer and more loving. We managed to find time to be with each other almost every week. I called her nightly. I had gotten into the habit of taking a walk after dinner every night. There was a convenient phone booth at the entrance to Lenox Hill Hospital on Lexington Avenue, a few blocks away from my apartment. Each night I would walk to the hospital armed with an ample supply of quarters to call her (this was before the cell phone era).

However much I loved Mary, keeping Hassie in the dark about my affair disturbed me profoundly. We had been peaceably married for almost thirty years. Our lives had settled into a stable pattern. We cared about each other, even though we had different conceptions of married love. For Hassie, love was not a verbal matter; words didn't count. Doing things together, especially things involving the family, was what counted.

My conception of love was not marital togetherness; it was more intimate, more erotic, more verbal, more physically demonstrative.

I hated the deceit involved in carrying out a clandestine affair. Hassie sensed that something was amiss. I would not have been surprised if she suspected that I was having an affair and didn't want to hear about it. If so, I was sure she wouldn't bring up her uneasiness on the likely premise that whatever was going on would surely pass. (We hardly ever talked about personal things.)

I was convinced that Mary's biological clock would set a time limit to our affair. If she wanted to have children, she couldn't stay with me for too many more years. Sometimes at four in the morning—the hour of dread—I wondered if I might lose both women.

That wouldn't have surprised me. The childhood traumas of my mother's death and the foster home experiences that followed had left me with a nightmarish conviction of abandonment as my fate in life.

The age issue between Mary and me came to a head in the spring of 1986, shortly after I had returned from a trip to the Soviet Union. Mary and I had missed each other intensely over the three-week separation. We had each written long daily letters to the other, but for some reason this particular separation had proven especially poignant.

On a long walk a week or so after I returned from my trip, Mary said she wanted to explain once and for all how she felt about the age gap and why she felt the way she did.

She said that with my encouragement she had dated a number of men of her own age over the past few years. All of them, she said, had been preoccupied with their futures and careers. She found this completely understandable; indeed, it reflected her own preoccupations and state of mind.

Somehow, she said, the relationships with her age peers didn't radiate the same warmth as ours did. She realized that it was the fact that we were *not* at the same stage of life that appealed to her. She said that she flourished in the attention and caring and nurturing that I gave her, and she had come to cherish and depend upon it.

She admitted that her work at the Public Agenda had disappointed her. She was, she said, sick with worry that she was letting me down because my expectations for her were so high. But as someone who valued honesty with one's self, she was surprised—and relieved—to realize that she really wasn't a career person after all. She knew that I had reached the life stage of no longer climbing the socioeconomic ladder. I didn't have anything to prove to the wider world, and I did have a lot of love to give to her, which is what she genuinely wanted.

She didn't know what was going to happen to us because she didn't think I would ever leave my wife. But she was sure that our age difference couldn't matter less; or if it did, it had a positive meaning for her, not a negative one.

What she wanted more than anything else in life, she said, was to be nurtured and cared for—for us both to love and be loved.

Caught Unprepared

IT TOOK A LONG time for the full significance of Mary's words to sink in. She was saying two different things. One was the surface message that our age disparity shouldn't affect our relationship. I came to accept this message with a feeling of relief. I didn't like the idea of a quasi-parental relationship to Mary.

The other message was deeper and harder to absorb. Mary was also telling me not to treat our age gap as an insurmountable obstacle to our being together in the future. She was assuming that I wouldn't leave Hassie—in her view, the only genuine obstacle standing in our way. But she was also saying that if I ever did decide to do so, she wanted to share her life with me, not with some young Catholic go-getter.

This deeper message "threw me for a loop" (in one of my dad's favorite phrases). It made me realize that I could no longer evade the issue of our possible future together by hiding behind our age difference. I knew that I loved Mary and that tensions between Hassie and me were growing stronger by the day. But I didn't see how I could abandon someone whose loyalty and fidelity had been beyond reproach.

My love affair with Mary had now taken a turn that stirred in me an agonizing conflict. Having lived for three years in France, where extramarital affairs were no big deal, I knew how strongly cultural relativity shaped sexual morality. As a confirmed outsider, cultural disapproval didn't particularly trouble me.

My guess was that to Hassie's way of thinking, a transient love affair would not be a sufficient reason for separating. Marriage was marriage; unless it was marred by violence, you stuck it out no matter what. For many years our relationship had worked smoothly. Sure, there were tensions between us, as between any husband and wife. But strong bonds also held us together.

Mary and I realized that the months ahead would be a time of painful struggle as we sought to resolve our dilemma. She said that she regretted placing the burden of decision on me, but that she had already made up her mind. She put her faith in Saint Jude—the Catholic saint of lost causes.

Not only did I love Mary as I had never loved anyone before, without qualification, I also knew that she genuinely loved me. I had learned to trust her. I knew that she was always truthful about her feelings. It had taken me a long time, but I had finally come to accept the reality that her love for me was not just a transient infatuation. It was the real thing.

What was so different about Mary? Why did she defy the odds that prevailed against such a desirable woman falling in love with me? Was it because, appearances to the contrary, she really felt she couldn't attract eligible young men? Did Michael do such a number on her that she had given up on herself and decided to compromise and settle for me? Did she have a deep psychological problem such as a fixation on father figures?

Given her eagerness to marry and have babies, why had she waited for me patiently for years, and why was she willing to wait more years (not always patiently) living with the uncertainty that in the end she might lose me?

Who was this Mary whom I had come to love so dearly that I was ready to turn my life upside down to be with her? What was special and different about her?

Superficially, she didn't seem particularly special. She was tall, slender, blonde, leggy, and near-beautiful. She had a radiant smile that was contagious. It conveyed warmth, enthusiasm, sociability, and an eagerness to please. She was instantly friendly—the opposite of the guarded reserve and sophistication I associated with most of the women I'd known who had gone to Radcliffe and other elite Eastern colleges.

She laughed a lot, loved to chat with people, and was gung ho for any interesting new project someone wanted to launch. She was curious to try anything new just once. She didn't want any life experience to go by untasted.

At the same time, she cherished her solitude. She always had a huge backlog of projects ready to tackle when she was alone—books to read, needlepoint to finish, clothes and appliances to fix (she was extremely adept at doing so), photograph albums to organize (she loved to take pictures, but procrastinated in organizing them), poetry to write, cards and gifts to buy or make for her many beloved nephews.

The qualities in her that I most admired were what made her special. First and foremost came her remarkable emotional maturity. She was steadfast: her bonds with those close to her were strong and enduring. She was honest and straightforward about expressing her feelings. I recall no exception to her honesty in relating how she felt, even when she had to admit to negative feelings such as being jealous, resentful, envious, or self-contradictory. Indeed, she had a visceral need to express her feelings. She was unable to keep them bottled up, and I saw evidence of this.

Understanding relationships was her passion, and she brought to it an uncanny awareness of her own deepest feelings. It took me a long time to appreciate that once she had given herself, there was no going back for her—no second thoughts, no buyer's remorse, no backtracking when it came to emotional commitment. Nothing could be more reassuring for me.

She knew what she wanted, and she was willing to accept all the tradeoffs and sacrifices that might be required to have it. In the interest of maintaining and strengthening our closeness, she was always quick to accept responsibility for something that may have gone awry. And she was unabashedly affectionate and demonstrative in her expressions of love.

I have emphasized the positive, as one should expect from a doting lover. But she readily acknowledged her own flaws and failings. She was fussy about clothes. Though necessarily frugal, she loved good clothes and she always looked fresh and well-groomed.

Though fastidious in her own personal cleanliness and appearance, she was totally untidy about things. She sometimes appeared to me to be a vision of loveliness in a setting of utter chaos.

She was also moody, with PMS and migraines and the vicissitudes of daily life all taking their toll. Part of her moodiness was due to a tendency to become overwhelmed when too many things piled up for her to attend to. Since she had a strong sense of responsibility and liked to do things right, she lost her composure when there were just too many things for her to do.

Perhaps her greatest vulnerability was her tendency to give too much of herself to others and then to feel resentment when she felt they were taking advantage of her. She never absorbed the reality that while people may initially express gratitude for what you do for them, the gratitude soon wears off and they begin to take your efforts on their behalf for granted. She was right about other people taking her helpfulness and efforts on their behalf for granted, but she never learned to hold back. She was incapable of doing so.

How Do I Defend Myself without a Shell?

MARY INSISTED THAT I give the marriage with Hassie every possible chance. I tried to do so, but it was too late. My love affair with Mary had been no casual sexual fling. It had developed and matured over a long period of years, spreading out over the decade of my sixties. The time left for us to be together before I was an old man or a dead one was shrinking every year. I finally confided to Hassie that I loved Mary and wanted to marry her.

After months of indecision, Hassie and I agreed to a trial separation. I moved from our posh East Side cooperative to a small rental apartment on the extreme West Side, not far from Mary's apartment.

Months into my separation from Hassie, Mary wrote to me, as she often did when I was travelling on business: "It's such a difficult thing for you to do…. There is still a chance that you could start a whole new relationship with her—one with some version of the intimacy and caring that we experience. If I had one wish granted to me today it would be to catapult the both of us about a year into the future—having gone through your divorce, going public, and my family adjusting to this new situation. I can dream about the impossible, can't I?"

A year passed and Hassie and I were separated but not divorced. For me, that year was one of extraordinary intensity, compounded of joy, guilt, and transformation. The source of the joy was obvious.

Subject only to the constraints of our two jobs and my heavy travel schedule, I was free to be with Mary whenever we wished, and we cherished every minute of our time together.

The psychological transformation was a novel experience, full of unfamiliar feelings. For virtually all of my life—from age eight to age sixty—I had lived with one constellation of feelings and experiences. Now for the first time in more than fifty years that constellation was breaking up. It felt like the tectonic plates of my being were slowly shifting. The shift was a positive one: it expressed what I had long desired. But while it was happening, I felt totally vulnerable and exposed.

In describing the feeling to Mary, I said that I felt like a turtle that had lost its protective shell. The shell may have been battered and bruised but it had become part of me. It had protected me for a very long time. Losing it was like losing a limb.

The shell comprised many layers built up laboriously over decades. The first layer developed in the foster homes to which I was sent after my mother's death. It formed in reaction to a change in my environment that distressed me deeply. Whatever my misbehavior, my own parents had accepted me totally and unreservedly. They created an environment of love and tolerance in which I thrived. With the foster families, I had to learn to live with their grudging willingness to tolerate me only if I toed a line that kept moving with each new foster home. I came to feel like an un-cherished outsider, and I developed a shell to protect myself.

As I moved from one foster home to another, I was determined to avoid the trap of self-pity. I refused to live life as a resentful and helpless victim. Searching for satisfaction outside of family life, I found myself retreating into the life of the mind. I became as self-sufficient as I possibly could, and I learned to keep my feelings to myself. The shell thickened.

In the army, and afterwards in college and graduate school, I grew yet another layer of protective shell. I became resigned to my seeming inability to attract the most desirable women—the kind who didn't need to compromise in their choice of men. Later on, I found myself withdrawing from the battle of the sexes, because I lacked the will to prevail: somehow, it seemed dangerous for me to engage, much less to win. In the quest to find both satisfying work and love, I had given up on unconditional love and compensated by over-emphasizing work.

Each of these developments fit together in a pattern that worked for me...up to a point. The pattern functioned as long as I could keep from being tempted by the kind of love that I so deeply yearned for. It was easy to keep temptation at bay because the women to whom I was attracted showed no special interest in me.

But then, along came Mary.

Mary's apartment was a ten-minute subway ride north of mine. We had dinner together almost every night, and on weekends we often rented a car and searched out beautiful places to explore. Mary particularly loved inns or hotels with fireplaces, and I promised her that someday we would have a fireplace of our own.

Every day it became more apparent that we were right for each other. My new freedom energized me. I stopped feeling that I was entering old age and instead started to count my many relatives who were blessed with longevity and typically survived into their late eighties, nineties and even their hundreds.

I knew that my father had been sexually active until his late eighties. His doctor said that he died of prostate cancer. But I think he died because the prostate cancer had rendered him impotent, which he found unacceptable.

Mary and I constantly talked about getting married, but we had to wait until my divorce was final, which didn't happen until 1989. And then a new obstacle arose. My daughter Nicole was engaged to be married, and it would have been inconsiderate to upstage her. Nicole's support through this trying time was very important to me. I loved my daughter and didn't want to embarrass her or make her uncomfortable.

Once my divorce did become final, Mary stopped fretting that I might go back to Hassie. While she was finding it ever harder to keep postponing our marriage, she agreed with me that it would be better to wait until Nicole got married.

She said that waiting would be less of a strain on her if we bought a house. I agreed immediately. We had been spending a number of weekends in Connecticut and found it quite agreeable. A number of my friends had country houses in Connecticut and we looked for a house in the small town of Sherman within driving distance of most of them.

We settled on a fairly large house at 21 Holiday Point Road (with several fireplaces).

We were married at the end of September 1991 by both a priest and a rabbi in a small stone church about twenty miles north of Sherman. The church had not been used for a number of years. It was damp from non-use but it had comfortable benches and no religious symbols.

It was one of those magical New England days with just a touch of fall in the air. Nicole posed for pictures with Mary; I posed for pictures with Mary's mom and dad, who seemed to accept me despite being twice Mary's age, Jewish, and divorced. It was an auspicious beginning.

The question I posed in the title of this chapter was: how do I defend myself without a thick shell? I now knew the answer.

There was no longer any need to do so.

Together

WE LAUNCHED OUR MARRIED life with a honeymoon in France and northern Italy. I took Mary to all my old Paris haunts—the Sorbonne, the Île Saint-Louis, the Luxembourg Gardens, the Picasso Museum, my favorite Left Bank bistros, and the hotel on the Rue Servandoni where I lived for most of my first two years in Paris, up the street from the Church at Saint-Sulpice. My French friends, Rosine Bernheim and Claude Cremieux, put us up in their respective guest quarters. They greeted Mary with warmth and friendship, for which I was enormously grateful.

We flew to Rome, rented a car, and toured Northern Italy, taking a side trip to Assisi. Mary had a strong desire to visit the Basilica of Saint Francis, one of the gentle saints to whom she had developed a strong personal attachment.

When we returned home we settled into a comfortable routine of spending midweek in our New York apartment and long weekends in Sherman. Our house had a large pool and an outdoor grill that we used until the days grew too short and cold. We walked a lot, visited friends in nearby towns, shopped and cooked together, listened to music, read to each other, and played chess, computer games, and flute-piano duets. My flute and Mary's piano playing were less than virtuoso quality, so we avoided difficult classical music and played popular tunes, which we hugely enjoyed.

I spent weekend mornings writing. To my surprise, I wrote some of my best work in this fashion. It proved to me that writing need not be a consolation for misery, and that one did not have to be unhappy in order to be creative.

Those few years of our marriage were the happiest years of my life. It had taken me until my retirement age to find peace of mind and sustained love.

One of my few sources of discomfort in those years came from my learning how to be happy. It sounds bizarre. What kind of idiot needs to learn how to be happy? And why in the world should this learning be a source of discomfort?

In the first months of our marriage, I continued to experience a deep emotional insecurity. At some unconscious level, the dread of abandonment and rejection persisted. I kept being surprised to find myself reacting with anger or suspicion or withdrawal to some imagined slight.

Mary's nephew, Darren, came to visit us, and I found myself full of jealous anger at the "inordinate" (in my mind) amount of attention that Mary was giving him. I got irritated when Mary was late, or when I felt she was spending too much time with her pottery. My feelings were easily hurt by casual offhand remarks.

Indeed, it turned out that I *was* insecure without my defensive shell.

I thought that I had fully recovered from my old habit of withdrawing into myself and digging a moat of reserve to protect myself. But it's not easy to undo old brain synapses, especially when they have been reinforced over and over again.

Fortunately for me, Mary understood. She knew that I had shed my turtle-like shell in the interests of creating intimacy and emotional trust between the two of us. She realized how difficult it was for me to give up my familiar old defenses, however dysfunctional they may have been.

She was uncanny in her mood-detecting abilities. She would coax me into admitting that I was responding inappropriately to some truly trivial incident.

Abandoning these defenses served us well. It is true that we had grown ever closer and more intimate with each other for years before we were married. But learning to live with each other day in and day out was a different matter. In some respects, it was harder: neither of us had an alternative existence to fall back upon. In most ways though, it was easier. We now had the time we needed to work things out and to come to understand each other better. I often felt that I was reliving my childhood and adolescence, with a far better outcome.

In addition to being happy, those years were also rich in self-discovery. They helped me practice a different kind of examined life, one that was much less intellectual than in earlier years. It was more practical, more down to earth, more emotional. And probably more valuable.

Here is a brief excerpt from a letter I sent to Mary on Valentine's Day, 1995:

I know that officially we have been married only for three years, but emotionally I feel I've always known you and that we have been together for a long, long time. The age difference has its disadvantages, especially now as I sashay into my seventh decade with an incessant "what-did-you-say?" Some of the senses may be waning, but not my unabated love for you. My hope is that years and years from now I'll make my exit by lunging for you from my wheel chair.

The day after I gave Mary this Valentine's Day card, February 15, 1995, Mary and I flew to California. I was scheduled to give a talk in Los Angeles on February 17, and we decided to stop in San Diego en route to spend a day with my friend, T. George Harris, the editor of *Psychology Today*. We arrived in San Diego at about nine in the evening local time. We rented a car at the airport and started to drive to George's house.

Mary was driving, as usual. It was quite dark at the airport, and we had difficulty reading the traffic signs. I had my head buried in the map trying to figure out the best route to take. I heard Mary say, "I think I see the sign for the exit."

That was the last time I ever heard her voice. Apparently she did not see the red light just ahead of her, and as she drove on toward the exit, a truck barreled into her side of the car. I was knocked unconscious, with a concussion and few broken ribs. I was later told that the car was so badly totaled that we both had to extricated from it using what are called "the jaws of life"—a huge metal pincer that pulled the two of us from the wreck.

My only memory of the accident is waking up in a hospital bed and groggily asking the nurse, "Where is my wife?"

Mary had been killed in the car crash.

I slipped back into misery and unconsciousness.

Picking Up the Pieces

I WILL FOREVER BE grateful for the outpouring of warmth and support I received from my family and friends after Mary died. Two kinds of support were particularly helpful. The first came from my cousin Leon Shapiro (my age) and his young bride, Laurie, who was Mary's age and her friend. Once my ribs and head were healed and I was released from the hospital, I travelled to Florida to stay with them.

Their winter apartment in Fort Lauderdale, Florida, was tiny and I was always in the way. Leon, though known for his impatience, proved a model of constraint. I was an intrusive houseguest, constantly imposing on their privacy—a semi-basket case: nervous, sad, restless, anxious, bewildered. They both displayed remarkable patience and support.

After a few weeks I pulled myself together and returned to my apartment in New York. At a moving memorial service for Mary in New York, my friend and former co-worker, Barbara Lee, was particularly warm and sympathetic. That was the second form of life-saving support.

I had had a close but proper relationship with Barbara when she worked for my firm. Both of us were married at the time and observed an appropriate distance. She was now divorced. Barbara had left our firm several years earlier to work in the communications department at CBS. She invited me to dinner at her apartment and I gratefully accepted.

I dated her with some frequency thereafter but I was grieving Mary and not ready to make any new commitments. For the next year or so I lived the improbable life of an "eligible bachelor." I was invited to dinner parties and dates solely on the basis of being an available single male. The fact that I was over seventy years old at the time didn't seem to count as an obstacle. I dutifully—and hopefully—accepted all invitations on the vain expectation that Mary might miraculously reincarnate herself, even though I knew the quest was futile.

I became somewhat promiscuous as a way of keeping my grief at bay, if only for short periods of time. After each fling I returned to the comfort of Barbara. She was very understanding and accepting. She was particularly helpful in supporting me in my work. I knew that the only way I could manage my grief was to keep busy. Constant activity is my habitual lifestyle, and I soon reverted to this familiar pattern.

I busied myself finishing my book, *The Magic of Dialogue*, which I had started to write when Mary was still alive. As soon as it was published, I started on another book. At the same time I continued working for my firm and for the Public Agenda. Gradually, Barbara and I drifted into an exclusive relationship and moved in together.

Barbara was of invaluable help in managing some big changes in my life. One of these was selling my house in Sherman, Connecticut. It was a big house, inseparable in my mind from Mary who had found it, furnished it, cherished it, and shared it with me.

An even bigger change was my decision to leave New York. I had never considered myself a true New Yorker. My Boston roots and accent were a permanent and—to my non-Bostonian friends—amusing feature of my persona. I hated the noise of New York. It was incessant and inescapable. I hated the frenetic busyness where people were preoccupied with their jobs and careers. While I dreaded the prospect of leaving my East Coast friends and family (Nicole, my son-in-law David, and my granddaughter Rachel), I was convinced that Mary's death required me to make a decisive break with the lifestyle I had enjoyed with her.

Barbara and I briefly considered moving to Florida. We gave it a try and decided, in Gertrude Stein's memorable phrase, that there was no *there* there. It was a place you go to retire. I was ready to move but not to retire.

I began to think of La Jolla in Southern California, the place of Mary's accident, as a potential destination. My good friend George Harris lived there. The University of California at San Diego, one of the country's leading research universities, was a definite attraction, and I hoped that I might find ways of relating to it. The idea of taking refuge in a university town held great appeal for me.

La Jolla also appealed to Barbara, who made a special trip to find a place for us to live. She succeeded in finding a splendid small house along the shores of the Pacific, just a few miles north of San Diego proper.

I bought the house without seeing it. And so we moved out of New York to California, though Barbara kept her apartment in Greenwich Village, which she greatly cherished (and used frequently even after we moved).

Our lives in La Jolla were stable and comfortable. Several years after Barbara and I settled there, we drifted into marriage.

My marriage to Barbara shared some of the same characteristics as my marriage to Hassie. My marriages to both women were the traditional type, featuring a strong division of labor and a determined protection of personal autonomy. Like most highly accomplished people, Barbara cherished her own autonomy. I respected her independence, and retained my own as well.

My life on La Jolla Shores in California was characterized by an unsettling restlessness of spirit. I missed my East Coast friends and family. In particular, I missed watching Rachel, my granddaughter, grow up. I kept looking for things to keep me busy and occupied. I couldn't keep busy enough.

For example, I became interested in investing in the stock market. Because I had been so busy with writing, I had initially used professional advisors for managing the money I had received from the sale of my firm, Yankelovich, Skelly and White. But during the dot-com bubble of 2000, my professional advisors lost so much of my money that I considered doing my own stock picking. I had had a lot of experience with stock investing on corporate boards of directors. I figured that I couldn't do a worse job than my advisers were doing.

Once I started to pick and choose stocks on my own, I discovered that I enjoyed doing it, and that I seemed to have a flair for it. I had read somewhere that the renowned British economist, John Maynard Keynes, had gotten rich by spending an hour or so before breakfast every day buying and selling stocks.

If he could do it, why couldn't I? At least I could try.

To my surprise, I found that its complexity fascinated me. It was challenging to try to understand how the crosscurrents of primitive emotions like investor fear and greed interacted with impersonal macro-economic trends and also with technical market factors such as the effect of huge hedge fund trading practices.

The switch from hiring advisors to do-it-yourself investor was successful beyond my expectations. I saved myself a lot of money in fees, indulged my new hobby and made money both for myself and for the friends who began to use me as their unpaid investment advisor.

During this same period I also renewed many of my ties in the world of international social science. One highlight was my visit to Sweden where I was invited to deliver the annual Hans Zetterberg lecture. Hans was a prominent sociologist both at Columbia University here in the United States and also in his native Sweden. He was also a good friend. To his delight, the lecture in his honor was given while he was still alive to enjoy the accolades heaped on him.

I was also invited to attend a conference in Bremen, Germany, convened by a select group of European social scientists. At the end of a highly stimulating meeting, we decided to meet annually in one or another nation represented by the group. The nations included Germany, France, Italy, Great Britain, Switzerland, and the United States. These annual junkets in various countries continued for years. They were among the most genial and enjoyable experiences of those years.

In La Jolla, I made a batch of new friends, some my own age, and some a generation younger.

I began to form some relationships at UCSD, at first with the Extension Division. The head of that division, Mary Walshok, had been quite hospitable when we first moved to La Jolla. Walshok and I formed a unit within her division to conduct studies of how young people from impoverished backgrounds could achieve the kind of access to the internet that was routinely available to middle- and upper-income young people.

I formed a close bond with two UCSD leaders my own age. Herb York, a world famous physicist was one of them. Herb had been a Defense Department official who had served as UCSD's first chancellor. The former president of Columbia University, William McGill, who was then teaching and advising at UCSD, was the other. We decided we would give a course together, but our plans were undercut by McGill's unexpected death.

The dean of the division of social sciences, a cognitive scientist named Jeff Elman, invited me to become a member of the division's advisory committee, and I accepted enthusiastically. I became a firm supporter of his division and when the opportunity arose I used some of my stock market gains to fund an endowed chair, the Yankelovich Chair in Social Thought. My goal was to encourage the social scientists to do interdisciplinary research rather than the more fashionable single-discipline research.

Jeff and I also worked together to build the Yankelovich Center for Social Science Research. Its goal is to encourage faculty and students to pursue both the kind of pragmatic, problem-solving research that addresses the nation's most urgent problems as well as the kind of highly theoretical research the faculty generally favors. The new center is actively engaged in research to revitalize the nation's faltering social mobility system and to help its schools do a better job in training and educating students from disadvantaged households.

I also started a new for-profit research firm, called Viewpoint Learning, Inc. The firm, which I cofounded with Steven Rosell, an extraordinarily intelligent scholar, specialized in conducting citizen dialogues as well as dialogues between leaders and citizens.

Most research with the public is fairly superficial—ranging from brief telephone interviews to participation in experiments that make limited demands on people's time. Our dialogues were far more demanding. Typically, they involved a minimum eight-hour day of discussion, sometimes spilling over into a second or third day.

Viewpoint Learning's purpose was to provide participants with a disciplined setting and framework that would permit them to deliberate with one other on complex societal problems. We weren't interested in people's raw, unreflective opinions; opinion polls gave us plenty of that kind of information. We wanted to give policy-makers feedback on the public's considered judgment, after people had engaged in serious deliberation and been exposed to a variety of viewpoints.

In our dialogues we addressed a wide array of questions. How can we achieve better preschool education for our children? What can we do to reduce the damage of human-made climate change? How can hospitals do a better job caring for patients in the last weeks of life?

These are the kinds of complicated issues that can benefit from dialogue that requires participants to listen attentively to others and to think hard before making up their own minds.

The new firm did a huge amount of prep for each dialogue, laying out the hard choices of each issue and its pros and cons. For several years, Steve, myself, and a gifted executive named Heidi Gantwerk had managed the new firm. But once I entered my eighties, I decided to retire completely from active engagement, leaving the management to Steve and Heidi.

The firm thrived until Steve suffered a serious stroke. While Steve underwent a lengthy recovery (which was ultimately successful), our other colleagues, including Isabella Furth and Reagan Espino, helped to insure that the firm's project commitments were completed skillfully and professionally.

SELECTED PHOTOGRAPHS

Dan and Nicole, 1970

Dan and Nicole, 1988

Dan and Nicole, 1992

David, Rachel, and Nicole, 2002

Dan and Rachel, 2004

Libby Schenkman with her family

Seated L to R: husband Walter, daughter Fay, Libby,
son-in-law Wayne

Standing: granddaughter-in-law Susan and grandson Max

Mary, Leon, and Laurie, 1993

L to R: Warren Bennett, Ray Selser, Dan, Art Borochoff
Cambridge MA, 1943

Liège, Belgium, 1944

Liège, Belgium, 1944

Handwritten on back: "Julius and myself posing in
front of the PX. Cute, isn't he?"

Liège, Belgium, 1944

Handwritten on back: "Rather good picture, eh? Fellow with
me, Jerry Merrit by name, quite an agreeable
and intelligent character."

Mary and Dan in Sherman, Connecticut
1993

The house in Sherman

Mary at the Berlin Wall, 1992

With Florence Skelly and Arthur White, early 1970s

At the Kettering Foundation with Gerald Ford,
Jimmy Carter, and David Mathews
Dayton, OH, 1990

With Georgi Abartov
(Director of Center for Soviet/American Studies)
Moscow, 1990

With social sciences group, Bremen, 1993

Dinner with Walter Cronkite , 1994

With Bill and Judith Moyers

With Cyrus Vance, 2001

Public Agenda 40th Anniversary
2015

Taking Stock

AS I LOOK BACK over the long trajectory of my life, I am struck by several pervasive themes that have shaped my most vivid experiences.

The first relates to my determination to avoid repeating my father's soul-crushing economic defeat. His experience of the Great Depression filled me with a dread of being powerless or victimized. The goal of avoiding exploitation motivated me far more powerfully than the positive pull of worldly success. I have clung to a persistent optimism and a proactive stance in confronting the randomness of events.

Another theme has been my ambivalent fascination with philosophy. Despite its failure to deliver on some of its most weighty promises, its perspective has helped me to achieve a sense of balance. It would be a fatal mistake, I believe, for people to shove philosophic inquiry aside as a useless relic of the past.

The most pervasive theme of all has been my search for love. For decades I settled for substitutes for the love I desperately sought but couldn't find. Luckily for me, these substitutes worked reasonably well: they saved me from depression and they gave meaning and structure to my young adult and middle years, until I found the real thing when I was nearly sixty years old.

Escaping my father's fate

I knew my father as two different people: as a cheerful, gregarious, story-telling, loving, indulgent dad, but also as a defeated soul whose spirit was crushed by external forces. The external forces were momentous ones: the premature deaths of two wives, being unable to support his family because of the Great Depression, and being economically dependent on an exploitative landlord.

Even though we never lived together after my ninth birthday, I always enjoyed a close, warm, loving relationship with him. It was a huge source of satisfaction to me as well as to him that I was able to support him for the last twenty years of his long life (he lived to almost ninety years of age). He always said that those last years were his most peaceful and serene.

I identified with him closely and was, I think, traumatized as a child by those occasions that he was obliged to work for his landlord for penurious and exploitative wages. I was frustrated at what I felt, even at that early age, was his passivity in accepting his misfortunes. He seemed to believe that there wasn't anything he could do about them.

I was determined that this would never happen to me, whatever I had to do to prevent it. Even as a child, my father's pain and humiliation stabbed at the core of my being.

When I was growing up my family never knew people of great wealth. I had uncles who made a good living for their families; that kind of normalcy felt comfortable for me. But I recall no childhood fantasies of great wealth and worldly success (as distinct from fantasies of achievement in the world of thought). I was gripped by an iron determination to avoid working for anyone who was exploitative. I would find a way of making a living without being dependent on anyone else, and I would make things happen and not just accept them.

This theme of avoiding exploitation, becoming proactive, and escaping economic dependence pervaded my life. I wasn't worried about austerity. I knew it first-hand and knew I could cope with it. Money didn't call out to me. But autonomy and taking the initiative did.

From an early age, I became convinced that life is full of random and unpredictable twists and turns. Some were disastrous while others opened up promising new vistas and possibilities.

Never knowing what to expect had its unsettling aspects. But it kept gloom away. Gloom settles in mainly when you are caught in a rotten situation and see no prospect of change. I have fallen into this trap only a few times in my life. Most of the time, I have been optimistic that something new and astonishing was bound to happen.

The economist John Maynard Keynes has labeled this kind of optimism "animal spirits. " To many people this kind of positive energy comes naturally as part of their genetic heritage. Unfortunately, this inborn vitality can be damaged or destroyed in the early years of life, especially if parenting is bad.

I had the good fortune to enjoy warm and caring parenting in those critical early years of childhood, leaving my optimism intact. Even my mother's death, my family's dissolution, and other destabilizing random events did not destroy it.

I knew, however, that if I remained passive I could readily suffer my father's fate of being overwhelmed and defeated by circumstances. I felt I had to gain some degree of control over my life. I knew that randomness could defeat me without preventive initiative and energy on my part. So I learned to become proactive and entrepreneurial. I was always willing—and eager—to intervene in fate and try something new.

It started with the foster home experiences. Some of the foster homes were disagreeable, but the prospect of escaping to a new one always remained an exciting possibility.

Being admitted to the Boston Latin School and Harvard also seemed like random events, but good ones—strokes of incredible good luck that came out of the blue. The Boston Latin School launched me on the path to social mobility; Harvard advanced it, in addition to being an intellectual's inexhaustible feast.

Taking the risks of action became an ingrained habit:

- When I became discouraged with philosophy at Harvard after the war, I switched to the social sciences.
- When I grew fed up with academic life in Cambridge, I went to live in Paris.
- In New York, in my search for financial independence, I founded the Door Store.
- I finally ended my intolerable marriage to Marti and formed a stable family life with Hassie that lasted for thirty years.
- In the midst of a recession and without capital, I took a chance at starting my own consulting and research firm.
- When the opportunity arose I leapt into the field of public opinion polling with the *New York Times* and *TIME* magazine.
- With Cyrus Vance I founded the non-profit Public Agenda.
- I cofounded Viewpoint Learning to experiment with new forms of dialogue with the public on important national issues.
- Most recently, I funded the Yankelovich Chair in Social thought and the Yankelovich Center for Social Science Research at UCSD.

This list only scratches the surface of times I took the initiative in coping with life's randomness.

Finding Closure in Philosophy

MY AMBIVALENT FASCINATION WITH PHILOSOPHY

I was surprised to discover that philosophy continued to engage me long after I had abandoned it as a career—not obsessively, but as a tension I was determined to resolve.

As I grew older, other tensions in my life lost some of their intensity. I was no longer compelled to fill every moment of silence with music, as I had done throughout most of my life. On the contrary, I sought out and cherished periods of solitude and silence.

The urge for recognition also subsided. I no longer had a need to dominate the conversation when I was with people discussing public issues. I learned to enjoy sitting back and heeding the views of others.

But my interest in philosophy—and my curiosity about where it fit both in my own life and in the general scheme of things—continued to scratch away at my consciousness. I was also aware of the conflict presented by my dual interest in existentialism as a personal philosophical framework and pragmatism as a general social philosophy.

I found resolution about these puzzling and conflicting aspects of philosophy through reading the writings of the American pragmatic philosopher, Richard Rorty—a controversial figure in American intellectual history. Rorty was a few years younger than me, but he seemed to have experienced the same frustration with his confrontation with so-called "analytic philosophy" in graduate school.

This school of academic philosophy had evolved out of a movement known as "logical positivism." It was dismissive of all branches of philosophy except those using logical analysis and argumentation to understand the pathways to knowledge. It had ambitious pretensions to make all other forms of philosophy seem trivial and lacking in rigor. It was contemptuous of people like myself who looked to philosophy for ways of living.

The dominance of logical positivism and analytic philosophy had pushed me to abandon philosophy as a career. But these forces had a quite different impact on Rorty. Instead of driving him out of philosophy, they led him to devote himself to mastering their intricacies.

From my perspective, it was highly likely that Rorty would eventually turn against analytic philosophy because of its almost comic pretentiousness. And when he did finally turn, he became analytical philosophy's fiercest critic. In philosophical circles, he enjoyed considerable credibility because he was attacking analytic philosophy as a knowledgeable and respected insider, rather than an easy-to-ignore outsider like myself and others who had abandoned philosophy once it became a narrow technical discipline.

Rorty made a sharp distinction between Philosophy with a capital *P* and philosophy with a lowercase *p*. Capital-*P* Philosophy represents the grand tradition that reaches all the way back to Plato. The Platonic tradition regards philosophers as enjoying a special, almost priest-like status that gives them a privileged perspective when it comes to understanding the nature of Truth. Rorty found it laughable that analytic philosophers could assign this high priest-like status to their trivial lawyerly arguments.

Rorty called for replacing capital-*P* Philosophy with lowercase-*p* philosophy, where the search for philosophical understanding need not be conducted exclusively in the form of legalistic argumentation.

To find a conception of truth to fit with this small-*p* philosophy, Rorty turned back to the unfashionable American tradition of philosophical pragmatism, particularly the work of John Dewey. Pragmatism holds that we are all creatures of evolution who use language and our minds to survive and flourish in a sometimes harsh and overwhelming world. We learn how to cope with life through constant doing, and we learn from one another, sometimes harmoniously, often in dispute, but without the need for a special class of Philosophers to tell us what is and isn't Truth.

Rorty's effort to revive pragmatism derived from his profound agreement with its core principle, namely, that the purpose of knowledge is to not discover an abstract entity called Truth but to cope successfully with life.

He was much clearer about what he rejected in the Platonic tradition of Philosophy than what he encompassed in small-*p* philosophy. I suspect that his preoccupation with the destructive pretensions of analytic philosophy created a blind spot in him when it came to appreciating the distinctive down-to-earth skills of small-*p* philosophy.

It has taken me much of my life to grasp what these skills are, where and how they fit with other disciplines, and why they are important, indeed indispensable, to the success of a democratic political system "of the people, by the people, and for the people."

Like Dewey, Rorty conceived of democracy as people working side by side to strengthen communal living and solve communal problems. My own concept of democracy is an adaptation of the Dewey/Rorty version, with a special role for the practice of dialogue.

People tend to use the word *dialogue* loosely to convey a variety of forms of conversation and interaction. But I use the term to identify a form of deliberation where people make a special effort to heed and absorb the views of other participants—to gain a gut understanding of where other people are coming from. The objective of this kind of dialogue is to enhance mutual understanding.

I see philosophy playing an important role in keeping our democracy flourishing, and I see dialogue as a way to practice philosophy. Dialogue highlights the importance of communal deliberation in insuring that the voting public acts with sound judgment. Philosophy permits our institutions to ground their rationale on thoughtful dialogue, rather than mindless raw opinion.

These days, most people don't pay much, if any, attention to philosophy. Widely regarded as a relic of the past, academic philosophy may retain some residual historic interest. But it is almost never a source of practical inspiration for people as they struggle with life's day-to-day problems.

When I finished my military service, I thought of pursuing philosophy as a calling as well as a way of earning a living. I abandoned this ambition only when I realized that philosophy, as practiced in today's universities, could not keep the promises that originally drew me to it. Many individuals, like myself, are attracted to philosophy because it promises gifts of great value to their lives.

Historically, philosophy has promised its devotees at least three enormous gifts:

- Going all the way back to Socrates, philosophy has promised guidance and answers to how best to live one's life.
- It has promised absolute standards against which to measure truth, knowledge, and other core values.
- Until it was eclipsed by the spectacular success of science, philosophy had promised to yield substantive knowledge about the way the world works.

It was these promises that seduced philosophers into regarding themselves as a kind of priesthood, standing apart from and above other scholars and disciplines, as judges and keepers of the flame.

My futile search for these promised gifts in contemporary philosophy brought about a major detour in my choice of my life's work. If the negative aspect of my encounter were the whole story, I would have lost interest in philosophy decades ago. I was fully prepared to cut my losses and walk away. With so many splendid possibilities for thought and reflection available, there was no need to hang onto those that, for whatever reason, failed to fulfill their potential.

But I have maintained a passionate interest in philosophy because, despite its academic distortions, it does have great gifts to convey, though they are not the overtly promised ones.

In recent decades, some philosophers have begun to accept the unpalatable reality that academic philosophy cannot conceivably live up to its grandiose historic pretensions. As a consequence, some thinkers have proclaimed "the end of philosophy." Others have tried to salvage something from the wreckage. This epic struggle forms a fascinating chapter in the history of ideas.

For me personally, the struggle is not an abstract, arms-length exercise. It has been a constant and ever-present theme in my life. Despite philosophy's failure to deliver on its historic promises, I have returned again and again to drink from the well.

I don't think I have done so out of obtuseness, stubbornness, or blindness. At any stage of my life, I would have been willing to sideline philosophy. Indeed, I did so for years at a time. But I kept being drawn back to it because I gradually came to realize that philosophy does have distinctive benefits to offer, though these are neither easy to describe nor effortless to achieve.

Fortunately, there exists a long tradition of "practical philosophy" that has the potential to make philosophy valuable to all thoughtful Americans. Its origins go all the way back to Aristotle.

Aristotle wrote extensively about four ways of thinking and knowing. He drew careful distinctions among raw, impulsive opinions (*doxa*), well-founded scientific knowledge (*episteme*), technical and administrative methods of thinking and doing (*techne*), and practical judgment or wisdom (*phronesis*).

He was convinced that each of these forms of thinking have their proper role to play in the life of the community. But in recent centuries, scientific knowledge and technical methods (*episteme* and *techne*), have taken center stage. In principle, there is also a role for opinion (*doxa*) in the democratic process. But practical judgment and wisdom (*phronesis*) have been marginalized. They are sometimes acknowledged as relevant to certain walks of life (e.g., business). But they are typically absent from the scientific quest for truth and knowledge.

For me as an outsider without a professional obligation to teach philosophy, the gift of practical judgment has served as a valuable guide to living. This aspect of philosophy has played a major role in my life.

Here are some of the practical judgments that come from my philosophical reflection over the span of a long life:

- Don't skip any of life's stages, even if out of sequence
- Find your own way to practice the examined life
- Make philosophical thinking a habit
- Create pockets of freedom for yourself
- Be self-expressive in ways that contribute to others
- Accept that you are less rational than you think you are
- Do not fight being an outsider. Relish it!
- Acquit with honor
- Rank intellectual honesty high on your core values
- Be willing to take a lot of responsibility for others
- Pursue stewardship as a personal as well as a social value
- Leave a heritage: do something for future generations
- Give special attention to the act of founding
- Take responsibility for the well-being of our democracy
- Never give up on seeking unconditional love

Significantly, a number of individual philosophers have redis-covered the importance of practical philosophy in public and pri-vate life. Philosophers like Dewey, Habermas, Rorty, Arendt, Kuhn, and MacIntyre have recognized that to function effectively, prac-tical judgment must involve dialogue and deliberation within the larger community. (In my own writings I have labeled this capability "public judgment.") Philosopher Hans-Georg Gadamer goes one step further and deeper when he says that the processes of judgment, interpretation and deliberative choice are central to the human con-dition (he calls the process hermeneutics).

The tradition of practical philosophy does still exist, though it is too often obscured by the seemingly more scientific traditions of analytic philosophy and the philosophy of language. These dominat-ing schools of thought are invariably presented in a confusing cloud of technical jargon, inaccessible to the average reader. As long as they continue to dominate academic philosophy, students and outsiders will find it difficult to discover the great gift of practical philosophy.

I would like to end this chapter with a brief comment on the per-plexing question of why wisdom-seeking philosophy, based on prac-tical judgment, is more important today than in earlier epochs of American life.

In recent years, American society has taken ever greater risks with our culture. In the pursuit of individualism, our cultural norms have loosened rules of conduct and the constraints of our social ethics. Our culture no longer provides the ethical guidance that cul-tures should provide.

The only way we can maintain stability and high ethical standards in such a nonconformist society is if the majority of our citizens and experts maintain a high level of sound judgment. But we can't do this unless we place a higher value on practical wisdom, as distinct from raw opinion and technology-based solutions.

The great majority of Americans have come to believe that our nation is on the wrong track and is becoming ever more polarized. And it is true that thoughtless raw opinion seems to rule the day. The only way we can strengthen our democracy is to find new ways for citizens and leaders to engage in the kind of deliberative processes that displace raw opinion with sound judgment.

We don't have to be pretentious and call this process by the technical names that philosophers use, like hermeneutics (Gadamer) or communicative action (Habermas) or representative thinking (Arendt). We can continue to think of it as plain-vanilla common sense. But we must recognize that it is growing ever more elusive and that it doesn't happen by itself. Greater reliance on sound judgment can get us back on the right path.

A New Love

THE TRAUMA OF MY beloved mama's death when I was barely eight years old and the decade-long wandering from one foster home to another left me with an aching nostalgia for a certain kind of mutual love. As I grew into adulthood, I realized that it wasn't maternal love I craved, but an adult form of love that would be intimate, mutually nurturing, and unconditional. I sought it out in one relationship after another, decade after decade, but failed to find it until I approached retirement age.

One reason for my failure was a profound lack of confidence that I was worthy of it. Low self-confidence is an insidious force; it weakens all close bonds. I was acutely aware of the paradox that when it came to friendships or work or coping with life's practical twists and turns, I had confidence galore. But when I sought mutuality in love I was haunted by the fear that I was somehow undeserving.

This lack of confidence had negative consequences. It led me to develop and hide behind a strong inner reserve. I was unable to shed the turtle-like protective shell I had grown until my relationship with Mary was quite far advanced—in my mid to late sixties, an age when many people are withdrawing from life.

Fortunately, there was at least one positive consequence of this lack of self-confidence. I kept busy looking for practical substitutes for the missing love. I refused to drift into self-pity, depression and anger at the world just because I couldn't have what I wanted.

The life of the mind became a home and a refuge for me. I found thinking about things and wondering how the world works a wonderfully intriguing preoccupation. I became a compulsive reader, devouring all manner of books, articles, and other forms of writing.

Also, for some odd reason, my lack of self-confidence in matters of love did not carry over to friendships with women. Throughout my life I have enjoyed a range of deep friendships with both men and women. Many men find it difficult to develop intimate, non-erotic relationships with women. Happily, I have enjoyed at least a half-dozen truly close, non-erotic friendships with strong, compelling, remarkable women.

After Mary died, I gradually gave up on ever again finding the kind of love Mary and I had shared, a love in which one relinquishes autonomous aspects of one's selfhood—a love that creates mutual emotional dependency.

In contrast to many conventional marriages, my bond with Mary had been the rare form of relationship where the two individuals virtually merge. It is a form of mutual nurturing that is hard to describe and define. But when you are lucky enough to find yourself in that type of relationship you know it and you know how different it is from the more familiar forms of marriage.

Even though I no longer actively sought to recreate the kind of love that Mary and I enjoyed, I now knew what it was like. When, quite unexpectedly, the promise of it happening again presented itself, I could not help but respond to it.

In my first years in La Jolla, I knew her simply as "Laura," the wife of my best friend locally, "Chuck" Nathanson.

I was awed by the strength of the love relationship that bound Laura and Chuck together. They had been married for thirty years and it was obvious that their joy in each other's company had remained undiminished throughout all of those years.

Both were busy professionals. Chuck was on the faculty at UCSD and the director of a not-for-profit organization called the San Diego Dialogue—an institute devoted to improving cross-border relations with Mexico.

Laura was a pediatrician with a reputation for caring for her patients far beyond the call of duty. She was beloved by many of her young patients and their families.

Chuck and Laura also enjoyed an exceptionally close bond with their grown daughter, Sara, who was about to be married and start her own family.

Then, suddenly, Chuck fell gravely ill. He died in his early sixties, his illness exacerbated by a serious misdiagnosis. Laura fell into a deep grief and intensity of mourning that threatened her own health.

Some months after Chuck died, Laura and I started to have occasional lunches and dinners together. I found myself falling in love with her. Like Mary, she knew a lot more about love and loving than I did. In temperament and appearance she and Mary were quite different, but they shared in common an understanding of, and a need for, a true loving relationship of mutual nourishing.

Ironically, I had had to wait until my senior years to discover what love meant for me and how intensely I valued it over everything else. In the past three decades, I have fallen deeply in love not just once but twice. First with Mary, who died after three all-too-brief years of marriage. And then, unexpectedly, Laura entered my life. I have dared to follow my heart, even at the cost of hurting and disrupting the lives of those I deeply cared about.

Barbara and I underwent a painful separation. The reason we officially separated was not incompatibility. It was that by a freak of chance, when I wasn't looking, I almost miraculously found someone with whom I developed the same special kind of bond of love that had formed the core of my relationship to Mary.

My paths to love were paved with guilt and angst. But deep down, I have no regrets or second thoughts about acting on them.

Laura and I are as happy with each other as were Mary and I, and Chuck and Laura. The same powerful bond of love holds us in its grasp and flourishes.

Looking back over my life, I believe I have devoted much of my productive energies to three main themes:

- Avoiding economic dependency and maintaining an optimistic and activist outlook in the face of chaos and randomness
- Searching for substitutes for love and then rejoicing late in life when I found the genuine article
- Keeping faith with the long tradition of the "examined life": understanding the centrality of sound judgment to philosophy, and how to achieve it.

So ends my story...up to now.

Dan and Laura, 2012

Other Books by Dan Yankelovich

Wicked Problems, Workable Solutions: Lessons from a Public Life. Lanham, Maryland: Roman & Littlefield, 2015.

Toward Wiser Public Judgment. Nashville: Vanderbilt Univeristy Press, 2011. With Will Friedman.

Profit With Honor: The New Stage of Market Capitalism. New Haven: Yale University Press, 2006.

Uniting America: Restoring the Vital Center to American Democracy. Editor, with Norton Garfinkle. New Haven: Yale University Press, 2006.

The Magic of Dialogue: Transforming Conflict into Cooperation. New York: Simon & Schuster, 1999.

Beyond the Beltway: Engaging the Public in U.S. Foreign Policy. Editor, with I.M. Destler. New York: W.W. Norton and Company, 1994.

Coming to Public Judgment: Making Democracy Work in a Complex World. Syracuse: Syracuse University Press, 1991.

Starting with the People. Boston: Houghton Mifflin Company, 1988. With Sidney Harman.

The World at Work: An International Report on Jobs, Productivity and Human Values. Octagon Books, 1985.

New Rules: Searching for Self-fulfillment in a World Turned Upside Down. New York: Random House, 1981.

The New Morality: A Profile of American Youth in the Seventies. New York: McGraw-Hill, 1978.

Work, Productivity and Job Satisfaction. New York: Harcourt Brace, 1975. With Raymond A. Katzell and others.

Changing Values on Campus: Political and Personal Attitudes of Today's College Students. New York: Washington Square Press, 1973.

Ego and Instinct: The Psychoanalytic View of Human Nature-Revised. New York: Random House, 1969. With William Barrett.